I0820293

A DICTIONARY OF TOLKIEN

To my daughter, Tarot

Thunder Bay Press
An imprint of Printers Row Publishing Group
9717 Pacific Heights Blvd, San Diego, CA 92121
www.thunderbaybooks.com • mail@thunderbaybooks.com

Artwork, design & layout copyright © Octopus Publishing Group 2024
Text copyright © David Day 1993, 2001, 2013, 2014, 2019, 2024

All rights reserved. No part of this publication may be reproduced, distributed, or transmitted in any form or by any means, including photocopying, recording, or other electronic or mechanical methods, without the prior written permission of the publisher, except in the case of brief quotations embodied in critical reviews and certain other noncommercial uses permitted by copyright law.

Some or all of the material in this book originally appeared in *A–Z of Tolkien*, *A Tolkien Bestiary* and/or *Tolkien: An Illustrated Encyclopedia* © Octopus Publishing Group 1979, 1991, 1993

Printers Row Publishing Group is a division of Readerlink Distribution Services, LLC.
Thunder Bay Press is a registered trademark of Readerlink Distribution Services, LLC.

Correspondence regarding the content of this book should be sent to Thunder Bay Press, Editorial Department, at the above address. Author inquiries should be addressed to Pyramid, an imprint of Octopus Publishing Group Ltd., Carmelite House, 50 Victoria Embankment, London, EC4Y 0DZ, www.octopusbooks.co.uk

THUNDER BAY PRESS
Publisher: Peter Norton
Associate Publisher: Ana Parker
Editor: Dan Mansfield

PYRAMID
Publisher: Lucy Pessell
Designer: Isobel Platt
Editor: Feyi Oyesanya
Assistant Editor: Samina Rahman
Production Manager: Allison Gonsalves
Cover illustration: Allan Curless

For illustration credits, refer to page 254-5

Library of Congress Control Number: 2024930928

ISBN: 978-1-6672-0774-2

Printed in Hui Zhou, China
Second printing, December 2024. TEN/12/24
28 27 26 25 24   2 3 4 5 6

This book has not been prepared, authorized, licensed or endorsed by J. R. R. Tolkien's heirs or estate, nor by any of the publishers or distributors of the book *The Lord of the Rings* or any other work written by J. R. R. Tolkien, nor anyone involved in the creation, production or distribution of the films based on the book.

A DICTIONARY OF TOLKIEN

DAVID DAY

THUNDER BAY
P·R·E·S·S
San Diego, California

J. R. R. Tolkien

A NOTE ON THIS EDITION

A *Dictionary of Tolkien* (2015) was first published as *An A–Z of Tolkien* and *The Tolkien Companion* (1993). A compilation of black and white art, and text drawn from *A Tolkien Bestiary* (1979) it is an illustrated guide to Middle-earth and the Undying Lands for the general reader with a complete listing of all its nearly 200 races and species; as well as over 300 biographical and geographic entries. It is not meant as a substitute for the reading of Tolkien's novels and posthumous works; nor is it meant to provide complete annotations to their multiple indices with their many thousands of names of lesser-known persons, places, and things.

It all began with the enormous investment in original art exclusively commissioned for the publication of *A Tolkien Bestiary* (1979) as the first ever fully illustrated reference work on J. R. R. Tolkien. *A Tolkien Bestiary* appeared just two years after the posthumous publication of J. R. R. Tolkien's *The Silmarillion*: a book that for the first time gave readers of *The Hobbit* and *The Lord of the Rings* some indication of the immense scope of Tolkien's mythology and cosmology. Subsequently, new original artwork was created for *Tolkien: The Illustrated Encyclopedia* (1992), and for *The World of Tolkien: The Mythological Sources of Lord of the Rings* (2002).

A Dictionary of Tolkien and its companion volume, *An Atlas of Tolkien,* were the first two books of a uniformly designed seven-volume reference library; *The Illustrated World of Tolkien* (2019) was published to celebrate and offer a retrospective of 40 years of the work of established artists and fresh new talents while *The Illustrated World of Tolkien: The Second Age* (2023) delves into the lesser-known parts of Tolkien's legendarium.

This special edition of *A Dictionary of Tolkien* has been expanded to include new and original art, as well as work from some of the many artists who have contributed to the books published within the past decade. It publishes alongside a special edition of *An Atlas of Tolkien.*

INTRODUCTION

If you've never heard of J. R. R. Tolkien and know absolutely nothing about his most famous books *The Hobbit*, *The Lord of the Rings* and *The Silmarillion*, the only possible explanation is that you have spent your entire life living at the bottom of a coal pit on the other side of the galaxy. Even for those who have never read a word of his writing, Tolkien's influence has been inescapable. The virtual inventor of the epic fantasy novel, there have been literally thousands of 'sword and sorcery' imitators who have come after him with a veritable avalanche of books and films.

John Ronald Reuel Tolkien was born of British parents in Bloemfontein, South Africa on January 3, 1892. Orphaned in childhood, he survived the carnage of the Great War and went on to a career as a noted Anglo-Saxon scholar at Oxford before becoming the author of imaginative fiction. As authors go, Tolkien was a late-starter. Although he was a relatively youthful 45 when his first work of fiction, *The Hobbit*, was published, it was not until 1954, when he was 62, that his second novel, the epic fantasy, *The Lord of the Rings*, was published. He never published another novel during his lifetime, but in the 19 years between the publication of *The Lord of the Rings* and his death in 1973, he became one of the most celebrated and widely-read authors of the twentieth century.

Today, Tolkien's Hobbits are as convincing a part of the English heritage as leprechauns are to the Irish, gnomes are to the Germans, and trolls are to the Scandinavians. Indeed, many people are now unaware that Hobbits were invented by Tolkien, and assume that, like fairies and pixies, they have, more or less, always been with us. However, Hobbits are not the only creations of Tolkien's mind that have invaded our world. Orcs, Ents and Balrogs have also found their way through; and the Elf, Dwarf, Dragon and Wizard are very different creatures today because of Tolkien.

So great was Tolkien's enthusiasm for creating and inhabiting his invented world that it can convincingly be argued that the undoubted literary merit of Tolkien's epic tale of *The Lord of the Rings* was a secondary concern. Important as the novel is, any analysis of Tolkien's life and work will show that his greatest passion and grandest ambition was focused on the creation of an entire mythological system.

Tolkien once wrote about his motivation for creating his mythical world of Middle-earth: 'I was from early days grieved by the poverty of my own beloved country: it had no stories of its own, not of the quality that I sought, and found in legends of other lands. There was Greek, and Celtic, and Romance, Germanic, Scandinavian, and Finnish, but nothing English, save impoverished chapbook stuff'. Later, in a personal letter, Tolkien further explained his efforts: 'I had a mind to make a body of more or less connected legend, ranging from the large and cosmogonic, to the level of romantic fairy-story . . . which I could dedicate simply: to England; to my country'.

The degree to which Tolkien actually succeeded is remarkable. Today, Tolkien's invented mythology in the popular imagination has to a considerable degree become that of England. He has been translated into every major language, and many of his characters and creatures have come to inhabit the world of popular culture everywhere.

A Dictionary of Tolkien was written in celebration of this aspect of J. R. R. Tolkien's genius. It was compiled and designed as a compact and easy-to-use guide to Tolkien's world. The purpose is to inform and entertain those readers who wish to use *A Dictionary of Tolkien* to help them in their personal exploration of the extraordinarily complex invented world and mythology of Middle-earth and the Undying Lands.

A Dictionary of Tolkien is a complete dictionary of all flora and fauna in Tolkien's writings. It describes every species and sub-species of flower, tree, plant, all birds, beasts, insects and every kind of spirit, spectre, ghost, demon and monster. It is also a complete guide to all the races, nations and tribes of Men, Elves, Dwarves, Hobbits, Ents, Maiar and Valar that ever populated Tolkien's world of Arda.

Furthermore, *A Dictionary of Tolkien* serves as a selective biographical dictionary and geographical gazetteer. It is a Who's Who of the major characters of his epic world, and an A to Z of all the prominent cities, countries, mountains, forests, rivers, lakes and seas of Middle-earth and the Undying Lands.

For those readers wishing to discover more of Arda's complex 37,000-year history and geographic evolution through its Ages of Creation, Ages of Lamps, Ages of Trees of Light, Ages of Stars and Ages of Sun, it might interest them to investigate this dictionary's companion volume, *An Atlas of Tolkien.*

It is hoped that the combination of the book's remarkable illustrations and its detailed text will make *A Dictionary of Tolkien* both a useful and an entertaining reference work for any reader interested in J. R. R. Tolkien's epic world.

CHRONOLOGY

1892 John Ronald Reuel Tolkien born 3rd January of British parents in Bloemfontein, South Africa. Brother, Hilary, born 1894.

1895 Mother (Mabel Tolkien) takes children back to Birmingham, England. Father (Arthur Tolkien) dies in South Africa.

1900 Ronald begins to attend King Edward's Grammar School.

1904 Mother dies of diabetes, aged 34.

1905 Orphaned boys move to Aunt's home in Birmingham.

1908 Ronald begins first term at Oxford.

1913 Ronald takes Honours Moderations exams.

1914 Ronald is betrothed to childhood sweetheart Edith Bratt. Great War declared. Returns to Oxford to complete his degree.

1915 Awarded First Class Honours degree in English Language and Literature. Commissioned in Lancashire Fusiliers.

1916 Married Edith Bratt. Goes to war in France. Sees action on the Somme as second lieutenant. Returns to England suffering from trench fever.

1917 While convalescing begins writing *The Silmarillion*.
Birth of first son, John.

1918 Promoted to full lieutenant, posted to Staffordshire. War ends. Returns with family to Oxford, joins staff of *New English Dictionary*.

1919 Works as a freelance tutor in Oxford.

1920 Appointed Reader in English Language at Leeds University.
Birth of second son, Michael.

1924 Becomes Professor of English Language at Leeds. Third son, Christopher, is born.

1925 Tolkien and E. V. Gordon publish *Sir Gawain and the Green Knight*. Tolkien elected Professor of Anglo-Saxon at Oxford.

1926 Friendship with C. S. Lewis begins.

1929 Fourth child, Priscilla, is born.

1936 Tolkien completes *The Hobbit*. Delivers his lecture, *Beowulf: The Monsters and the Critics.*

1937 *The Hobbit* is published. Tolkien begins to write a sequel, which eventually becomes *The Lord of the Rings.*

1939 Tolkien delivers his lecture *Fairy Stories*. Works on *The Lord of the Rings* fitfully throughout the war years.

1945 War ends. Tolkien elected Merton Professor of English Language and Literature at Oxford.

1947 Draft of *The Lord of the Rings* sent to publishers.

1948 *The Lord of the Rings* completed.

1949 Publication of *Farmer Giles of Ham.*

1954 Publication of *The Lord of the Rings, Volumes One and Two.*

1955 Publication of *The Lord of the Rings, Volume Three.*

1959 Tolkien retires his professorship.

1962 Publication of *The Adventures of Tom Bombadil.*

1964 Publication of *Tree and Leaf.*

1965 American paperback editions of *The Lord of the Rings* are published and campus cult of the novel begins.

1967 Publication of *Smith of Wootton Major*, and *The Road Goes Ever On.*

1968 The Tolkiens move to Poole near Bournemouth.
1971 Edith Tolkien dies, aged 82.
1972 Tolkien returns to Oxford. Receives CBE from the Queen.
1973 September 2, J. R. R. Tolkien dies, aged 81.

POSTHUMOUS PUBLICATIONS

1976 *The Father Christmas Letters.*
1977 *The Silmarillion.*
1979 *Pictures by J. R. R. Tolkien.*
1980 *Unfinished Tales of Númenor and Middle-Earth.*
1981 *The Letters of J. R. R. Tolkien.*
The Old English 'Exodus'.
1982 *Mr Bliss.*
Finn and Hengest.
1983 *The Monsters and The Critics and Other Essays.*
The History of Middle-Earth: The Book of Lost Tales.
1984 *The History of Middle-Earth: The Book of Lost Tales – Part two.*
1985 *The History of Middle-Earth: The Lays of Beleriand.*
1986 *The History of Middle-Earth: The Shaping of Middle-Earth.*
1987 *The History of Middle-Earth: The Lost Road and Other Writings.*
1988 *The History of Middle-Earth: The Return of the Shadow.*
1989 *The History of Middle-Earth: The Treason of Isengard.*
1990 *The History of Middle-Earth: The War of the Ring.*
1992 *The History of Middle-Earth: Sauron Defeated.*
1993 *The History of Middle-Earth: Morgoth's Ring.*
1994 *The History of Middle-Earth: The War of the Jewels.*
1996 *The History of Middle-Earth: The Peoples of Middle-Earth.*
2007 *The Children of Húrin.*
2009 *The Legend of Sigurd and Gudrun.*
2013 *The Fall of Arthur.*
2014 *Beowulf: A Translation and Commentary.*
2015 *The Story of Kullervo.*
2016 *The Lay of Aotrou and Itroun.*
2017 *Beren and Lúthien.*
2018 *The Fall of Gondolin.*
2021 *The Nature of Middle-earth.*
2022 *The Fall of Númenor.*

A

Aglarond

The great caverns beneath Helm's Deep and the fortress called Hornburg where one of the crucial battles of the War of the Rings was fought. Here the Rohirrim horsemen had their strongest fortifications and under King Théoden they defeated the forces of the evil wizard, Saruman. The caverns themselves were of ancient origin and believed to have been delved in the Second Age of the Sun by the Númenóreans. Aglarond is Elvish for 'Glittering Caves' and this vast glittering complex of caverns was one of the wonders of Middle-earth. After the War of the Ring, Gimli the Dwarf (one of the Fellowship of the Ring) returned to Aglarond with many of the Dwarves of Erebor. Gimli became the Lord of the Glittering Caves and in the Fourth Age this became the most powerful Dwarf kingdom in Middle-earth. Under Gimli's leadership, the Dwarves of Aglarond became famous as the master smiths of Middle-earth.

Ainur

In the very beginning there was Eru, the One, who dwelt in the Void, and whose name in Elvish was Ilúvatar. As is told in the 'Ainulindalë', Thoughts came forth from Ilúvatar to which He gave eternal life through the power of the Flame Imperishable. Ilúvatar named these creations Ainur, the 'holy ones'. They were the first race and they inhabited the Timeless Halls that Ilúvatar had fashioned for them.

ARGONATH The huge statues were of the first kings of Gondor, Isíldur and Anárion.

The Ainur were great spirits and each was given a mighty voice so that he could sing before Ilúvatar for His pleasure. When He had heard each sing, Ilúvatar called them to Him and proposed that they should sing in concert. This was what the tales call the Music of the Ainur, in which great themes were made as individual spirits sought supremacy or harmony according to their nature. Some proved greater than others; some were powerful in goodness, some in evil; yet in the end, though the battle of sound was terrible, the Music was great and beautiful. From this harmony and strife Ilúvatar created a Vision that was a globed light in the Void. With a word and the Flame Imperishable Ilúvatar then made Eä, the 'World that Is'; Elves and Men later named it Arda, the Earth. The Music soon became the Doom of Arda and the fate of every race was bound to it, save that of the late-coming race of Men, whose end nobody but Ilúvatar knew.

So it was that after Arda was made, some of the Ainur went down into this newly created World, where they were known as the Powers of Arda. Later they were thought by Men to be gods. Those who were good among them were guided by their knowledge of the Will of Ilúvatar, while others strove to fulfil their own ends. Whereas in the Timeless Halls they had been beings of pure spirit, within Arda they were limited in power by choosing to inhabit the bounds of Time and the small space of the World. Further, within Arda they took on separate shapes, each according to his nature and the elements he loved, and, though not bound to a visible form, they most often wore these shapes as garments, and in later Ages they were known to Elves and Men in these forms.

In the 'Valaquenta' a part of the long history of the Ainur who inhabited Arda and shaped the World is written. It tells how the kingdoms of Almaren, Utumno and Angbad were built in Middle-earth; and how the kingdom of Valinor was made in the Undying Lands of Aman. It speaks also of how the Ainur brought forth Light and the Count of Time, and how there were terrible wars among them that shook Arda; and it gives the names and forms of many of the mightiest of the race.

In Arda the Elves divided this race into the Valar and the Maiar. Those of the Ainur counted among the Valar are: Manwë, the Wind King; Varda, Queen of the Stars; Ulmo, Lord of the Waters; Nienna, the Weeper; Aulë, the Smith; Yavanna, Giver of Fruits; Oromë, Lord of the Forest; Vána, the Youthful; Mandos, Keeper of the Dead; Vairë, the Weaver; Lórien, Master of Dreams; Estë, the Healer; Tulkas, the Wrestler; Nessa, the Dancer; and Melkor, later named Morgoth, the Dark Enemy.

Many of the Ainur were counted among the Maiar, but only a few are named in the histories that have come down to Men; Eönwë, Herald of Manwë; Ilmarë, Maid of Varda; Ossë, of the Waves; Uinen, of the Calm Seas; Melian, Queen of the Sindar; Arien, the Sun; Tilion, the Moon; Sauron, the Sorcerer; Gothmog, Lord of the Balrogs; and Olórin (Gandalf), Aiwendil (Radagast), Curunír (Saruman), Alatar and Pallando – the Wizards. In the histories of Middle-earth there also appear others who may have been Maiar; Thuringwethil, the Vampire; Ungoliant, the Spider; Draugluin, the Werewolf; Goldberry, the River-daughter; and Iarwain Ben-adar (Tom Bombadil).

As has been said, only some of the Ainur went down to Arda. A greater part has always lived in the Timeless Halls, but it has been foretold that at the World's End the Valar and the Maiar shall rejoin their kindred in the Timeless Halls, and among those who return will also be the Eruhíni, the Children of Ilúvatar, who came forth upon Arda. Once again there shall be Great Music: this shall be mightier than the first. It shall be unflawed, filled with wisdom and sadness, and beautiful beyond compare.

Alfirin

One of the many sad songs sung by the Grey-elves of Middle-earth tells of a plant called Alfirin. Its flowers were like golden bells and it grew on the green plain of Lebennin near the delta lands of the Anduin, the Great River. The sight of them in the fields, with the sea-wind blowing, would tug at the hearts of the Eldar and awaken the sea-longing that always drew these Children of Starlight westwards, over Belegaer, the Great Sea, to where their immortal brethren lived. In the minds of Elves, the Alfirin were like the great gold bells of Valinor in miniature, which always toll upon the ears of the Blessed in the Undying Lands.

Almaren

The Isle of Almaren, in the midst of a great lake in Middle-earth, was the first dwelling-place of the gods of Middle-earth, the Valar, during the Age of the Lamps. It was an idyllic island realm filled with godly dwellings and temples. However, it was destroyed when the rebel Vala, Melkor, made war on the others, destroyed the Two Lamps and cast Middle-earth down into darkness.

Alqualondë

City and port of the Teleri Elves in Eldamar, on the coast of the Undying Lands. The Teleri were the last of the Three Kindred of Elves to make their way out of Middle-earth during the Ages of the Stars. These were the Sea-Elves, Elves who above all others love the sea and know its ways best. These are the greatest of sailors who were taught the art of ship building by the sea gods. And so, on the seas about Eldamar, the Teleri sail their ships built in the shapes of the swans of Ulmo the Sea Lord. And this is the reason for the Elvish name of their principal city of Alqualondë, which means 'swan haven'. For Alqualondë was a magnificent city of marble and pearl built beneath the stars on the shore of the Undying Lands in a great natural harbour which shelters their vast fleet of swan ships. It can only be entered through the arching sea-carved stone gate of their haven.

Aman

The great western continent which is the Undying Lands of the immortal Valar and the Eldar. Aman in Quenya Elvish for 'blessed', and until the downfall of Númenor and the Change of the World, it lay far to the west of Middle-earth over Belegaer, the Great Sea. After that cataclysm, Aman was torn away from the sphere of the world, so that those who sailed from Middle-earth after the Second Age of the Sun could only reach the Undying Lands on the magical ships of the Sea Elves. These miraculous ships alone are granted the power to sail the vast abyss that lies beneath the mortal and immortal lands.

Amanyar

In the time of the Trees of the Valar, many of the Elven peoples made the Great Journey from Middle-earth to the continent of the Undying Lands, which is also known as Aman. Thereafter, in the Ages of Stars and Sun, Elves also came to Aman and all those who reached the Undying Lands, soon or late, were named the Amanyar, 'those of Aman'.

Amon Amarth

Also called Orodurin, Amon Amarth is an Elvish name meaning 'Mount Doom', a volcanic mountain on a barren plain in the evil land of Mordor. It was in the fires of the Cracks of Doom on Amon Amarth that Sauron first forged the One Ring. And it was back to this mountain of destiny that the Ringbearer Frodo Baggins the Hobbit brought the Ring in order to destroy it, and bring an end to the power of Sauron, the Dark Lord.

Amon Hen

The 'hill of the eye', one of the three peaks at the end of the long lake called Nen Hithoel on the Anduin River. The other two were Amon Llaw, or the 'hill of the ear', on the eastern bank, and Tol Brandir, or Tindrock, an unclimbable island pinnacle that stood in the centre of the lake. Amon Hen and Amon Llaw had on their summits two magical thrones built to watch the borderlands of Gondor. These stone thrones were called the 'Seat of Seeing' on Amon Hen and the 'Seat of Hearing' on Amon Llaw. During the War of the Rings, the Fellowship of the Ring made their way to Amon Hen. There, Frodo Baggins sat upon the Seat of Seeing and discovered its magical properties by suddenly being able to see telescopically for hundreds of miles in all directions.

Amon Lhaw

The 'hill of the ear', one of the three peaks at the end of the long lake Nen Hithoel on the Anduin River. It was one of the two watchtowers of the marchlands of Gondor, the other being Amon Hen, the 'hill of the eye'. On the summit of Amon Lhaw was the 'Seat of Hearing', a throne comparable to the 'Seat of Seeing' on Amon Hen. It is presumed that upon this throne, one may hear all the enemies of Gondor conspiring against her.

Amon Rûdh

The 'bald hill' in West Beleriand, south of the Brethil Forest and between the Narog and Sirion Rivers. The caverns cut into Amon Rûdh were the last home of the Noegyth Nibin, or Petty Dwarves, which *The Silmarillion* tells, had so diminished in numbers by the fifth century of the First Age of the Sun, that there were only three surviving: an ancient dwarf named Mîm and his two sons. It was also the hiding place of the hero Túrin Turambar. Amon Rûdh was called the Bald Hill because it was rocky and without any vegetation, except the red flowers of the hardy seregon or bloodstone plant.

Amon Uilos

Literally means 'hill of ever snow white'. It is one of the many names for Taniquetil, the highest mountain in the Undying Lands. It is the Olympus of Arda where Ilmarin, the great halls of the gods Manwë and Varda are built.

Amroth

Elven King of Lothlórien. Amroth was the son of Amdir, and ruled from 3434 of the Second Age until 1981 of the Third Age. Amroth fell in love with the Elf maid Nimrodel, and was the star-crossed lover who was the subject of many songs. He once lived on the hill of Cerin Amroth in Lothlórien but in the year 1981 he went to Dol Amroth and awaited his lover, so they might sail to the Undying Lands. However, Nimrodel lost her way and perished, and Amroth threw himself from his white ship into the sea.

Anárion

Dúnedain king of Gondor. Anárion, with his father Elendil and brother Isildur, escaped the Downfall of Númenor, and founded the kingdoms of Gondor and Arnor in 3320 of the Second Age. They were among the chief enemies of Sauron, the Ring Lord, in the Second Age. With the Elf King, Gil-galad, they formed the army of the Last Alliance of Elves and Men. The Alliance was successful in destroying Sauron's power, but Anárion was killed by a stone hurled down on him from the Dark Tower of Mordor.

Ancalagon

Dragon of Angband. Ancalagon was the first and greatest of the Winged Dragons. Called Ancalagon the Black, he was bred in the Pits of Angband by Morgoth the Dark Enemy in the First Age of the Sun. The name itself meant 'rushing jaws' and when he was first released on the world in the Great Battle, his vast shape blotted out the light of the sun. For a time Ancalagon and his legions of Winged Fire-drakes looked as if they would overcome the Valar but at a critical moment the giant Eagles and Eärendil, the Mariner, in his magical flying ship, entered the fray and slew Ancalagon the Black. So great was the Dragon's weight that when he fell the towers of Thangorodrim were destroyed and the vast Pits of Angband burst beneath him.

Andor

Andor means the 'land of the gift' and is one of the Elvish names for Númenor, the Atlantis of the Arda. This is the great island kingdom that at the end of the Second Age of the Sun was swallowed up in to Belegaer, the Great Sea.

Andram

A massive escarpment wall that ran from west to east across central Beleriand. Its name means 'long wall' and it served to divide north and south Beleriand. It ran from Nargothrond in the far west to Ramdall, the 'wall's end', in East Beleriand, and was breached in only two places. In the west, the River Narog cut a fantastically deep gorge through the Andram, and twenty-five leagues to the east of the Narog the great river Sirion hurled itself over the sheer escarpment in one of the mightiest falls in Middle-earth, only to vanish into deep caverns beneath the Andram.

Andúnië

The earliest chief city of the great island kingdom of Númenor that during the Second Age of the Sun was found in the middle of Belegaer, the Great Sea, and between Middle-earth and the Undying Lands. Andúnië

was a haven on the westernmost part of Númenor, and its name means 'sunset'. Its people were the most faithful to the old ways of the Númenóreans, and later founded the Dunedain kingdoms of Gondor and Arnor on Middle-earth.

Angband

Utumno was the first and chief underground kingdom of the satanic Valarian Melkor, but in the ages of darkness that followed the destruction of the Lamps of Valar, Melkor built a great armoury and underground fortress in the north of Beleriand called Angband, the 'iron prison'. At the end of the First Age of Stars Utumno was destroyed and Melkor put in chains, but though its main defences were broken, the pits and dungeons of Angband were not torn up during the War of Powers. For four ages of starlight while Melkor was captive, his minions and evil spirits, led by his captain, Sauron, hid themselves in the depths of Angband. So when Melkor rose again, destroyed the Trees of the Valar and stole the Silmarils, he fled once more to Angband. Calling his demons to him, he rebuilt Angband, vaster and stronger than before. Above the Angband he then raised the three-peaked volcanic mountain called Thangorodrim as a great battlement. In Angband, throughout the First Age of the Sun and the War of the Jewels, Melkor ruled and bred his demons and such monsters as his mighty Dragons. Attacked many times, Angband was not taken until the War of Wrath and the Great Battle. It took all the power of the vast hosts the Valar, Maiar and Eldar to break down its defences, crush its demons and cast Melkor out into the void. So great was the battle, that not only was Angband destroyed, but all the land of Beleriand was swallowed up by the western sea.

ANDRAM Its name means 'long wall' and it served to divide north and south Beleriand.

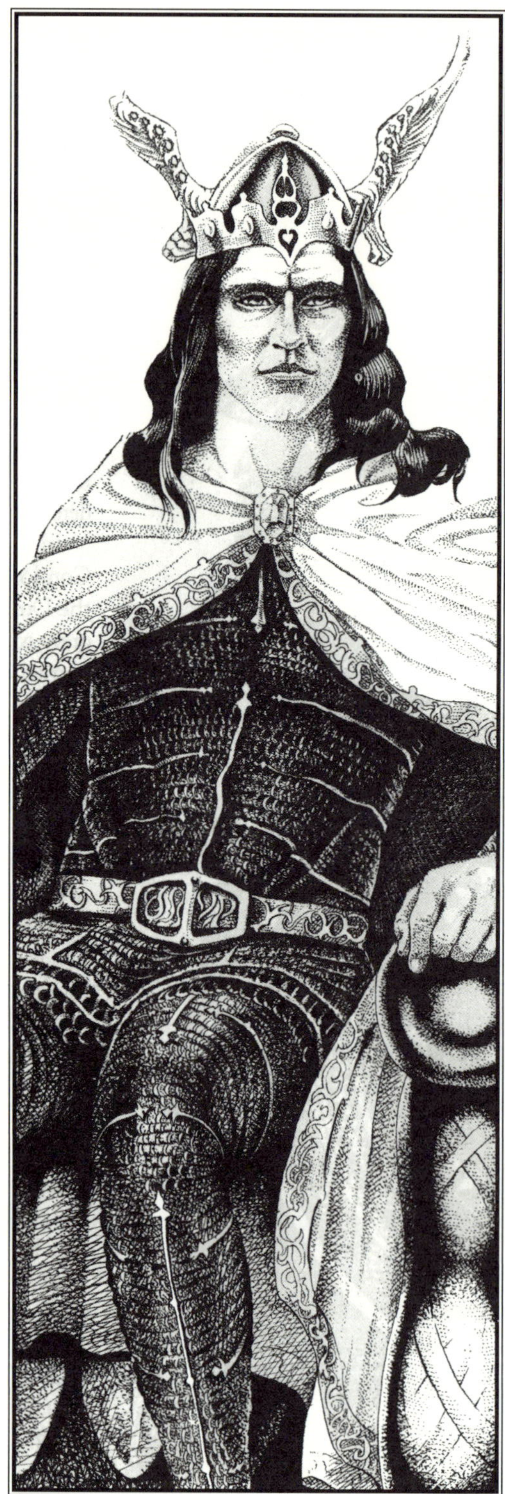

Angmar

The Witch-kingdom of Angmar in the northern part of the Misty Mountains arose in the year 1300 of the Third Age of the Sun. Its capital was Carn Dûm, and it was populated by Orcs and the barbarian Hillmen of the Ettenmoors. Its ruler was called the Witch-king of Angmar, but in reality he was the Lord of the Nazgûl and the chief servant of Sauron, the Dark Lord. For nearly 700 years the Witch-king ruled and Angmar made constant war on the Dúnedain Kingdom of the North in Arnor. Arnor was finally destroyed in the year 1974, but in 1975, a combined army of Gondor Men and Elves defeated the Witch-king's army at the Battle of Fornost, then went on to lay waste to all of the kingdom of Angmar.

Apanónar

When the Sun first rose on Arda and its light shone in the land of Hildórien in eastern Middle-earth, there arose a race of mortal beings. This was the race of Men, who were also named the Apanónar, which means 'afterborn', because they were not the first speaking people to come to Arda. Elves, Dwarves, Ents and the evil races of Orcs and Trolls had been in the World for many Ages before Men arrived.

Aragorn I

Dúnedain chieftain of Arnor. After the North Kingdom of the Dúnedain was destroyed by the Witch-king of Angmar in 1974 of the Third Age, the heirs to this lost kingdom were thereafter known as the Chieftains of the Dúnedain, and of these there were sixteen. The fifth was Aragorn I. Little is recorded of those dark days, except that after ruling for eight years as Chieftain, in 2327 he was slain by wolves in Eriador.

ARAGORN II The last Chieftain of the Dúnedain of the North after he was crowned King Elessar of the Reunited Kingdom of Gondor and Arnor.

Aragorn II

Dúnedain chieftain of Arnor. At the time of the War of the Ring, Aragon II was the sixteenth and last chieftain of the Dúnedain. Born in 2931 of the Third Age, Aragorn was raised by Elrond the Half-Elven in Rivendell. When Aragorn was twenty he met Elrond's daughter, Arwen, and the couple fell in love. However, Elrond would not permit marriage until Aragorn became the rightful king of Arnor and Gondor. To this end, Aragorn travelled widely and fought for the rights of the Free Peoples. He went by many names: Thorongil, Elfstone, Elessar and Strider. As a Dúnedain lord, Aragorn was blessed with a lifespan three times that of other Men. In 2956, he met Gandalf the Wizard and they became friends and allies. In 3018, he came to Bree where he met the Hobbit Ringbearer, Frodo Baggins, and in Rivendell he became one of the Fellowship of the Ring. After Gandalf was lost to the Balrog in Moria, Aragorn became the leader of the Fellowship. In the War of the Ring, Aragorn played a prominent role in routing Saruman's army at Hornburg. He commanded the Dead Men of Dunharrow and captured the fleet at Pelargir. His arrival with new allies at the Battle of Pelennor Fields saved Gondor, and he commanded the Army of the West at the Black Gate of Mordor. After the war, Aragorn became King Elessar ('Elfstone') of the Reunited Kingdom and married Arwen. During the next century of his reign, Aragorn extended his kingdom to most of the Western lands of Middle-earth. With Arwen, he had several daughters and one son, Eldarion. After Aragorn's death in 120 of the Fourth Age, his son became king of the Reunited Kingdom, ruling long and well.

Aratar

Among the Powers of Arda there are the Valar, eight of whom are named the Aratar, the 'exalted'. Their might far exceeds that of all others in the Undying Lands. The Aratar are: Manwë, the Wind King and Varda, Queen of the Stars, who both live on Taniquetil in Ilmarin, the 'mansion of the high airs'. Two others, called Aulë the Smith and Mandos the Doomsman, live in halls beneath the Earth, while Yavanna, who is Queen of the Earth, and Oromë, the Forest Lord, live on the open land. Another is Ulmo, the Lord of the Waters, who inhabits the seas. The last Aratar is Nienna the Weeper, whose home is a great house in the West from which she looks upon the Door of Night.

Arda

The High Elven name for the whole world as it was conceived by Ilúvatar and shaped by the Valar. It included both the mortal lands of Middle-earth and the immortal realm of the Undying Lands.

Argonath

Literally the 'royal stones', but also called the Gates of the Kings or the Gates of Gondor, the Argonath was a pair of massive carvings cut into the high cliffs on either side of a gorge that fed into a lake above the great falls of Rauros on the Anduin River. The huge statues were of the first kings of Gondor, Isildur and Anárion, and were carved into the living rock in the year 1340 of the Third Age to mark the northern limit of the kingdom of Gondor.

Arien

Maia guardian of the Sun. The radiant Arien was a Maia maiden spirit of fire who once served Vana the Ever-young in the gardens of Valinor. However, after the destruction of the Trees of Light, Arien took the single surviving fruit of the Golden Tree and, in a vessel forged by Aulë the Smith, carried it through the heavens. As the guardian of the Sun, Arien is the best-loved of all the Maiar spirits by mortal Men.

Armenelos

The capital city of Númenor, Armenelos was built on the slopes of Meneltarma, the highest mountain of the island kingdom. Sometimes called Armenelos the Golden, it contained the court of the kings of Númenor, and by the power of cunning evil, overcame and corrupted the king, causing the destruction of Númenor.

Arnor

Founded in the year 3320 of the Second Age of the Sun by Elendil the Númenórean, Arnor was the first kingdom of the Dúnedain on Middle-earth. Elendil ruled in Arnor as High-king of the Dúnedain, but sent his sons south to found Gondor, the realm of the Dúnedain of the South. Arnor's first capital was Annúminas, on the shores of Lake Evendim; by 861 Fornost had become its major city and capital. It was in that year that Arnor was split up into three kingdoms – Arthedain, Cardolan and Rhudaur – by the three sons of Eärendur, its tenth king. In the year 1300 there arose to the north-east of Arnor the evil Witch-kingdom of Angmar. For nearly seven hundred years the Lord of the Nazgûl, who was known only as the Witch-king, made war on the Dúnedain of Arnor. By 1409, the kingdoms of Cardolan and Rhudaur had been destroyed, but the Dúnedain of Arthedain fought on another six centuries. Finally, in the year 1974, Arthedain was overrun by the Orc legions and barbarian hordes of the Witch-king. Though the line of its kings was unbroken in the scattered remnant of its people, the kingdom of Arnor ceased to exist. It was not right until the end of the War of the Ring, when Aragorn, the last Chieftain, became High King of all the Dúnedain, that Arnor was reclaimed and restored to its former power and glory.

ARMENELOS Armenelos was built on the slopes of Meneltarma, the highest mountain of the island kingdom.

Arwen

Elven princess of Rivendell. Arwen was the daughter of Elrond Half-elven and Queen Celebrian. Born in the year 241 of the Third Age of the Sun she was considered the greatest beauty of her time. She was known as Evenstar by Elves, and often called Undómiel, or 'evening maid' by Men. For nearly three thousand years she lived in Rivendell and Lothlórien. In 2951, she met and fell in love with Aragorn, the heir to the Dúnedain kingdom. In 2980 they became betrothed, but Elrond forebade this marriage until Aragorn became king. Aragorn's deeds in the War of the Ring resulted in fulfilment of Elrond's conditions, and Arwen became Aragorn's queen. For Arwen, this was a brave choice, for through this marriage she chose to share the ultimate fate of all mortals. She bore Aragorn several daughters and one son, and they reigned happily and well until Aragorn's death in the year 120 of the Fourth Age. The following year Arwen went back to Lothlórien where she chose to die on Cerin Amroth, where she and Aragorn had been betrothed.

Asëa Aranion

From the land of the Númenóreans, a herb of magical healing powers came to Middle-earth. In the High Elven tongue this herb was named Asëa Aranion, the 'leaf of kings', because of the special powers that it possessed in the hands of the kings of Númenórë. More commonly, Elven-lore used the Sindarin name, Athelas; in the common Westron tongue of Men it was Kingsfoil.

Ash Mountains

The realm of Sauron, the Lord of the Rings, was called Mordor. It was a dark and evil land protected by a great horseshoe of mountains. The mountains that made up the northern border of Mordor were called the Ash Mountains, which in the Elvish was Ered Lithui. These mountains appear to have been totally impassable, except where they met the Shadowy Mountains – the Ephel Dúath – which formed the western and southern parts of Mordor's defences. The narrow gap where the two mountain chains met was Morannon, the Black Gate, the main point of entry into Sauron's Realm.

Atanatári

Of the race of Men, there were those who, in the First Age of the Sun, came from the East of Middle-earth, went West and North, and came to the realm of Beleriand where the Noldor and Sindar Elves lived. The Noldor named these Men the Atanatári, the 'fathers of Men', though more often this name took the Sindarin form, which is Edain.

These men learned great skills from the wise Elves who had recently come from Aman, the Land of Light, and had themselves been taught by the Powers of Arda, the Valar and the Maiar, whom Men greatly feared and worshipped as gods.

So the Atanatári were truly the fathers of their race, for though, later, other Men came from the East, where they had learned much from the Dark Elves of those lands, their lore was as nothing when compared with that learned by the Atanatári from the Calaquendi. For this reason the Atanatári were destined to become the teachers of all their people in the Ages of Sun that were to follow. Much that has been counted great and noble in all Men has its source in these ancestors.

Atani

Of all Men in the First Age of Sun the mightiest were the Atani of the Three Houses of Elf-friends, who lived in Beleriand. Even by the measure of the Eldar the deeds of these mortals during the War of the Jewels were great. Much is told in the 'Quenta Silmarillion': how Húrin killed seventy Trolls and endured the tortures of Morgoth; how Túrin slew Glaurung, Father of Dragons; how Beren cut a Silmaril from Morgoth's crown; and how Eärendil the Mariner sailed the skies in his jewelled ship. And through the Atani, Men were first ennobled by the mixture of Elven-blood, for three times in the First Age an Atani lord wed an Elf-princess: Beren wed Lúthien, Tuor wed Idril and Eärendil wed Elwing. Thus the Atani were the noblest and strongest of Men, who created powerful kingdoms, and taught much that they learned from Elves to their descendants and to the lesser Men that came after.

However, the name Atani was given to the Men of the Three Houses only for a brief time by the Noldor. Its true meaning is 'Secondborn', which is what all the race of mortals who arose in the East of Middle-earth were called. For as Elves, who came into the World at the time of the Rekindling of the Stars, were named the Firstborn, so Men, who came at the time of the Rising of the Sun, were named the Secondborn – the Atani.

In time, however, the name Atani faded altogether, for the Quenya tongue of the Noldorin Elves was not widely used in Mortal Lands. The Men of the Three Houses became the Edain in the more common Sindarin language of the Grey-elves, and it is under that name that the greater part of the tales of these Men in the lost lands of Beleriand are told.

Athelas

Among the many tales in the 'Red Book of Westmarch' is recorded a part of the Grey-elven rhyme concerning the healing herb Athelas. The meaning of the rhyme has in the passing of Ages been lost to the understanding of all but the wisest of Men, though by the time of the War of the Ring it remained a folk cure for mild ailments of the body.

In the terrible days of that war Aragorn, son of Arathorn, who was a true descendant of the kings of Númenórë from where the magical woodland herb had come, came to the kingdom of Gondor. It is told in tales that Aragorn, who had the healing hands of these kings, broke the long-leafed herb into cauldrons of steaming water and released its true power. The fragrance of orchards, the coolness of mountain snow, and the light of a shattered star poured into the dark rooms where the victims of poisoned wounds and black sorcery lay, until they stirred again with life and youth, and the long trance that had held them in sway broke before it had taken them to an evil death.

So Athelas was named Kingsfoil, the 'leaf of kings', by Men and its use by a true king of Númenórë was a sign of the end that would soon come to that greatest evil of Mordor, east of Gondor, which threatened all who inhabited Middle-earth.

Aulë

Vala called 'the Smith', but also called the Maker of Mountains, for Aulë did more than any of the Valar in the Shaping of Arda. He made the Lamps of the Valar, and forged the vessels that hold the Sun and the Moon. Aulë is the master of all crafts, and the deviser of all metals and gemstones. By the Dwarves he is known as Mahal, meaning 'the Maker', for it was he who conceived and fashioned their race from earth and stone. And it was he who taught the Noldor Elves about the making of gems and carving of stone. The mansions of Aulë are to be found in central Valinor. His spouse is Yavanna the Fruitful.

Avallónë

The port and city of the Teleri Sea Elves on the Lonely Isle of Tol Eressëa in the Bay of Eldamar. It was here during the Third Age of Stars that the Teleri first learned to build ships, and it was from this port that they sailed at last to the shore of Eldamar in the Undying Lands. During the Second Age of the Sun, it was from the lamplit quays of Avallónë that the Sea Elves most often sailed to the land of Númenor with their many gifts and blessings which so enriched the lives of the mortals of that blessed realm. It was claimed that from the highest peak of Númenor, the keen-eyed could see that city's glittering lights, and the massive white tower at its heart.

AULË Aulë is the master of all crafts, and the deviser of all metals and gemstones.

Avari

At the Time of Awakening, all Elves lived in the East of Middle-earth near Orocarni, the Mountains of the East, on the shore of Helcar, the Inland Sea. But in time the summons of the Valar came and all the Elves had to make a choice between starlight and the promise of a land of eternal light. Those who chose eternal light and set out on the Great Journey were named the Eldar, while those who remained were called the Avari, the 'unwilling'.

The Avari became a less powerful people, for their land became barbarous with Dark Powers and evil races, and so the Elves dwindled and hid themselves. They became as shadows and sprites that mortal eyes could not perceive. They lived always close to the wooded land, built no cities and had no kings. Later, in the years of Sun, the Avari were named Silvan or Wood-elves, and some of them wandered westwards and became involved in the great affairs of their Eldar kindred under whom they grew prosperous and strong for a while, before dwindling once again.

Avathar

That southern part of the continent of Aman in the Undying Lands that lay between the Pelóri Mountains and the Sea. Avathar means 'shadows', for indeed it was a dark, cold desert region. In this shadowland, Ungoliant the Great Spider lived until she was summoned by the evil Melkor and came forth and destroyed the Trees of the Valar.

Azaghâl

Dwarf king of Belegost. Through the Ages of Starlight and the First Age of the Sun, King Azaghâl's realm in the Blue Mountains of Beleriand was famous for the forging of the finest steel blades and the best Dwarf-mail armour the world had ever seen. These arms were put to the test during the terrible Battle of Unnumbered Tears, when only Azaghâl's Dwarves could withstand the blaze of Dragon fire. It was the bravery and strength of King Azaghâl alone that caused the Dragons to retreat.

For though it cost him his life, Azaghâl drove his sword deep into the belly of Glaurung, the Father of Dragons, and forced him to withdraw from the field of battle.

Azanulbizar

The once fair pass outside the gates of Khazad-dûm was called Azanulbizar. Since the destruction of the Dwarf kingdom at the hands of the Balrog, the pass, along with the kingdom (later called Moria), suffered many evils. Once beautiful and sacred, it was the source of the Silverlode River and contained Mirrormere, the lake of vision and prophecy. Towards the end of the Third Age of the Sun it was a dark and threatening place ruled by evil powers and in the year 2799 was the battleground of the final bloody conflict in the War of the Dwarves and the Orcs. Called Dimrill Dale by Men, by the time of the Fellowship of the Ring it was a wasteland buffer between Moria and the Golden Forest of Lothlórien. The Fellowship of the Ring travelled through Azanulbizar on their way to the Elf refuge in the Forest of Lothlórien.

Azog

Orc king of Moria. Azog ruled the hordes within the old Dwarf realm of Moria. He was a particularly large and obnoxious Orc, possibly one of the Uruk-hai, a breed of Orkish soldiery. He was responsible for the murder and mutilation of the Dwarf King Thrór in 2790 of the Third Age. Azog's murder of Thrór led to the bloody War of Dwarves and Orcs, and in 2799, the final struggle of the Battle of Azanulbizar, in which the Orcs were annihilated. In revenge for the mutilation of Thrór, Azog was decapitated by Dáin Ironfoot and his severed head impaled on a stake.

Bag End

Bag End was considered by Hobbits to be one of the finest hobbit-holes in the whole of Hobbiton, if not the entire Shire. Built in the twenty-eighth century of the Third Age, at the end of Bagshot Row, it was the home of three generations of Bagginses: Bungo, Bilbo and Frodo. In 3018, when embarking on the Fellowship of the Ring, Frodo sold Bag End to Lobelia and Lotho Sackville-Baggins. From September 3019, during the last months of the War of the Ring, it became the headquarters of Saruman the evil wizard during his brief reign of terror over the Shire. After Saruman's destruction, Bag End was given back to Frodo Baggins by Lobelia. When Frodo Baggins departed from the shores of Middle-earth on an Elven ship bound for the Undying Lands, Bag End became the home of Sam Gamgee, his family and his heirs.

Balar

In its beginning the Isle of Balar was a part of Tol Eressëa, the floating island that was the ship of Ulmo the Ocean Lord who used it to take the Teleri into the Undying Lands. However, in the Bay of Balar off the coast of Beleriand, the island ran aground, and that part called Balar broke off and remained. Balar was favoured by the servant of Ulmo, Ossë the Master of the Waves, and its shores were famous for their wealth of pearls. The island became a part of the domain of Círdan and the Falathrim, and during the Wars of Beleriand it became a refuge for first the Sindar, and then the Noldor under Gil-galad. At the end of the War of Wrath at the end of the First Age of the Sun, Balar, along with the rest of Beleriand, is believed to have sunk beneath the sea.

Balchoth

In the time of Cirion, the twelfth Ruling Steward of Gondor, some fierce barbarian people lived in Rhovanion on the eastern borders of the realm. They were the Balchoth and they were part of the Easterling race. The Balchoth caused great terror in the southern Vales of Anduin, for their ways were evil and their deeds were directed by the Dark Lord Sauron, who resided in Dol Guldur in Mirkwood.

The savagery of the Balchoth was legendary and their numbers were very great. In the year 2510 of the Third Age, the Balchoth barbarian tribes launched a huge fleet of boats upon the Great River and at last crossed into the realm of Gondor. They despoiled the province of Calenardhon and slaughtered its people, until they were set upon by the Men of Gondor in a mighty army led by Cirion. Yet, a black army of Orcs came from the mountains and attacked the Men of Gondor from behind. In that darkest moment aid came to the Men of Gondor: the Rohirrim sent into battle a great force of cavalry that routed both Balchoth and Orc. This was the Battle of the Field of Celebrant, at which the power of the Balchoth was broken for ever. The barbarian army was annihilated and no history tells of the fierce Balchoth after that day. They were a vanquished people and they soon disappeared completely from the lands of Middle-earth.

Balin

Dwarf of Thorin and Company. Balin was born in the Kingdom under the Mountain at Erebor in 2763. However, in 2770 Smaug the Dragon drove all his people out. In 2790, Balin followed King Thrain II into the bloody War of Dwarves and Orcs, after which he settled for a time in a Dwarf-colony in the Blue Mountains.

In 2841, Balin began an ill-fated quest with King Thrain II to return to Erebor. This journey resulted in the disappearance and eventual death of Thrain II. Balin returned to the Blue Mountains. Exactly a century later, he set out with Thorin and Company in the successful Quest of Erebor, which resulted in the slaying of Smaug the Dragon and the re-establishment of the Kingdom under the Mountain. In 2989 Balin left Erebor in an attempt to re-establish a Dwarf-kingdom in Moria. For five years Balin struggled against the Balrog and his Orkish hordes, but finally he and his followers were overwhelmed and slain.

Balrogs

The most terrible of the Maiar spirits who became the servants of Melkor, the Dark Enemy, were those who were transformed into demons. In the High Elven tongue they were named the Valaraukar, but in Middle-earth were called Balrogs, the 'demons of might'.

Of all Melkor's creatures, only Dragons were greater in power. Huge and hulking, the Balrogs were Man-like demons with streaming manes of fire and nostrils that breathed flame. They seemed to move within clouds of black shadows and their limbs had the coiling power of serpents. The chief weapon of the Balrog was the many-thonged whip of fire, and, though they also carried the mace, the axe and the flaming sword, it was the whip of fire that their enemies feared the most. This weapon was so terrible that the vast evil of Ungoliant, the Great Spider that even the Valar could not destroy, was driven from Melkor's realm by the fiery lashes of the Balrog demons.

Most infamous of the Balrog race was Gothmog, Lord of the Balrogs and High Captain of Angband. In the Wars of Beleriand three High Elven-lords fell beneath the whip and black axe of Gothmog. After the Battle under Stars, Fëanor, the most renowned of Elven-Kings, was cut down by Gothmog at the very doors of Angband. In the Battle of

BALROGS The most terrifying of all demons. Balrogs were Maiar fire spirits corrupted by Melkor the Dark Enemy. These huge demons had manes of fire and nostrils that breathed flame.

the Sudden Flame, he slew Fingon, High King of the Noldor. Finally, again in the service of Noldor, Gothmog led the Balrog host and its Troll-guard and marshalled the Orc legions and the Dragon brood, before storming and sacking the kingdom of Gondolin and killing Ecthelion, the Elf-lord. But it was here at the Fall of Gondolin, in the Square of the King, that Gothmog met his end, by the hand of Ecthelion, whom he himself had just slain.

In each of Melkor's risings and in each of his battles, the Balrogs were among his foremost champions, and so, when the holocaust of the War of Wrath ended Melkor's reign for ever, it largely ended the Balrogs as a demon race.

It was said that some fled that last battle and buried themselves deep in the roots of the mountains, but after many thousands of years nothing more was heard of these evil beings and most people believed the demons had gone from the Earth for ever. However, during the Third Age of Sun the deep-delving Dwarves of Moria by accident released an entombed demon. Once unleashed, the Balrogs struck down two Dwarf-kings, and, gathering Orcs and Trolls to aid them, drove the Dwarves from Moria for ever. As is told in the 'Red

Book of Westmarch', the Balrog's dominion remained uncontested for two centuries, until he was cast down from the peak of Zirak-zigil by the Wizard Gandalf after the Battle on the Bridge of Khazad-dûm.

Banakil

It was not until the first thousand years of the Third Age of the Sun had passed in the Vales of Anduin, east of the Mountains of the Mist, that men first became aware of the Banakil, the 'Halfling' race called the Hobbits. Smaller than Dwarves and shy of other races, they lived quietly and no history tells of their beginning before this time. Though they were of little importance to Elves and Men, the 'Red Book of Westmarch' tells how their deeds determined the wars of the mightiest that inhabited Middle-earth in the Third Age. Under the name Hobbit they became far-famed in the songs and tales that tell of the great War of the Ring, which ended the evil dominion of Sauron, the Dark Lord of Mordor.

Barad-dûr

The greatest fortress-tower on Middle-earth during the Second and Third Age of the Sun was Barad-dûr in the evil land of Mordor. Called the Dark Tower by Men and Lugbúrz by Orcs, it was built after the first millennium of the Second Age by Sauron, with the power of the One Ring. For over two thousand years of the Second Age, Barad-dûr was the centre of the Ring-Lord's evil empire, but in the year 3434 it was besieged by the combined forces of Elves and Dúnedain. After a seven-year siege, in the year 3441, the tower was captured and Sauron overthrown. For the next twenty-nine centuries of the Third Age, Barad-dûr was a massive ruin, but because it was made by the sorcerous powers, its foundations could not be destroyed while the One Ring survived. So, when Sauron at last returned to Mordor in the year 2951 of the Third Age, he was able to rebuild and restore the Dark Tower to its former power. It now appeared invincible. However, Sauron had not counted on the discovery of the Ring. In the year 3019, the One Ring was destroyed in the fires of Mount Doom, and the very foundations of Barad-dûr cracked and collapsed. With the One Ring unmade Sauron's powers were utterly destroyed and the tower of Barad-dûr fell into a pile of rubble.

Bard the Bowman

Man of Dale and Dragon Slayer. Born and raised among the Lake Men of Esgaroth, Bard was an exile of Dale, which had been destroyed by Smaug, the Golden Dragon. He was a strong and grim-faced Man who claimed descent from a famous archer called Girion of Dale. In 2941 of the Third Age, while the city fathers fled for their lives, Bard used his archer's skills to strike the mighty Smaug beneath his armour in his one vulnerable spot. He then led the army of Men to victory in the Battle of Five Armies. After that battle, Bard used a part of the Dragon's golden hoard to rebuild both Esgaroth and Dale. He became the first in a long line of kings of Dale. He died in the year 2977 and was succeeded by his son, King Bain.

Bardings

Among the strong Northmen who lived between Mirkwood and the Iron Hills, there were those who, in the last century of the Third Age of the Sun, were called the Bardings. Previously these people had been known as the Men of Dale and had inhabited the wealthy city of Dale below the Lonely Mountain. But, when the Dragon Smaug came to the Lonely Mountains, Dale was sacked and the people fled. The Lake Men of Esgaroth gave them sanctuary for almost two centuries. In that time, among these exiles of Dale rose the heir to the king who was called Bard the Bowman. He was a great warrior and a grim and strong man. When the Dragon of the Lonely Mountain attacked again, it was Bard who shot the beast through the breast with a black arrow and freed the land.

So Bard became the ruler of his people and, with a portion of the wealth of the Dragon's hoard, he rebuilt Dale and once again made a rich kingdom around it. Thus, in honour of this hero, all the people of Dale from that time bore his name.

Barrow Downs

The downlands east of the Shire and the Old Forest were called the Barrow Downs because of the great barrow graves built there. Considered by many during the Third Age to be the most ancient burial ground of Men on Middle-earth, they were revered by the Dúnedain of Arnor. There were no trees or water on the downlands, only grass covering dome-shaped hills that were ringed and crowned with stone monoliths. During the wars with the Witch-king of Angmar, the last of the Dúnedain of Cardolan found refuge for a time among the barrows. However, by 1636 the barrows became haunted by evil spirits called Barrow-wights, demons sent out from the Witch-king's realm of Angmar to do what evil they could. These undead spirits made the Barrow Downs a dread and fearful place. Into such a haunted land, in the year 3018 of the Third Age, came the Ringbearer, Frodo Baggins. But for the intervention of the strange forest spirit Tom Bombadil, the Hobbit adventurer would certainly have lost his life to the evil beings of the Barrow-downs, and the Quest of the Ring would have come to an early end.

Barrow-wights

West of the Brandywine River beyond the Old Forest were the Barrow-downs, the most ancient burial ground of Men in Middle-earth. There were no trees or water there, but only grass and turf covering dome-shaped hills that were crowned with monoliths and great rings of bone-white stone. These hills were the burial mounds that were made in the First Age of Sun for the Kings of Men. For many Ages the Barrow-downs were sacred and revered, until out of the Witch-kingdom of Angmar many terrible and tortured spirits fled across Middle-earth, desperately seeking to hide from the ravening light of the Sun. Demons whose bodies had been destroyed looked for other bodies in which their evil spirits could dwell. And so it was that the Barrow-wights, the Undead, who animated the bones and jewelled armour of the ancient Kings of Men who had lived in this land in the First Age of the Sun.

The Barrow-wights were of a substance of darkness that could enter the eye, heart and mind, or crush the will. They were form-shifters and could move from shape to shape and animate whatever life-form they wished. Most often a Barrow-wight came on the unwary traveller in the guise of a dark phantom whose eyes were luminous and cold. The voice of the figure was at once horrible and hypnotic; its skeletal hand had a touch like ice and a grip like the iron jaws of a trap. Once under the spell of the Undead the victim had no will of his own. In this way the Barrow-wight drew the living into the treasure tombs on the downs. A dismal choir of tortured souls could be heard inside the Barrow as, in the green half-light, the Barrow-wight laid his victim on a stone altar and bound him with chains of gold. He draped him in the pale cloth and precious jewellery of the ancient dead, and then ended his life with a sacrificial sword.

In the darkness these were powerful spirits; they could be held at bay only with the spell of strong incantations. They could be destroyed only by exposure to light, and it was light that they hated and feared most. The Barrow-wights were lost and tortured spirits and their last chance to remain on Earth depended on dark security of the burial vaults. Once a stone chamber was broken open, light would pour in on the Barrow-wights and they would fade like mist before the sun and be gone for ever.

Bats

Of the many creatures that Melkor the Dark Enemy bred in darkness, the blood-sucking Bat was one. No story tells whether they were made from bird or beast but they were always known to be servants of evil. The lusts and habits of the Bat were well suited to evil purposes and tales tell how even the mightiest of Melkor's servants used the Bat shape in times of need. Such was the form of Thuringwethil the Vampire, 'woman of secret shadow', and Sauron himself changed into a great wide-winged Bat when he fled after the Fall of Tol-in-Gaurhoth. The story of the Hobbit also tells how, at the Battle of Five Armies in the Third Age of the Sun, black storm clouds of Bats advanced in open war, with legions of Orcs and Wolves, to battle against Men, Elves and Dwarves.

Belain

Within Arda since its beginning there was a race of guardians who were known as the Valar in the High Elven tongue. The Grey-elves of Beleriand knew them as the Belain, which means the 'powers'.

Belegaer

The vast western sea which separated Middle-earth from the Undying Lands was called Belegaer, Elvish for the 'Great Sea'. The domain of the Vala Ulmo the Ocean Lord, and the Maia Ossë of the Waves and Uinen of the Calms, Belegaer extended from Helcaraxë in the north (the 'grinding ice' bridge that once joined the two continents) to the limits of Arda in the south, with Númenor in the centre.

Belegost

One of the two great Dwarf kingdoms built in the Blue Mountains of Beleriand during the Second Age of Starlight, Belegost is Elvish for 'mighty fortress'. In Khuzdul, the language of the Dwarves, it was called Gabilgathol,

BARROW-WIGHTS Undead evil spirits who haunted the Barrow-downs. They animated corpses of long-dead men, or bewitched unlucky travellers into entering tombs on the downs, where they were slain.

or Mickleburg. The Dwarves of Belegost were the first to enter Beleriand, and they were among the finest smiths and stone-carvers of Middle-earth. They were the first Dwarves to forge chain-mail. They traded their incomparable steel weapons with the Sindar and, commissioned by the Grey Elf King Thingol, they carved that most beautiful of realms, the Thousand Caves of Menegroth. In the War of the Jewels, the Dwarves of Belegost won great fame. They alone in the Battle of Unnumbered Tears could withstand the blaze of Dragon-fire because they were a race of smiths used to heat and on their helms they wore flame-proof masks of steel that protected their faces. Though the king of Belegost, Lord Azaghâl, was slain in this battle, he wounded Glaurung and forced the Father of Dragons and all his Dragon brood to flee the battleground. Yet, valiant and steadfast as the Dwarves of Belegost were, when the War of Wrath was ended, their kingdom, along with all of Beleriand, was overwhelmed and swallowed up by the sea. Those few who managed to survive fled eastward and found refuge in the mansions of Khazad-dûm.

BELEGAR The domain of the Vala Ulmo the Ocean Lord, and the Maia Ossë of the Waves and Uinen of the Calms.

Beleriand

Until its sinking at the beginning of the Second Age of the Sun, Beleriand was to be found west of the Blue Mountains in the extreme northwest part of Middle-earth. All the Eldar passed through Beleriand during the Great Journey, but the Teleri lingered there the longest while they awaited Ulmo the Ocean Lord to take them to the Undying Lands. Indeed, not all of the Teleri departed. The Sindar or Grey Elves of Doriath and the Falas remained behind and through all the Ages of Starlight built wonderful kingdoms there. Also out of the East came another remnant people of the Teleri, the Laiquendi Elves, who settled in the riverlands of Ossiriand just east of the Blue Mountains. Later still, during the First Age of the Sun, the Noldor Elves who returned from the Undying Lands built the kingdoms of Nargothrond, Himlad, Thargelion, Dorthonion, Gondolin, Mithrim Dor-lómin, Nevrast and East Beleriand. Besides the Elven people there were the two Dwarf realms of Nogrod and Belegost, several wandering tribes of Men, and finally the invading forces of Orcs, Balrogs, Dragons and other monsters from out of Morgoth's evil kingdom of Angband. It was these terrible invasions of Morgoth that eventually brought to ruin every one of the Elven Kingdoms during the War of the Jewels. This resulted in the War of Wrath, wherein the Valar themselves came to destroy Melkor, but in so doing all of Beleriand was broken apart and swallowed up by the western sea.

Beorn

Northman, Beorning chieftain. Beorn's people inhabited the northern Anduin valley between the Misty Mountains and Mirkwood during the last centuries of the Third Age. He and his woodsmen guarded the Ford of Carrock and the High Pass from Orcs and Wargs. Beorn was a huge, black-bearded Man who wore a coarse wool tunic and was armed with a woodsman's axe. He was a berserker warrior who had the gift of the 'skin changer': that is, transforming into the form of a bear. In the year 2941, Beorn gave shelter and protection to Thorin and Company, and later fought with them in the Battle of Five Armies. In that battle Beorn took on his bear shape and slew scores of Orcs.

Beornings

In the Third Age of the Sun there was a race of solitary Northmen who guarded the Ford of Carrock and the High Passes in Rhovanion from the Orcs and Wargs. These people were the Beornings, and they were black-haired, black-bearded Men clothed in coarse wool garments. They carried the woodsman's axe and were gruff, huge-muscled but honourable. They were named after a fierce warrior called Beorn, who was a mighty man and a skin-changer. By some spell he could shift form and become a great bear. In terror of this bear-man the Orcs and Wargs of the Misty Mountains kept from his road.

Where Beorn learned the trick of form-shifting is not known, but he was a distant blood relation of the Edain of the First Age, and the 'Quenta Silmarillion' relates how some of that race were skin-changers. Greatest of them was Beren, who, like Beorn, lived long alone in the forest and ate no flesh. As with Beorn, the beasts and birds came to Beren and aided him in his war with the Orcs and Wolves. In the Quest of the Silmaril it is told how Beren learned from the Eldar the art of form-shifting: presenting himself first in the shape of an Orc, and then as a great Wolf. So perhaps some of that magic was inherited by Beorn and his people, or perhaps it was as a result of living with bears for so long that Beorn learned this skill. Whatever the source, it is said that this trick of skin-changing was passed on to the heirs of Beorn through many generations. In the War of the Ring the Beornings led by Grimbeorn, son of Beorn, advanced fiercely with the Woodmen and Elves of Mirkwood, and drove evil from that place for ever. Because of the terrible strength and the berserk rage of the Beornings in battle, the legend of the bear-skin warriors lived long in the memory of Men.

Beren

Edain lord of Dorthonion. Beren was the son of Barahir, lord of the Edain. Born in the fourth century of the First Age, Beren was the sole survivor of the outlaws of Dorthonion, and the only person ever to cross the Mountains of Terror and pass through the vile realm of the Giant Spiders. Entering Doriath, Beren met and fell in love with Princess Lúthien, the daughter of King Thingol and Melian the Maia. Thingol forbade the marriage unless Beren brought him one of the Silmarils. Undaunted, Beren embarked on the Quest of the Silmaril. Captured and nearly slain by Sauron on the Isle of Werewolves, Beren was saved by Lúthien and Huan the Hound. Thereafter, Lúthien and Beren entered into Angbad, where Lúthien cast a spell of enchantment on Morgoth, and Beren cut a Silmaril jewel from his crown. But as they fled, the Wolf of Angband bit off Beren's hand, and swallowed both the hand and the Silmaril it held. Beren and Lúthien escaped to Doriath, but Huan the Hound of the Valar hunted down and slew the Wolf. Recovering the jewel, Beren survived just long enough to put the Silmaril into Thingol's hand. With the death of Beren Lúthien soon wasted away and died of grief, but she persuaded Mandos, the Lord of the Dead, to give both herself and Beren a second mortal life on Middle-earth. This was granted and they returned to live quietly in Ossiriand until the beginning of the fifth century. Only once did Beren venture away, and that was to avenge the death of Thingol and recover the Silmaril.

Bifur

Dwarf of Thorin and Company. Bifur went on the Quest of Erebor which, in 2941 of the Third Age, resulted in the death of Smaug the Dragon and the re-establishment of the Dwarf Kingdom under the Mountain. He survived the Battle of Five Armies; thereafter, he settled in the kingdom at Erebor.

Big Folk

To the small, shy race of the Hobbit, the ways of other races (except Elves) are thought to be coarse, loud and without subtlety. And though the affairs of other races might often threaten Hobbit lives, they seem little interested in the great nations of Men, and so Men of whatever origin are simply known to the Hobbits as the Big Folk.

Bilbo Baggins

Hobbit of the Shire. Born in the year 2890 of the Third Age, Bilbo was a bachelor Hobbit who lived in Bag End in the Shire. In 2941, Bilbo was lured away by a Wizard and thirteen Dwarves on the famous quest of Thorin and Company that, in 2941, led to the slaying of Smaug the Dragon and the re-establishment of the Dwarf Kingdom under the Mountain at Erebor. With a modest portion of the Dragon gold he won on his adventure, Bilbo returned to the Shire for some sixty years. On his adventure, Bilbo acquired a mysterious ring which had the power to make its wearer invisible. However, it was later discovered that this was, in fact, the One Ring that belonged to the Lord of the Rings. In the year 3001, Bilbo held a huge birthday party, then vanished before the eyes of the assembled host, leaving wealth, home and the One Ring to his young cousin and adopted heir, Frodo Baggins. Bilbo then went on to live a rather monkish life in Rivendell and for twenty years wrote poems, stories and Elf-lore, as well as his memoirs, entitled *There and Back Again* and his three-volume scholarly work, *Translations from the Elvish*. After the War of the Ring, at the age of 131 years, Bilbo sailed into the west with Frodo to the Undying Lands.

Black Númenóreans

In the 'Akallabêth' is told the story of the land of the Númenóreans, which flourished as the mightiest kingdom of Men upon Arda during the second Age of the Sun. But in the year 3319 of the Second Age it was cast down beneath Belegaer, the Western Sea, in other parts for ever. Most of the Númenóreans perished, but some had left Middle-earth before the Downfall and so survived.

One part of those who were saved from disaster was named the Black Númenóreans. These people made a great haven in a place named Umbar, which lay on the coastlands in the South of Middle-earth. The Black Númenóreans were a great sea power and for many centuries they raided and pillaged the coastlands of Middle-earth. They were allies of Sauron, for he came among them and corrupted them through their overweening pride and gave them many gifts. To three of the Black Númenóreans he gave Rings of Power, and these three were numbered among the wraiths who were called the Nazgûl. To two others, who were named Herumor and Fuinur, he gave other powers and they became lords among the Haradrim.

The Black Númenóreans often came north into the lands of Gondor and Arnor to test their strength against that other noble remnant of the Númenórean race, the Elendili, or Elf-friends. For as allies of Sauron the Black Númenóreans opposed all things Elvish and, above all, they hated these Men who they believed had betrayed Númenor and its king. The Black Númenóreans proved to be immensely strong and for more than a thousand years their pillaging was endured. But at last, in the tenth century of the Third Age, King Eärnil I arose in Gondor and reduced the sea power of the Black Númenóreans of Umbar to nothing and took the havens. Umbar became a fortress of Gondor, and, though in the years that followed the Black Númenóreans rose again, they were finally broken by Hyarmendacil of Gondor in the year 1050

BILBO BAGGINS Hobbit hero of the Quest of the Lonely Mountain which led to the slaying of Smaug the Dragon. Bilbo was the first Hobbit to possess the One Ring. He wrote many poems, stories and memoirs.

and never again were they rulers of Umbar. Thereafter, the wandering people of this strong race merged with the Haradrim and the Corsairs, and others lived in Morgul and Mordor. As is told in the 'Red Book of Westmarch', one became the spokesman of the Dark Lord and was named the Mouth of Sauron. But the end of the Third Age was also the end of the Black Númenóreans, for the gifts of power that Sauron gave them vanished with his fall, and the annals of the Fourth Age speak of these people no more.

Black Riders

In the centuries that followed the forging of the Rings of Power by the Elven-smiths and Sauron the Maia, nine Black Riders on swift black Horses appeared in Middle-earth. Few knew what manner of beings the Black Riders were, but the wise learned that they had once been Men, who by the power of the Rings had been turned to deathless wraiths. These Black

Riders were the mightiest of the Ring Lord Sauron's servants; in the Black Speech of the Orcs their name was Nazgûl.

Blue Mountains

The great mountain chain that marked the eastern border of the Elf lands of Beleriand was the Ered Luin, the Blue Mountains. These were the home of the twin Dwarf kingdoms of Belegost and Nogrod. However, after the end of the First Age of the Sun, when the Elf and Dwarf kingdoms of Beleriand were destroyed, all but a small part of the Blue Mountains sank into the sea. Even that part of the Blue Mountains that remained above the sea was cleft in two by the Gulf of Lune. Here the master of the Falathrim Elves of Beleriand, Lord Círdan, built the Grey Havens, the last harbour of the Eldar upon Middle-earth. And on that small remaining piece of Beleriand west of the Blue Mountains, called Lindon, was the kingdom of Gil-galad, the last High-King of the Eldar on Middle-earth. Right through the Third Age, Lindon survived as an Elf land and the Blue Mountains remained a homeland and refuge for several kingdoms of the Dwarvish peoples.

Boars

The hunting of Boars was a sport among Elves and the Men of Arda. Even Oromë the Valarian huntsman, who was Lord of the forest, would chase these tusked beasts of the woodlands with hounds and Horse.

Most famous of the tales of the hunted Boar is the one record in the 'Annals of the Kings and Rulers', which tells how a king of Rohan died on a wild Boar's tusks. Folca of the Rohirrim was a mighty warrior and hunter, and thirteenth in the line of kings, but the beast named the Boar of Everholt that he pursued was fierce and huge. So, when the contest was joined in the Firien Wood beneath the shadow of the White Mountains, there was loud battle in which both hunter and hunted were slain.

Bofur

Dwarf of Thorin and Company. Bofur was one of the company which, in the year 2941 of the Third Age, embarked on the Quest of the Lonely Mountain. The quest eventually resulted in the death of Smaug the Dragon and the re-establishment of the Dwarf Kingdom under the Mountain. After Thorin's death, Bofur, with others of the company, swore allegiance to Dáin Ironfoot, and remained contentedly at Erebor for the rest of their lives.

Bolg

Orc king of Misty Mountains. Bolg of the North was the son of Azog, the Orc King who was slain by Dáin Ironfoot in the Battle of Azanulbizar at the end of the War of Orcs and Dwarves. Like his father, Bolg was a particularly large and powerful Orc, and therefore was probably one of that race of super-Orcs called the Uruk-hai. Bolg led a vast army of Orcs and Wargs into the Battle of Five Armies in the year 2941. It was during that battle that he was slain by Beorn, the Beornings' chieftain.

Bombur

Dwarf of Thorin and Company. In 2941 of the Third Age of the Sun, Bombur went on the Quest of the Lonely Mountain which resulted in the slaying of Smaug the Dragon and the re-establishment of the Dwarf Kingdom under the Mountain at Erebor. Bombur, like his companions Bifur and Bofur, was a Dwarf of Moria, but was not descended from Durin's race. Even during his prime, Bombur had always been a very fat Dwarf; however, later in life he became so enormously stout that he could not even walk, and it took six other Dwarves to carry him about. After the quest, Bombur remained at Erebor for the rest of his life.

Boromir

Dúnedain lord of Gondor. Eldest son of Denethor II, Ruling Steward of Gondor. Born in the year 2978 of the Third Age, Boromir was the tall and handsome heir to the Steward. In 3018, he valiantly led the defence of Osgiliath against Sauron's forces. After a prophetic dream that he shared with his brother, Faramir, he made his way to the Elf-kingdom of Rivendell and became a member of the Fellowship of the Ring. Enduring the many perils of the Fellowship's journey as far as the Hill of the Eye, near Rauros Falls, he was overcome by the desire to seize the One Ring, and tried to kill Frodo Baggins the Ring-bearer. Although Boromir soon repented, Frodo continued the Quest only with Samwise Gamgee as a companion. Shortly after, Boromir died in battle while gallantly defending the Hobbits Meriadoc Brandybuck and Peregrin Took from an Orc attack. Boromir was given a formal ship-burial over the Rauros Falls.

BLACK RIDERS The mightiest of the Ring Lord Sauron's servants; in the Black Speech of the Orcs their name was Nazgûl.

Brambles of Mordor

In the Black Land of Mordor was Gorgoroth, where the furnace and forge of the Ring Lord Sauron were housed. It was boasted that nothing grew upon that poisoned land, but as the 'Red Book of Westmarch' tells, some life did in fact dare to come forth from the harsh ground. In sheltered places twisted tree-forms and stunted grey grasses haltingly grew and though the leaves were shrivelled with sulphur vapour and maggot hatchings, nowhere on Middle-earth did brambles grow so large and fierce. The Brambles of Mordor were hideous with foot-long thorns, as barbed and sharp as the daggers of Orcs, and they sprawled over the land like coils of steel wire. They were truly the flowers of the land of Mordor.

Brandywine River

In the Third Age of the Sun, the Brandywine was one of the three great rivers of Eriador. It flowed from the hills and lake of Evendim that was once the heart of the lost kingdom of Arnor, southwestward past the Shire and the Old Forest through to the sea at the southern end of the Blue Mountains. It appears to have had only two crossings along its length: the Sarn Ford to the south of the Shire and the Bridge of Stonebows to the east of the Shire, just north of the Old Forest and on the Great East Road. In Elvish, the river is called Baranduin which means 'gold-brown river', in reference to its colour. The name Brandywine is a translation of the original Hobbitish name Branda-nîn, meaning 'border-water', as it marked the eastern border of the Shire. In time this name was corrupted to Bralda-hîm meaning 'heady ale', and thus the translated form, Brandywine.

Bree

Reputedly founded during the Second Age of the Sun by Men from Dunland, Bree was the main village of Breeland (the others being Combe, Archet and Staddle). It was to be found at the crossing of the Great East Road and the North Road, which was to the east of the Shire and in the heartland of what was once the kingdom of Arnor, and was home to around one hundred Hobbits and Men. By the time of the War of the Ring, Bree was much diminished in size and importance from the great days of Arnor. However, considering the scale of destruction of Arnor at the hands of the Witch-king of Angmar, it is surprising that Bree survived at all. This survival was no doubt due in part to the protection of the Rangers of the North, and in part to its naturally strategic position at the crossing of the two main trading route roads. To many who travelled these roads, Bree was most famous for the Prancing Pony Inn, the region's most ancient inn and the most likely place to catch up on all the news and gossip from places both near and far.

Brethil

In the lost land of Beleriand, there were once wide forests of birch trees. In the Sindarin language of the Grey-elves, the trees of these lands were called 'Brethil' and their beauty was much admired by those Elves.

C

Cair Andros

Fortified by Túrin II, the twenty-third ruling steward of Gondor, during the thirtieth century of the Third Age, Cair Andros was an island on the Anduin River just north of the White Tower that guarded entry into the lands of Gondor and Rohan. It was a spectacular island and fortress, shaped like a huge ship with a high prow heading upstream. The flow of the river breaking fiercely against this 'prow' explains the name, which means 'ship-long-foam'. During the War of the Ring, Cair Andros was fiercely defended by the Men of Gondor, but finally fell to the forces of Mordor. However, after the decisive Battle of Pelennor Fields and the retreat of Sauron's army, Cair Andros was retaken by Gondor.

Calacirya

Literally meaning 'light cleft' in the High Elven tongue, Calacirya was also called the Pass of Light for it was the only pass through the great Pelóri Mountains in the Undying Lands, and in the Ages of the Trees of Valar the blessed light of these trees flowed through this gap. The hill of Túna was set in the midst of this pass, upon which was built Tirion, the chief city of the High Elves of Eldamar.

Calaquendi

The 'Quenta Silmarillion' tells how those Elves who arose in Middle-earth came to the Undying Lands in the time of the Trees of the Valar. These pilgrim people were called the Calaquendi or Light Elves. For many Ages they lived in the Eternal Light of the Two Trees, and they were ennobled by that Light, strengthened in body, and filled with great knowledge by the teaching of the Valar and of the Maiar.

To compare the Calaquendi with the lesser Elves of Middle-earth was to compare diamonds with coal. The spirits of the Calaquendi were bright as the blades of their swords, and their souls strong and fierce as the naked flames that seemed to shine from their eyes. Before them, all but the mightiest of Melkor's servants stood in awe.

Caras Galadhon

Chief city of the hidden Elven kingdom of Lothlórien was Caras Galadhon, 'city of trees'. It was literally a city of elaborate tree-houses, or 'telain', built in a huge walled grove of giant silver-limbed mallorn trees in the heart of Lothlórien, and the highest ranking Elves remaining on Middle-earth during the Third Age. After the War of the Ring, when Galadriel left Middle-earth and Celeborn moved to East Lórien, Caras Galadhon was deserted by the Elves and the spell that magically protected it and all Lothlórien was no more.

Carcharoth

Wolf of Angband. Carcharoth, meaning 'the Red Maw', was the greatest Wolf of all time. Guardian of the gates of Angband who never slept, he was reared on living flesh by Morgoth during the First Age of the Sun. During the Quest of the Silmaril, Carcharoth bit off Beren's hand and swallowed both the hand and the Silmaril in it. The Elf-gem filled the beast with such a terrible fire that he ran amok, slaying everyone in his path. Horrifically, the burning jewel made his powers even greater than before. But finally, he met his equal: Huan, the Wolfhound of the Valar. In the battle that followed, Carcharoth mortally wounded Huan with his venomous fangs, but in the end he was himself slain, and the Silmaril cut out of his belly.

Celeborn

Elven king of Lothlórien. Celeborn was a Sindar prince of Doriath and kinsman of King Thingol. During the First Age of the Sun he wed the Noldor princess, Galadriel, who gave birth to their only child, Celebrian. When Beleriand was destroyed, Celeborn and Galadriel fled to Lindon until the eighth century of the Second Age, when they settled in the kingdom of the Elven-smiths of Eregion. Later, Celeborn and Galadriel founded Lothlórien in the Golden Wood on the Silverlode River. During the War of the Ring, Celeborn defended Lothlórien from three attempted invasions, then led his Elven army into Mirkwood and destroyed Sauron's stronghold of Dol Guldur. At the end of the Third Age, Galadriel sailed to the Undying Lands, but Celeborn remained behind. With Galadriel gone, Celeborn and his Silvan Elves left Lothlórien and founded East Lórien in the south of what was Mirkwood. Celeborn ruled East Lórien for some time but finally retired to Rivendell. Some time after, he is believed to have sailed to the Undying Lands.

Celebrant

Called the Silverlode in the Mannish tongue, and Kibil-nâla by the Dwarves, the Celebrant is the Elvish name, meaning 'silver course', for the river which flowed from the White Mountains through the pass of Azanulbizar, through the golden wood of Lothlórien and on into the Great River Anduin. During the Third Age of the Sun, the Fellowship of the Ring followed its course from the gates of Moria to the golden wood of Lothlórien.

Celebrían

Elven princess of Lothlórien. Celebrían was the only daughter of King Celeborn and Queen Galadriel. At the end of the first century of the Third Age of the Sun, Celebrían married Elrond Half-Elven of Rivendell. They had three children: Elladan, Elrohir and Arwen. In the year 2509 of the Third Age, while Celebrían was travelling from Rivendell to Lothlórien, her entourage was attacked by an evil band of Orcs. Although Celebrían was rescued by her brave sons, she sustained a poison wound which would not heal. She suffered her painful affliction for a year, but finally sailed to the Undying Lands where the Valar would cure her.

Celebrimbor

Elven king of Eregion. Born during the Ages of Starlight, Celebrimbor was a Noldor prince, the son of Curufin, and the grandson of Fëanor, who created the Silmarils. He fought in the War of the Jewels and the War of Wrath. In 750 of the Second Age, he founded the realm of the Gwaith-i-Mírdain, 'the Elven-smiths'. From the Dwarves he obtained mithril, and many other precious metals, and forged the finest weapons and jewellery of the age. But, like Fëanor, Celebrimbor always sought to create something better and greater than any before him. It was his Elven-smiths who forged the Ring of Power. This was his downfall, for he did not know that the fair stranger, called Annatar, who aided in the forging of the Rings, was none other than Sauron, the Dark Lord. When Sauron forged the One Ring, Celebrimbor immediately realized his tragic mistake. The disastrous War of the Elves and Sauron followed, from 1693 to 1701, in which Eregion was destroyed, and Celebrimbor slain.

Cerin Amroth

In the Elven kingdom of Lothlórien there was a hill where the Elf King Amroth built his house during the Second Age of the Sun. Songs of the Elves tell how in sorrow for his lost love, the Elf maiden Nimrodel, Amroth threw himself from an Elven ship and drowned in the sea. By the end of the Third Age his house on the hill had long vanished, but it was considered an enchanted place full of the beauty and sorrow of star-crossed love. Covered with Elanor and

Niphredil flowers, it was here that Aragorn and Arwen were betrothed, and here that, after the death of her husband, Arwen herself came to die.

Círdan

Elven lord of Grey Havens. In the Ages of Starlight, Círdan became Lord of the Falathrim. Círdan means 'ship-maker', and his people were the first on Middle-earth to build ships. The harbours of Círdan survived through the Wars of Beleriand until 474, when Morgoth's Orc legions overran the Falas. However, Círdan withdrew to the Isle of Balar with his people. After the sinking of Beleriand, Círdan became the Lord of the Grey Havens. Considered one of the wisest of the Elves, he was given Narya, the Elf 'ring of fire' by Celebrimbor. At the end of the Second Age, Círdan joined the Last Alliance of Elves and Men, which resulted in the downfall of Sauron. Around the year 1000, he gave his ring to Gandalf the Wizard. In 1975 Círdan led a force of Elves and Men into the Battle of Fornost, and defeated the Witch-king of Angmar. At the end of the Third Age the Keepers of the Rings left Círdan's havens. Círdan himself remained there long into the Fourth Age, until the last Elves departed.

Cirith Gorgor

The Black Gate and the Towers of the Teeth were the mighty barriers built across the 'haunted pass' called Cirith Gorgor, which was the main entrance into Sauron's evil realm of Mordor. This was the largest pass into Mordor and the one most powerfully defended by Sauron during the Second and Third Ages. In both ages these massive

CELEBRIMBOR Celebrimbor was a Noldor prince, the son of Curufin, and the grandson of Fëanor, who created the Silmarils.

defences were eventually thrown down and the pass opened.

Cirith Ungol

In the Mountains of Shadow that form the western wall and border of Mordor there was one little-used and narrow pass called Cirith Ungol, the 'pass of the spider'. This secret pass was used by the Witch-king of the Nazgûl in the year 2000 of the Third Age when his forces poured out of Mordor and besieged Minas Ithil. In 2002, Minas Ithil fell and was renamed Minas Morgul, the 'tower of the wraiths'. For the next thousand years the pass was closed, for this was where the giant evil Spider called Shelob made her lair. Any who attempted to travel here were devoured by this monster. It was thought by Sauron that none might now enter his realm through this pass, but in the year 3019 the Hobbits Frodo Baggins and Samwise Gamgee, accompanied by Sméagol Gollum, overcame Shelob. They then defeated the powers of the triple-headed, evil-spirited guardian statues called the Watchers, and survived the ordeals of the Orc Tower at the crest of the pass. This was the last obstacle of Cirith Ungol, and the Hobbits at last made their way into the infernal land of Mordor.

Cold-Drakes

Of the Dragons that Morgoth brought forth from Angband during the First Age of the Sun, there were many breeds. Some were breathers of fire, others had mighty wings, but the most common were the Cold-drakes, who had no power of fire or flight but had great strength of tooth and claw and a mighty armour of iron scales. The Cold-drakes were a terror to all races who opposed them in that First Age, and they wrought untold destruction on the lands of Middle-earth. At the end of the Age nearly all the Dragon race and most of Morgoth's servants perished during the Great Battle in the War of Wrath.

In the Third Age of the Sun, the histories of the Westlands tell how many Cold-drakes arose once again in the wastelands of the North and went to the Grey Mountains. Dwarves had come to these mountains for they were rich in gold, and in the twentieth century of this Age the Cold-drakes followed, seeking the Dwarf-hoards and prepared for war, and though the Dwarves battled bravely, they were outmatched and the Cold-drakes wantonly stalked and slaughtered their foes. A prince of the Men of Éothéod – one named Fram, son of Frumgar – came and slew Scatha the Worm, the greatest Dragon of that land, and the Grey Mountains were cleared of Dragons for five centuries. Yet the Cold-drakes came again to the mountains in the year 2570. One by one the Dwarf-lords fell to them: the last was the Dwarf-king named Dáin I of Durin's Line, and he and his son Frór were slain by a great Cold-drake within their very halls. So the last of the Dwarves fled from the Grey Mountains, leaving reluctantly all their gold as the Dragon's prize.

Corsairs

In the Third Age of the Sun the dreaded Corsairs of Umbar tyrannized the coastlands of Middle-earth for many centuries. The sight of their black-sailed dromonds always filled the peoples of Middle-earth with fear, for they held many warriors and were driven by the power of slaves pulling many oars.

The Númenóreans were the founders of Umbar in the Second Age of the Sun, but in time they succumbed to evil and, after the Downfall of their land into the Western Sea, some remained in Umbar and were named the Black Númenóreans. They were an evil sea power. Yet in time the kings of Gondor

CORSAIRS Pirates of the southern land of Umbar. Their strong kings, Black Númenóreans, fell under the evil power of Sauron and made constant war on Gondor. Corsair ships had both oars and distinctive black sails.

came against them, and in 1050 of the Third Age, the power of the Black Númenóreans was broken for ever and Umbar became a fortress in Gondor's realm.

But there was always strife with the Haradrim, who often attacked Umbar, and also there was rebellion within Gondor itself, until finally the rebels of Gondor, the Haradrim and those few of the scattered Black Númenóreans who remained, conquered Umbar with many great ships and restored its power. So it was, from the fifteenth century until the War of the Ring, that these people were named the Corsairs of Umbar and were always counted among the chief enemies of the Dúnedain of Gondor and Arnor.

The 'Red Book of Westmarch' tells how in the last century of the Third Age, the Dúnedain chieftain 'Aragorn', son of Arathorn, proved to be the chief architect of the downfall of the Corsairs. For this fierce warrior led the Dúnedain of Gondor into the havens of Umbar. There he slew their captain and set a torch to their fleet. In the year of the War of the Ring itself, Aragorn brought a phantom army out of Dunharrow to the Corsairs' black ships at Pelargir. And with these Dead Men of Dunharrow, Aragorn once again routed the Corsairs in what was their final defeat, for the chieftain took all their ships from them.

With this action he both broke the power of the Corsairs and turned the tide of the War of the Ring. Aragorn used the black ships of the Corsairs to bring the allies of the Dúnedain victoriously into the Battle of Pelennor Fields.

Crébain

Tales tell of a breed of large black Crows that lived in Dunland and the Forest of Fangorn in the Third Age of the Sun. These birds were named Crébain in the language of the Grey-elves, and they were servants and spies of evil powers. During the War of the Ring they searched far and wide over the lands of Middle-earth for the bearer of the Ruling Ring.

Crows

Crows were always the chief carrion birds of Middle-earth and they carried a reputation of being allied with Dark Powers. Men called them birds of ill-omen, for it was thought they spied over the land and brought tales to evil beings, who plotted deeds of ambush and slaughter. So it was that these carrion birds profited by bearing tales, for on the bloody work of these evil armies of Orcs the Crows often feasted.

As was common among birds of Middle-earth, the Crows spoke a dialect of bird-tongue, although it was the opinion of Dwarves, who knew the language, that their discourse was as ill-disposed as that of the evil race of Orcs.

Culumalda

In the wooded province of North Ithilien, in the realm of Gondor, was the Isle of Cair Andros, which, like an anchored ship, rested in the River Anduin. On this island grew the fairest of the trees of Ithilien. They were called Culumalda, which was 'golden red', for such was the hue of their foliage. To Elven people their beauty was as a faint memory of Laurelin, that great Tree of the Valar in the Undying Lands, which was brilliant beyond imagining and which also bore the name Culúrien meaning both 'gold' and 'red'.

D

Dagorlad

During the Second and Third Ages of the Sun, just to the north of the Black Gate through the Mountains of Mordor and south of the evil swampland of the Dead Marshes, there was a wide, treeless plain called the Dagorlad, which in Elvish means 'battle-plain'. In the year 3434 of the Second Age, this was the site of a mighty battle (called the Battle of Dagorlad) in which the Last Alliance of Elves and Men overthrew Sauron's army before going on to destroy the Black Gate and the Dark Tower of Mordor itself. During the Third Age the Dagorlad was the scene of many battles between the armies of Gondor and invading Easterlings. Especially notable were the battles with the Easterlings called the Wainriders in 1899 and 1944. During the War of the Ring, Sauron chose not to do battle there, allowing the Captains of the West to approach the gates of Mordor before turning his vast army loose in the vain hope of driving them back onto the Dagorlad and slaughtering them there.

Dáin I

Dwarf king of Grey Mountains. Dáin I was born in the year 2440 of the Third Age of the Sun, and became king of the Grey Mountains in the year 2585. Shortly after, Dragons invaded the gold-rich Dwarf-realm and Dáin I – along with his son Fror – was slain by a Cold Drake while making a last valiant stand at the gates to his own halls.

Dáin II

Dwarf king of Erebor. Called Dáin Ironfoot, he was born in 2767 of the Third Age of the Sun in the Iron Hills. In his youth he established a name as a great warrior by slaying Azog, the Orc king of Moria, during the Battle of Azanulbizar in 2799. Six years later, he became Lord of the Iron Hills. In 2941, Dáin II led his army into the Battle of Five Armies and was one of the victorious commanders. After Thorin Oakenshield died of wounds sustained during the battle, Dáin Ironfoot was named his rightful heir, and became the King under the Mountain. He ruled there until the War of the Ring in 3019, when he was slain during the Battle of Dale.

Dale

One of the many settlements of Northmen west of Mirkwood in Rhovanion was the ancient city-kingdom of Dale, just south of the Erebor, the Lonely Mountain. Like all Northmen, the inhabitants of Dale were related to the Edain of the First Age, and although it is not known when Dale was founded, it is believed to have been of very ancient origin. As a city, however, it ceased to exist after the year 2770 of the Third Age, when the terrible winged dragon, Smaug the Golden, burned it to the ground and seized all its treasures. Vengeance for this deed came in the year 2941, when Smaug was slain by a descendant of the kings of Dale, called Bard the Bowman.

In the years that followed, Bard rebuilt Dale and became the first in its new line of kings. With the restoration of its treasures and those of the Dwarf Kingdom under the Mountain at Erebor, Dale became prosperous once again. Danger came when Easterling barbarians attacked Dale and drove its inhabitants to find refuge with their allies, the Dwarves of the Lonely Mountain.

After the fall of Sauron's empire in Mordor, the allied forces of Dwarves and Men broke the siege of Erebor and drove the Easterlings from Dale and all its lands to the south and east. After the war, and well into the Fourth Age, Dale appears to have been a prosperous and independent kingdom allied with the Reunited Kingdom of the Dúnedain.

Dark Elves

Those numbered among the Dark Elves were all the Elven-folk who never beheld the ennobling Light of the Trees of the Valar. These were the Avari – the Silvan Elves of the East and those of Mirkwood and Lothlórien – and the Eldar who never completed the Great Journey to the Undying Lands – the Nandor, the Laiquendi (Green-elves), the Falathrim and also of the Sindar (Grey-elves) – who inhabited Beleriand until the end of the First Age of the Sun, when all the Elf-realms of that place were lost in the sea.

The Dark Elves, or 'Moriquendi' in the Elven tongue, were counted a lesser people than the High Elves of Eldamar, who were the Vanyar, Noldor and Teleri. Yet by the reckoning of Men these Dark Elves were magical and brilliant beings. For they were immune to pestilence and aged not with the passage of time. They were wiser, stronger and fairer than Men and their eyes always shone with the light of the Stars. In the first years of the Sun, it was these Elves who taught all Men speech and many other arts and skills, that they might live in Middle-earth and raise themselves above the station of beasts of the wilderness.

The Nandor and the Laiquendi both were said to have learned powers of woodlore greater than any other living creatures. The Falathrim were the first shipbuilders of Middle-earth and the finest mariners. The Sindar, who were ruled by a High Eldar king and a Maia queen, built the fairest kingdom on Middle-earth and performed noble deeds counted great even by the measure of the High Elves.

In the Second Age of the Sun, after the sinking of Beleriand new Elf-realms were created by the High Elves of Middle-earth and many Silvan Elves came to them out of the East and the North. Of these new realms, those of Lindon, Rivendell, Mirkwood and Lothlórien survived until the Fourth Age. But, as the 'Red Book of Westmarch' tells, the High Elves in the Fourth Age took the white Elven ships to the Undying Lands. And though Dark Elves long remained in Middle-earth, all their realms faded and they became a wandering folk of ever diminishing power.

Dead Marshes

Northwest of the Mountains of Mordor, between the wetlands of the Anduin River below the Rauros Falls and the Dagorlad battle plain, was a haunted and desolate place called the Dead Marshes. Through three thousand years of the Third Age, the wetlands of the Dead Marshes spread eastward and swallowed up that part of the battle plain which contained many of the graves of Men and Elves who died during the Battle of Dagorlad at the end of the Second Age. In the Third Age, after the Battle of Camp in 1944, much of the Wainrider army was driven into the Dead Marshes and perished. It was through these marshes that the Hobbit Frodo Baggins – with Samwise Gamgee and Sméagol Gollum – was forced to travel on his quest during the War of the Ring, and it was here that they found the horrible phantoms of the Mere of Dead Faces, where animated spirits of long-dead warriors appeared in its swampy, haunted pools.

Dead Men of Dunharrow

In Mortal Lands of Arda there were many spirits who, because of some righteous curse or evil act of sorcery, were bound to Arda longer than was their right. The Barrow-wights and the mighty Ringwraiths were such beings; other unquiet souls inhabited the Dead Marshes, where floods disturbed the graves of Men and Elves who had fallen at the Battle of Dagorlad near the Black Gate of the evil land of Mordor.

The 'Red Book of Westmarch' also tells of those known as the Dead Men of Dunharrow, who haunted the labyrinths of the ancient citadel of Rohan. These were once Men of the White Mountains who in the Second Age of the Sun had sworn allegiance to the king of the Dúnedain but, in time of war, broke that oath and betrayed him to the Dark Lord Sauron. Thereafter, all the warriors of the Men of the White Mountains were cursed as oath-breakers and became wandering ghosts who could find no rest.

For all the years of the Third Age of the Sun these Men haunted the Paths of the Dead above the mighty hold of the Dunharrow, and all who entered the corridors were driven mad with fear and were lost. But in the last years of that Age one who could command them came from the northern wilderness. He was Aragorn, son of Arathorn, the rightful heir of the king of the Dúnedain. He summoned the Dead to fulfil the oath they had broken long ago. And indeed they appeared, pale riders on pale Horses, yet they proved to be a mighty battalion of mighty Men. They rode with Aragorn to Pelargir and made war on the Corsairs of Umbar on land and sea, and they slew them and made them flee in terror. Thus the Dead Men of Dunharrow gave victory to Aragorn – the heir to the Dúnedain kings – and were redeemed by this act. Their souls were released and, before the eyes of the great living Men, the vast form of a great pale army faded as mist in a wind at dawn.

DEAD MARSHES Northwest of the Mountains of Mordor was a haunted and desolate place called the Dead Marshes.

Deep Elves

Of all the Elves the most famous in the songs of Men are the Noldor, who are called Deep Elves because of their great knowledge of the crafts taught them in the Undying Lands by Aulë, the Smith of the Valar and Maker of Mountains. In Eldamar, these Elves greatly loved to build with stone and they delved deep into the mountains for it. They were first to find the bright Earth-gems and they were first to devise the Elf-gems that were brighter still.

The Deep Elves were well known to Men, for alone of the Calaquendi they returned to Middle-earth after the coming of Men and performed great deeds, for both good and evil. These Elves wrought the Great Jewels – the Silmarils – and also made the Rings of Power. The greatest wars ever known to Men were fought over these works.

Denethor I

Dúnedain lord of Gondor. Denethor I became the Tenth Ruling Steward of Gondor in 2435 of the Third Age. During Denethor I's rule, Sauron spawned that evil race of super-Orc known as the Uruk-hai, and in the year 2475 they overran Ithilien and sacked Osgiliath. Denethor's son, Boromir, resolutely led an army against Sauron's Uruks and was able to retake Osgiliath. Unfortunately, in the struggle the city was almost entirely destroyed and its stone bridge broken. Denethor I died in the year 2477.

Denethor II

Dúnedain lord of Gondor. Denethor II, son of Ecthelion II, ruled Gondor from 2984 until the War of the Ring in 3019. He was the twenty-sixth and last Ruling Steward of Gondor. In 2976 he married Finduilas, the fair daughter of the Prince of Dol Amroth. Finduilas gave birth to two sons, Boromir and Faramir, but died after only a dozen years of marriage. Although once a noble and wise man, after Finduilas' death, Denethor II became an increasingly solitary and secretive ruler. Knowing that the final confrontation with Sauron would come during his time, he trusted few others and excluded both Aragorn and Gandalf as counsellors. Bravely and rather unwisely, he often looked into the Palantír (or 'Seeing Stone') in the White Tower. Although he undoubtedly gained knowledge that helped him prepare Gondor for the oncoming war, the stone caused him to age and finally had a corrupting influence on him. When his eldest son, Boromir, died in the Ring Quest, and Faramir lay in a coma brought on by the Black Breath of a Ringwraith, Denethor's iron will was at last broken. In mad despair he attempted to take both his own life and that of Faramir. Gandalf was able to intercede and prevent Faramir from being burnt alive, but he was unable to stop the grief-crazed Denethor from immolating himself.

Dior

Elven king of Doriath. Son of Beren and Lúthien, grandson of King Thingol and Queen Melian, Dior had the blood of three races in his veins: Edain, Eldar and Maiar. Born and raised in Ossiriand in Beleriand around 470 of the First Age, he married the beautiful Sindar princess, Nimloth, and she gave birth to three children: Elréd, Elurín and Elwing. In 505 Dior became king of Doriath after Thingol's murder and the sacking of Menegroth by the Dwarves of Nogrod. Upon the death of Beren and Lúthien, Dior inherited the Nauglamír, the necklace that contained one of the Silmarils. It was the necklace which was the cause of the treachery of the Dwarves. Soon after, the Noldor sons of Féanor, who considered the Silmaril their birthright, attacked Menegroth. In the ensuing battle both Dior and Nimloth were killed.

Dol Amroth

The tower, port and city of Dol Amroth was one of the five great cities of Gondor. It was the largest city in the fief of Belfalas. It was ruled by the princes of Dol Amroth, whose banners were blue and marked with a white ship and a silver swan. Dol Amroth was built by the legendary Elf-king Amroth, the star-crossed lover of the Elven princess, Nimrodel. Until Amroth's death in 1981 of the Third Age, the Elves of Lothlórien sailed out of Dol Amroth to the Undying Lands in their magical white ships.

Dol Guldur

During the Third Age of the Sun, when the vast forest of Greenwood the Great slowly became such a dark and haunted place that it was renamed Mirkwood, an evil fortress was built in its southwestern part. This was Dol Guldur, the 'hill of sorcery', and for a thousand years an evil power called the Necromancer lived there with legions of Orcs and many evil and haunting spirits. In the year 2063, the Wizard Gandalf entered Dol Guldur, but found its mysterious commanding demon had vanished. However, by the twenty-fifth century it had returned with much increased powers. It was not until the year 2850, when Gandalf again went to Dol Guldur, that he learned that Sauron the Ring Lord was the Necromancer. Sauron ruled from his hidden realm until 2941, when he found refuge in his mighty Dark Tower in Mordor. However, in 2951, three of Sauron's most terrible servants, the Nazgûl Ringwraiths, took command of Dol Guldur and used it as a base for campaigns of terror against the free peoples of the north. In the War of the Ring, the evil armies of Dol Guldur attacked both Lothlórien and the Woodland Realm, but were finally annihilated by the Elves of those realms. The walls of Dol Guldur were knocked down, and its pits and dungeons opened and cleansed of all evil.

Dori

Dwarf of Thorin and Company. Dori set out on the Quest of the Lonely Mountain in the year 2941 of the Third Age. The expedition eventually led to the slaying of Smaug the Dragon and the re-establishment of the Dwarf Kingdom under the Mountain. After the Quest, Dori swore allegiance to King Dáin Ironfoot and settled down in Erebor.

Doriath

In the Second Age of Starlight, the Grey Elf King Thingol and his Queen, Melian the Maia, founded the Sindar kingdom of Doriath in the great woodlands of Beleriand. Through four ages of stars, the Grey Elf lands of Doriath and the royal court in the Thousand Caves of Menegroth grew ever more prosperous and were the most beautiful and powerful on Middle-earth. However, during the First Age of the Sun, the lands of Beleriand proved to be the primary battleground between the Noldor Elves and Morgoth the Dark Enemy in the disastrous War of the Jewels. Wishing to keep the Grey Elves out of this conflict, Queen Melian the Maia wove a powerful spell of protection about the woodland kingdom of Doriath that prevented any evil being from entering and Doriath became known as the Hidden Kingdom. In this way, for the greater part of the First Age of the Sun, the Grey Elves of Doriath were safe from the ravages which eventually destroyed all the kingdoms of Beleriand. However, the Sindar were also caught up in the conflict when one of the Silmaril jewels came into King Thingol's possession. For the sake of this jewel, the Dwarves of Nogrod betrayed their allies and slew Thingol. With the death of Thingol, Melian left Middle-earth and her spell of protection fell away, and Doriath was invaded by Dwarves. The Sindar in Doriath rallied for a time under the rule of Thingol's grandson, King Dior, but the cursed possession of the Silmaril resulted in his death at the hands of the Noldor Elves. After Dior's death and the second sacking of Menegroth, the Grey Elves deserted the ruined realm of Doriath. When the War of Wrath ended the First Age of the Sun, Doriath, with all the other lands of Beleriand, sank beneath the sea.

Dorwinions

On the western shore of the Inland Sea of Rhûn there lived the Dorwinions. Of all Northmen, the Dorwinions were the most easterly, and they were far-famed as makers of the finest and strangest of wines. By trading with many of the people of Middle-earth the Dorwinions became prosperous, for even the fine sensibilities of the Elves were nourished by their wines.

Dragons

The 'Quenta Silmarillion' tells how, in the First Age of the Sun, Morgoth the Dark Enemy hid himself in the Pits of Angband and wrought his masterpieces of evil from flame and sorcery. The dark jewels of Morgoth's genius were the Great Worms called Dragons. He made great serpents that slithered, those that walked on legs and those that flew with wings like the Bat. Of each kind there were two types: the Cold-drakes, who fought with fang and claw, and the miraculous Urulóki Fire-drakes, who destroyed with breath of flame. All Dragons were the embodiment of the chief evils of Men, Elves and Dwarves, and so were great in their destruction of those races.

The Dragons were in themselves vast armouries that worked towards Morgoth's aims. The reptiles were of massive size and power and were protected by scales of impenetrable iron. Tooth and nail were like javelin and rapier, and their tails could crush the shield-wall of any army. The winged Dragons swept the land below them with hurricane winds, and the Fire-drakes breathed scarlet and green flames that licked the Earth and destroyed all in their path.

Beyond strength of arms, Dragons carried other more subtle powers. Their eyesight was keener than the hawk's and anything that they sighted could not escape them. They had hearing that would catch the sound of the slightest breath of the most silent enemy, and a sense of smell that allowed them to name any creature by the least odour of its flesh.

Their intelligence was renowned, as was their love of setting and solving riddles. Dragons were ancient serpents, and so were creatures of immense cleverness and knowledge but not of wisdom, for their intelligence had the flaws of vanity, gluttony, greed, deceit and wrath.

Being created chiefly of the elements of fire and sorcery, the Dragons shunned water and preferred darkness to the light of day. Dragon-blood was black and deadly poison, and the vapours of their worm-stench were of burning sulphur and slime. Their bodies glowed always with a hard, gem-like flame. Their laughter was deeper than well-shafts and made the very mountains quake. The eyes of the Dragon emitted rays of ruby light or in anger flashed red lightning. Their cruel reptilian voices were harsh whispers and, combined with the intensity of the serpent eye, invoked the Dragon-spell that bound unwary foes and made them wish to surrender to the beast's awesome will.

First of the Fire-drakes, the Urulóki, created by Morgoth in Angband, was Glaurung, Father of Dragons. After only a century of brooding and growing in the caverns, Glaurung in fiery wrath burst out from Angband's gates and came into a startled World. Though he was not of the winged race that would later arise, Glaurung was the greatest terror of his time and begat a legion of lesser Fire-drakes and Cold-drakes. He burned and savaged the land of the Elves in Hithlum and Dorthonion before being driven back by Fingon, prince of Hithlum. Morgoth, however, was displeased with Glaurung for his impulsiveness, for he had planned that the Dragon should grow to full power before revealing him to an unsuspecting World. To

Glaurung this attack was but mere adolescent adventure – a youthful testing of power. Terrible though it was to Elves, his strength was barely developed and his scale-armour was still tender to the assault of weapons. So Morgoth held Glaurung within Angband for another two centuries before he let the Urulóki loose. This was the beginning of the Fourth Battle in the Wars of Beleriand. It became known as the Battle of the Sudden Flame when Glaurung, the Great Worm, in full power led Morgoth's forces into battle against the High Elves of Beleriand. His great size and scorching fire cleared a path into the armies of the foe, and with Morgoth's demons, the Balrogs, and black legions of innumerable Orcs he broke the Siege of Angband and brought despair and desolation to the Elves.

In the Fifth Battle, called the Battle of Unnumbered Tears, Glaurung caused even more terrible destruction, as by now he had (in the mysterious way of Dragons) fathered a brood of lesser Fire-drakes and Cold-drakes to follow him in war. So a great army of Elves and Men fell before this onslaught, and none could withstand the Dragon-flame, except the Dwarves of Belegost, who had come to fight the common foe.

Morgoth used Glaurung as well to hold the territories he gained; but force in battle was not the only power this monster knew. He brought many under his sway with the binding power of his serpent eye and the hypnotic Dragon-spell.

Years after Glaurung had sacked and laid waste the kingdom of Nargothrond, the 'Narn i Hîn Húrin' tells how he was slain by the mortal Túrin Turambar. For this son of Húrin came on the Fire-drake by stealth and drove the sword Gurthang deep into the beat's underbelly, but, by the poison of the black blood and the venom of the Dragon's last words, Túrin Turambar was also killed.

Though Glaurung was named Father of Dragons, the greatest Dragon that ever entered the World was one named Ancalagon the Black. Ancalagon was the first of the winged Fire-drakes, and he and others of that breed came out of Angband like mighty storm clouds of wind and fire as a last defence of Morgoth's realm was made. 'Rushing Jaws' is the meaning of his name, and his ravening majesty devastated the army of the West in the Great Battle and the War of Wrath at the close of the First Age of Sun. This was the first the World had seen of winged Dragons and for a time Morgoth's foes were in retreat. Yet Eagles and all the warrior birds of the Earth came out of the West together with that great flying ship 'Vingilot' and the warrior Eärendil. The battle of these beings of the air lasted a long time, but at last Eärendil was victorious, and yet Ancalagon was cast down and the other Fire-drakes were slain or fled. So the War of Wrath ended and the power of Morgoth was broken for ever within this world. So great was the defeat of the Dragons in the Great Battle that it is not until the Third Age of the Sun that the histories of Middle-earth speak again of the Dragons. In that time they inhabited the wastes beyond the Grey Mountains of the North. And, it is said, their greed led them to the hoarded wealth of the Seven Kings of the Dwarves.

Mightiest of the Dragons of the Grey Mountains was one named Scatha the Worm who drove the Dwarves from their halls in fear and dread, but a prince of Men stood and gave battle. This was the warrior Fram, son of Frumgar, chieftain of the Éothéod, and Scatha was killed by the hand of this Man. Yet this was but temporary release from the terror that lurked in the mountains, for in time many Cold-drakes returned to the Grey Mountains. Though the Dwarves' defence was valiant and long, they were over-whelmed; one by one their warriors fell and the gold-rich Grey Mountains were left entirely to the Dragon legions.

In the twenty-eighth century of the Third Age, the chronologies of the Westlands tell how the greatest Dragon of the Age came from the North to the kingdom of Dwarves in

Erebor, the Lonely Mountain. This Fire-drake called Smaug the Golden was vast and Bat-winged and a fearsome bane to Dwarves and Men. With consuming Dragon-flame, Smaug ruined the city of the Men of Dale and broke the door and wall of the Dwarf Kingdom of the Lonely Mountain. The Dwarves fled or were destroyed and Smaug took the riches of that place: gold and gemstones, mithril and silver, elf-gems and pearls, the many-faceted crystals of emerald, sapphire and the brilliance of diamonds.

For two centuries Smaug ruled Erebor unchallenged. Yet, in the year 2941, a company of adventurers came to the mountain: twelve Dwarves led by the rightful king of Erebor, Thorin Oakenshield, and the Hobbit mercenary who was named Bilbo Baggins. They approached the Dragon by stealth and were amazed, for Smaug was huge beyond all that they had imagined and glowed golden-red with serpent rage. He was armoured as all of his race with scales of impenetrable iron, but in wariness he also protected his soft underbelly from assault: as he lay sprawled upon the wealth of his hoard he allowed diamonds and gemstones to imbed in his belly, and in this way armoured his only weakness. Yet, by cunning, the Hobbit, Bilbo Baggins discovered one point upon the broad breast of the beast that was not sheathed in jewels, where sharp steel might cut.

When Smaug was aroused by the adventurers he came out in wrath and loosed his fire on the land. In vengeance he came to Esgaroth on the Long Lake, for the Lake Men had aided the adventurers. Yet there lived a Northman, valiant and strong, named Bard the Bowman who, guided by the secret of the Dragon's weakness, drove a single black arrow into the beast's one vital place. Wondrously the great Dragon screamed and fell flaming from the sky. So died Smaug the Golden, mightiest Dragon of the Third Age.

It was rumoured that Dragons continued for many centuries to inhabit the Northern Waste beyond Grey Mountains, but no tale that has come to Men out of Middle-earth speaks again of these evil, yet magnificent beings.

Draugluin

Werewolf Lord of Tol-in-Gaurhoth. Draugluin was the sire and lord of the Werewolf race, which came out of Angband to terrorize the Elves. During the Wars of Beleriand, Draugluin and the greater part of his brood inhabited Tol-in-Gaurhoth, the 'Isle of Werewolves'. Under the command of Sauron, Draugluin led his Werewolves out time and again against Elvish forces. During the Quest of the Silmaril, after Beren and his companions were captured, Princess Lúthien with Huan, the Hound of the Valar, dared to challenge Draugluin. Draugluin joined battle with Huan on the bridge of Tol-in-Gaurhoth. He was at last overcome by Huan and crept away to die at the feet of Sauron. After Draugluin's death and Beren's release, both Lúthien and Beren used Draugluin's Werewolf skin to disguise themselves and enter Angband.

Druadan Forest

During the time of the War of the Ring, there was an ancient forest some thirty miles north-west of the White Tower of Gondor that was inhabited by a strange tribe of primitive people called the Woses. This woodland was called the Druadan Forest. By the Third Age, Druadan had come to mean 'wildman', but it was a corruption of Drúedain, the Elvish name for the Woses during the First Age of the Sun when they were allied with the Edain. After the War of the Ring in which the Woses aided the allies of Gondor against the legions of Sauron,

DRAGONS The most terrible monsters of Middle-earth. Some slithered like snakes, others walked on clawed feet, and still others flew with lizard wings. Some fought with tooth and claw – the greatest breathed flames.

King Elessar of the Reunited Kingdom gave control of the Druadan Forest to the Woses, commanding that no others may enter it unless they wished them to do so.

Drúedain

Drúedain or Drúath was the Grey-elf name for the primitive Wildmen of the forests, the Woses. By the Haladin they were called Drûgs, by the Rohirrim Rógin and by the Orcs Oghor-hai.

Dúlin

The most loved bird-song on Middle-earth is that of the nightingale, which the Grey-elves call Dúlin, the 'night-singer', and Tinúviel 'twilight-maiden'. For, like the Elves themselves, the nightingales are delighted by starlight and bring forth the most beautiful song and joy into a dark World.

Dumbledors

In the playful Hobbit poem 'Errantry', a part tells of a ferocious race of winged insects. They are named Dumbledors, but nothing more is told of their origin and history.

Dúnedain

The histories of the Dúnedain, the Men of Westernesse, begin at the start of the Second Age of the Sun, for the Dúnedain were the remnant of the Edain of the First Age. These people were honoured by the Valar and given a land that lay in the Western Sea between Middle-earth and the Undying Lands. This place was named Númenórë, Westernesse in the common tongue of Men. The history of the Dúnedain of that time is told in the 'Akallabêth' and in the tale of the Númenóreans, for the Dúnedain of Númenórë were known by that name. These people were mighty and their downfall was terrible when their land was plunged beneath the sea and the belly of the World was torn out. In that holocaust all the Númenóreans were lost, except those known as the Black Númenóreans, who in earlier times had gone to the southern haven of Umbar, and those known as the Elendili, who made the realms of Arnor and Gondor. So when the histories speak of the Dúnedain they most often mean the Elendili, whose name means 'faithful'.

The histories of Middle-earth tell how, in the year 3319 of the Second Age of the Sun, nine ships came upon a great wave out of the Western Sea. These were the ships of Elendil the Tall who, with his sons, brought the surviving faithful Dúnedain to Middle-earth. Elendil then made Arnor, the North Kingdom of the Dúnedain, and built Annúminas as its first city near the Elven lands of Lindon; while Anárion and Isildur went to the South and made Gondor, the South Kingdom of the Dúnedain, and built Osgiliath as its first city. In Arnor were the extensive provinces of Rhudaur, Cardolan and Arthedain; whereas in Gondor were the fiefs and territories of Anórien, Ithilien, Lebennin, Lossarnach, Lamedon, Anfalas, Tolfalas, Belfalas and Calenardhon.

The Dúnedain prospered peacefully for a century of that Age while they strengthened their new kingdoms, but another power was also growing. Out of Mordor came Sauron and the Nazgûl, and Orcs and Men of many races who were his thralls. So there was war once again, but a pact was made that in later times was named the Last Alliance of Elves and Men. Gil-galad, the last High King of the Elves on Middle-earth, led the Elves of Lindon, and Elendil commanded the Dúnedain. Sauron's servants fell before their strength and Sauron himself was forced into battle at last. And although Elendil, Anárion and Gil-galad were all killed, so too was the power of the Ringwraiths and Sauron ended. Isildur cut the Ring from Sauron's hand and Sauron, the Ringwraiths and all his servants went into the shadows. This was the war that ended the Second Age of the Sun. With Sauron gone, a time of peace was anticipated, but the Third Age was also doomed to end in bloody war, for Isildur did not destroy Sauron's Ring and within the Ring a terrible power remained. In the second year of the Third Age, Isildur was ambushed upon Gladden Fields, slain by black Orc arrows, and the Ring was lost in the River Anduin. So, as the 'Red Book of Westmarch' and the 'Annals of the Kings and Rulers' tell, though there was peace for a time, strife was doomed to return to the Westlands. The Dúnedain were attacked from all sides: Balchoth and Wainriders out of Rhûn; Black Númenóreans and Haradrim from the South; Variags from Khand; Orcs and Dunlendings from the Misty Mountains; Hillmen and Trolls from the Ettenmoors; and Ringwraiths risen once again in Mordor, Angmar, Morgul and Dol Guldur. So did the Third Age pass, with the Dúnedain warring with those who were driven by a single force that had at last regained a form and resided in the mighty tower of Barad-dûr in Mordor: Sauron the Ring Lord.

At times the Dúnedain grew still more powerful in those years and their lands increased far into Rhûn and Harad. But through the centuries they were like sea-cliffs, worn down by the tides: Arnor as a kingdom was broken apart, and in 1975 the last city of Arnor fell. Though an heir to the throne remained hidden in the land, this Dúnedain kingdom was completely lost. After that time, in the North, those who were rightful kings of the Dúnedain were only chieftains. In the South, though frequently besieged and threatened, most of the Dúnedain kingdom of Gondor remained intact and strong, yet the royal line was broken and the kingdom was ruled by Stewards.

Through the Third Age Sauron's power increased, until at last he came forth openly in war, determined to drive the Dúnedain and the Elves from the World and make Middle-earth his domain for ever. This was the War of the Ring, which ended the Third Age; and its history is told in the masterwork called the 'Red Book of Westmarch'.

In that War, among the Dúnedain of the North rose Aragorn, son of Arathorn, the one true heir of Isildur and rightful king of all the Dúnedain of Middle-earth. His knights were the Rangers of the North: horsemen armed with sword and spear in hooded travellers' cloaks of forest-green and high leather boots. Aragorn himself went about the land in this guise, weather-worn, yet strong, brave and keen of eye.

In that time he was called Strider, but in the many adventures of his long life he went by other names: he was Estel among the Elves of Rivendell in his youth, and Thorongil as the captain of Gondor who went to the South and destroyed the fleets of Umbar. During the War of the Ring he fought at the Hornburg, Pelargir, Pelennor Fields and before the Black Gate of Mordor itself.

He proved to be a true leader of Men and, as the heir of Isildur, was crowned King Elessar Telcontar, ruler of all the Dúnedain of the twin realms of Gondor and Arnor, after the War of the Ring.

Upon his succession Aragorn was totally transformed from rugged Ranger into a king, fierce and lordly yet glad, wise and Elven-eyed. He was enthroned and crowned beneath three banners, green, blue and sable: Rohan, Dol Amroth and Gondor. He wore the White Crown of the Dúnedain, the tall warrior's helm of mithril with white seabirds' wings of pearl and silver. A circlet of seven adamant gems was set around it, and a single Elf-gem on the crown glowed with a bright, clear light. Aragorn was compared with the noblest of the Númenóreans of old and even with the Elven-lords. Indeed, he took the Elf-princess Arwen Undómiel as his queen, and they ruled wisely over the Westlands long into the Fourth Age and brought peace to all the people of Middle-earth.

Dunharrow

One of the most ancient and mysterious fortress refuges on Middle-earth, Dunharrow was a part of Rohan during the War of the Ring. It was one of the main refuges during various wars for those in the vale of Harrowdale beneath it. Dunharrow appeared to be almost impossible to attack successfully as it was approached by a switch-back road up the steep cliffs of the mountains. Each switchback doubled sharply back on the lower one, and at each roadside turning were huge round stones in the shape of squatting pot-bellied men. It was a monumental piece of engineering, and snaked back and forth in a high pyramid of roads until it reached a wall of rock at the top through which a gap was cut and an incline leading onto the Hold of Dunharrow. This was a high, broad and well-watered alpine meadow on which many thousands could encamp themselves in times of war. Upon this plateau was a great corridor in the form of a long line of unshaped black standing stones which marched across the plain in a straight line leading toward the Dwimorberg, or the 'Haunted Mountain', and a black wall of stone pierced by the Dark Door. This led to a secret glen that was haunted by the spirits of the dead who prevented living men from crossing to the far side of the White Mountains by this abandoned pass. Dunharrow was built during the Second Age by the Men of the White Mountains who were ancestors of the Dunlendings, but who inhabited the land before the coming of the Men of Gondor. Although they later swore allegiance to Gondor, these people had already been corrupted by Sauron, and so in time of war betrayed their new allies. For the breaking of this oath, the spirits of these people were never allowed to rest and for all the years of the Third Age the ghostly army known as the Dead Men of Dunharrow haunted this part of Dwimorberg above Dunharrow which was called the Paths of the Dead. It was not until the arrival of Aragorn that the Dead Men were allowed to make amends and Dunharrow's haunting spirits were at last laid to rest.

Dunlendings

In the Second Age of the Sun, before the Dúnedain came to Middle-earth and made the kingdoms of Gondor and Arnor, there lived a tall, dark-haired people in the fertile valleys below the White Mountains. For many centuries, it is said, they developed a civilization apart from other people and built many great fortresses of stone. No history tells of the fate of these men of the White Mountains, yet they vanished and only those descendants named Dunlendings remained in their lands.

Long before the Dúnedain made the kingdoms of Gondor and Arnor, Dunlending power had dwindled. The people had become divided. Those who had remained in Dunharrow became allies of the Men of Gondor; others had wandered North and settled peaceably in the land of Bree. Yet most of the Dunlendings had retreated to the hills and plains of Dunland and had become a tribal herding people. Though they kept their language and remained fierce warriors, they became a barbaric folk.

In the twenty-sixth century of the Third Age, the Men of Gondor granted the Rohirrim a province called Calenardhon, but the Dunlendings considered it theirs by right. So these two people grew to hate one another, and in the year 2758 a Dunlending named Wulf led a great invasion of his people against the Rohirrim and was victorious. But this was at great cost, for in the next year the Rohirrim arose and drove the Dunlendings back into the hills, and Wulf the war lord was himself slain.

So it was that for nearly three centuries the Dunlendings remained in the hill lands and left the fertile valleys to the Rohirrim. Yet they did not forget their hurt, and the tall, dark Men of Dunland made an evil pact with the rebel Wizard Saruman, who had brought vast numbers of the Great Orcs (called Uruk-hai) into Isengard. And it is recorded that by some evil act of sorcery the Dunlendings were bred with the Uruk-hai, and evil offspring called Half-orcs were the result of this union. Half-orcs were black, lynx-eyed Men with evil Orkish features; combined with the Dunlendings and Great Orcs, the Half-orcs made a huge army of terrifying strength.

When the power of Gondor and Rohan seemed to wane, this army gathered in Isengard about the banner of Saruman's White Hand, to fight against the Rohirrim. The 'Red Book of Westmarch' tells how the fierce Dunlendings in tall helms and sable shields advanced to the Battle of the Hornburg at Helm's Deep with the Uruk-hai and Half-orcs.

But the Battle of the Hornburg was great disaster for the Dunlendings; they were overthrown and the fierce Uruk-hai and Half-orcs were annihilated. Those who were not slain could only sue for peace, promising never again to arise against their Rohirrim conquerors.

Durin I

Dwarf king of Khazad-dûm. Durin I was the first and eldest of the Seven Fathers of the Dwarves who were conceived by Aulë the Smith in the Ages of Darkness. King Durin I's realm was Khazad-dûm, the greatest Dwarf kingdom, which was found beneath the Misty Mountains. After the destruction of Beleriand at the end of the First Age of the Sun, the histories of Elves and Men primarily tell us of the Dwarves of Durin's line. Durin lived to such a great age that he was called Durin the Deathless. The name was also a reference to the belief that he would be reincarnated seven times as king of the people, and each time he would take the name of Durin.

DUNLENDINGS Tall, dark-haired people of Dunland who made an evil pact with Wizard Saruman and joined his Orc legions. In the Battle of Hornburg the Dunlendings were crushed and their power broken.

Durin II

Dwarf king of Khazad-dûm during the eighth century of the Second Age. During this time the Dwarves of his realm cut the caverns and tunnels of the realm all the way through the Misty Mountains, from east to west, and built the West-gate, allowing trade in precious materials with the Elven-smiths of Eregion.

Durin III

Dwarf king of Khazad-dûm. Durin III was the Dwarf king best known for his friendship with the Elven-smiths of Eregion during the sixteenth century of the Second Age. He was given the first of the Seven Dwarf Rings by Celebrimbor. Not long after, the War of Sauron and the Elves forced the Dwarves to close their doors on the world. Khazad-dûm became known as Moria, the 'dark kingdom'.

Durin VI

Dwarf King of Moria (Khazad-dûm). Born in the year 1731 of the Third Age, Durin VI was ruler of Moria in 1980 when his people were delving after a mithril lode deep beneath the roots of the Redhorn mountain. Tragically, they broke into a sealed chamber and released a horrific evil spirit called a Balrog. Both Durin VI and his son, Nain I, were slain by the demon during the following year, and the Dwarves were driven forever from Durin's kingdom.

Durin VII

Dwarf King of the Last Kingdom. Believed to be the seventh and last incarnation of King Durin, his coming signalled the last kingdom of Dwarves of Durin's line.

Dwalin

Dwarf of Thorin and Company. Dwalin was the son of Fundin and the brother of Balin. He went on the Quest of the Lonely Mountain that re-established the Dwarf Kingdom under the Mountain at Erebor, where he remained until the end of his life. It was the second such quest for Dwalin, for he had been a companion of King Thrain II, the Dwarf-king in exile, a century before, on the disastrous journey to Erebor which led to the king's capture and eventual death.

Dwarves

In a great hall under the mountains of Middle-earth Aulë, the Smith of the Valar, fashioned the Seven Fathers of Dwarves during the Ages of Darkness, when Melkor and his evil servants in Utumno and Angband held sway over all Middle-earth. Therefore, Aulë made Dwarves stout and strong, unaffected by cold and fire, and sturdier than the races that followed. Aulë knew of the great evil of Melkor, so he made the Dwarves stubborn, indomitable, and persistent in labour and hardship. They were brave in battle and their pride and will could not be broken.

The Dwarves were deep-delving miners, masons, metal-workers and the most wondrous stone-carvers. They were well suited to the crafts of Aulë, who had shaped the mountains, for they were made strong, long-bearded and tough, but not tall, being four to five feet in height. As their toil was long, they were each granted a life of about two and a half centuries, for they were mortal; they could also be slain in battle. Aulë made the Dwarves wise with the knowledge of his crafts and gave them a language of their own called Khuzdul. In this tongue Aulë was called Mahal and the Dwarves Khazâd, but it was a secret tongue unknown,

DURIN Durin I was the first and eldest of the Seven Fathers of the Dwarves.

but for a few words, to all but Dwarves, who guarded it jealously. The Dwarves always gave thanks to Aulë and acknowledged that by him they were given shape. Yet they were given true life by the power of Ilúvatar.

It is said that, once Aulë had made the Dwarves, he secretly hid them from the other Valar and thought himself and them hidden as well from Ilúvatar. Yet Ilúvatar was aware of Aulë's deed and judged that Aulë's act was done without malice, and thus He sanctified the Dwarves. Yet He would not permit that this race should come forth before his chosen children, the Elves, who were to be the Firstborn. So, though the Dwarves were full-wrought, Aulë took them and laid them deeply under stone, and in this darkness the Seven Fathers of Dwarves slept for many Ages before the Stars were rekindled and before the Time of the Awakening drew near.

So it was that the Elves awoke in Cuiviénen in the East in the First Age of Stars. In the years that followed the Seven Fathers of Dwarves stirred, and their stone chamber was broken open, and they arose and were filled with awe.

It is said that each of these Seven Fathers made a great mansion under the mountains of Middle-earth, but the Elven histories of these early years speak only of three. These were the Dwarf-realms called Belegost and Nogrod in the Blue Mountains, and Khazad-dûm in the

DWARVES The most wonderful stone-carvers and metal workers of Middle-earth. A powerful, rugged and long-bearded race, between four and five feet high, much used to working in mines and foundries.

Misty Mountains. The tale of Khazad-dûm is longest for this was the House of the First Father called Durin I and Durin the Deathless.

To the Elves of Beleriand in the Age of Stars the Dwarves of Belegost and Nogrod were a boon indeed. For they came into the realm of the Grey-elves with weapons and tools of steel and displayed great skills in the working of stone. And though the Grey-elves had not previously known of these people, whom they thought unlovely, calling them the Naugrim, the 'stunted people', they soon understood the Dwarves were wise in the crafts of Aulë, and so they also called them the Gonnhirrim, 'masters of stone'. There was much trade between Elves and Dwarves, and through this traffic both peoples prospered.

And though an ungainly people without graceful form, the Dwarves brought forth much beauty. Their mansions had grand halls filled with bright banners, armour, jewelled weapons and fine tapestries. Starlight shone down great light-wells and played upon mirroring pools and sparkling silver fountains. In echoing domes, by the light of crystal lamps, bright gemstones and veins of precious ores might be seen. In walls of jet polished like glass, dreaming marble forms were visible, and winding stair or twisting venue might lead to tall, fair tower or court of many-coloured stone. Tunnels led to courtyards and grottos with columns of alabaster, fluted by Time and the gentle promptings of Dwarf chisels.

In the Ages of Starlight, the Dwarves of the Blue Mountains fashioned the finest steel that the World had ever seen. In Belegost (which was also named Gabilgathol and Mickleburg) the famous Dwarf-mail of linked rings was first made, while in Nogrod (which was called Tumunzahar and Hollowbold) resided Telchar, the greatest Dwarf-smith of all time. At this time these Dwarves forged the weapons of the Sindar and built for the Grey-elves of King Thingol their citadel of Menegroth, the Thousand Caves, reputed to be the fairest of mansions on Middle-earth.

The War of the Jewels came in the First Age of the Sun and in it most of the Dwarves fought with the Elves against the servants of Morgoth. Of all Dwarves of that Age, greatest fame was won by King Azaghâl, the lord of Belegost. In the Battle of Unnumbered Tears only the Dwarves could withstand the blaze of Dragon-fire, for they were a race of smiths used to great heat, and on their helms they wore masks of steel that protected their faces from flames. Thus, the Dwarves of Belegost could stop the advance of the Dragon-horde, and though slain, King Azaghâl drove his sword into the belly of Glaurung, the Father of Dragons, and so Glaurung and his brood fled from the battle field.

Not all the deeds of the Dwarves in that Age were praiseworthy. For, it is told, the Dwarves of Nogrod desired the Silmaril, and for it they murdered King Thingol and sacked Menegroth. In turn the Dwarves were caught by the Laiquendi at the Ford of Gelion and the Silmaril was taken from them, and those who escaped the ambush were attacked by Ents and utterly destroyed. From the ending of the First Age of the Sun the histories of Elves and Men that speak of Dwarves tell primarily of those of Durin's Line who lived in Khazad-dûm. When the destruction of Beleriand came with the War of Wrath, the mansions of Nogrod and Belegost were broken and lost. The Dwarves of those kingdoms came into the Misty Mountains in the Second Age and made Khazad-dûm, that greatest mansion of Dwarves on Middle-earth, greater still. The vast halls filled with these prosperous people, whose craftsmen achieved matchless deeds and whose miners delved deep and long into the mountains' heart. In the Second Age many of the Noldorin Elves of Lindon entered into Eregion near the West Door of Khazad-dûm and made a kingdom so they might trade with the Dwarves for the precious metal, mithril, which was found in abundance there. These Elves were the Gwaith-i-Mírdain, who were called the Elven-smiths in later times. By the wisdom of these Elves and

Sauron's deceit, the Rings of Power were forged in this place. And though Dwarves were given seven of these Rings, they were not drawn into the terrible wars that followed until the end of the Second Age. In Khazad-dûm, the Dwarves closed the doors of their mansions to the troubles of the World. None could force an entry into their realm, but ever after it was thought to be a closed and dark kingdom, and so Khazad-dûm was renamed Moria.

Thus, the Dwarves of Durin's Line survived into the Third Age of the Sun, though by then they had seen their greatest days and the Dwarvish people had begun to dwindle. Yet Moria stood for five Ages of Stars and three of the Sun and until the twentieth century of the Third Age was still wealthy and proud. But in the year 1980, when Durin VI was king, the delving Dwarves quarried too deep beneath the mountains and released a great demon. This was one of Morgoth's Balrogs, and it came in wrath and slew King Durin and his son Náin and drove the Dwarves of Moria out for ever.

Durin's people were made a homeless, wandering folk, but in the year 1999 Náin's son, Thráin, founded the kingdom under the Mountain in Erebor. For a while Thráin and some of the people of Moria prospered, for Erebor, the Lonely Mountain, was rich in ore and stones. But Thráin's son, Thorin, left that place and in the year 2210 went to the Grey Mountains, where it was said the greatest numbers of the scattered Dwarves of Moria already lived. Here Thorin was accepted as king and with his Ring of Power his people grew wealthy again. After Thorin, his son, Gróin, ruled, then Óin and Náin II, and the Grey Mountains became famed for Dwarf-gold. And so, during the reign of Náin II's son, Dáin, out of the Northern Waste there came many Cold-drakes of the deserts. Lusting for the wealth of the Dwarves, these Dragons came prepared for war and they slew the Dwarves and drove them out of the Grey Mountains.

In the year 2590 the heir to Dáin I, Thrór, took part of the survivors of the Grey Mountain realm back to the kingdom under the Mountain in Erebor, while in the same year his brother, Grór, took those others who remained to the Iron Hills. And again, for a time, all these people prospered, for there was great trade between Dwarves, Men of Dale and Esgaroth, and the Elves of Mirkwood. Yet for Durin's Folk the peace was short-lived, for in 2770, during the long reign of Thrór, the greatest Dragon of the Third Age, the winged Fire-drake called Smaug the Golden, came to Erebor. None could stand before this great Dragon. He slew wantonly, sacked Dale and drove the Dwarves from the Mountain. There for two centuries Smaug remained, lord of the Lonely Mountain.

Again the Dwarves were driven from their homes. Some retreated into the Iron Hills colony for shelter, but other survivors followed King Thrór and his son, Thrain II, and grandson, Thorin II, in wandering companies.

In this period Thrór was slain by the Orcs of Moria and his body was mutilated and his severed head was delivered to his people. The Dwarves, who had already suffered grievously from various evil hands, felt they could not bear this last insult. All the Houses of Dwarves gathered together and they decided to wage a great war.

This was the terrible and bloody War of the Dwarves and Orcs. It raged for seven long years, and through all the Westlands the Dwarf army hunted out every Orc cavern and slew every Orc band, until at last it reached Moria's East Gate in the year 2799. Here was fought the Battle of Azanulbizar, which is famous even in the histories of the Elves. In that battle the Orcs of the North were all but exterminated by the Dwarves. Yet the Dwarves had little joy in their victory, for half of all their warriors perished in that war. Such a loss could never be regained by this already dwindling folk. Even in spoils and territory they gained little from this war, for, though the Orcs were slain, the Balrog still held Moria and Dragons occupied the kingdom under the Mountain in Erebor and the Dwarf-realms of the Grey Mountains.

The Dwarves returned to their kingdoms filled with sadness. The grandson of Grór, Dáin Ironfoot, returned to rule in the Iron Hills, while Thráin II with his son, Thorin II (now called Oakenshield), went west to the Blue Mountains and made a humble kingdom there. Yet Thráin II did not rule long, because while travelling he was captured by Sauron near Mirkwood and imprisoned in Dol Guldur. The last Ring of the Dwarves was taken from him and he was tortured to death.

Yet Thorin Oakenshield remained in the Blue Mountains, for he did not know the fate of his father. Many wandering Dwarves came to the Blue Mountains and his halls grew, but he was unhappy and desired to return to Erebor to the kingdom under the Mountain, which had been his grandfather's. With such thoughts still in his mind, Thorin Oakenshield approached the Wizard Gandalf in the year 2941 and they immediately fell to a plan of great adventure, which is told by the Hobbit Bilbo Baggins in the 'Red Book of Westmarch'. This one Hobbit and twelve Dwarves accompanied Thorin in his mission to regain his kingdom. The twelve were: Fíli, Kíli, Dori, Ori, Nori, Óin, Glóin, Balin, Dwalin, Bifur, Bofur and Bombur. As is told in the Hobbit's tale, Thorin achieved his quest. For, in the end, the Dragon Smaug the Golden was slain and Thorin II took possession of his rightful kingdom, although his grasp of it was brief. There followed the Battle of Five Armies, in which Orcs, Wolves and Bats battled against Dwarves, Elves, Men and Eagles. And though the Orkish legions were destroyed, so too was Thorin's brave warrior life ended.

This was not, however, the end of Durin's Line, for Dáin Ironfoot had come to the Battle of Five Armies with five hundred warriors out of

DWARVES Fierce and stubborn when provoked in battle, Dwarves were master forgers of arms and armour. The hero Gimlí, son of Glóin (illustrated), brandishes their favourite weapon, the battle-axe.

the Iron Hills and he was Thorin's rightful heir, being, like Thorin, a great-grandson of Dáin I. So Dáin Ironfoot became Dáin II and he ruled wisely until the last days of the War of the Ring, when he fell with King Brand of Dale before the gates of the kingdom under the Mountain. Yet this Dwarf kingdom withstood the attack by Sauron's minions, and Dáin's heir, Thorin III, who was also called Thorin Stonehelm, ruled there long and prosperously into the Fourth Age of the Sun.

The Dwarf Kingdom under the Mountain was not the last and only home of Durin's Folk in the Fourth Age. Another noble Dwarf, descended from Borin, brother of Dáin I, had founded a kingdom of Dwarves at the beginning of the Fourth Age, after the War of the Ring. This Dwarf was Gimli, son of Glóin; he had won great fame in the war and he had been one of the Fellowship chosen for the Quest of the Ring. He had acquitted himself well in all tasks and the song of his axe had been a terror to his foes at the Battles of the Hornburg, Pelennor Fields and before the Black Gate. At the War's end, Gimli had taken many of the Dwarves out of the kingdom under the Mountain into the wondrous caverns of Helm's Deep, and by all he was named lord of Aglarond, the 'glittering caves'.

For more than a century Gimli the Elf-friend ruled Aglarond, but after the death of King Elessar he allowed others to govern and went to the realm of his great friend Legolas, Elf-lord of Ithilien. Here, it is claimed, Gimli boarded an Elven-ship and with his companion sailed over the Great Sea of the West to the Undying Lands.

This is the last that the histories of Middle-earth tell of Dwarves. It is not known if their kingdoms survived the Fourth Age and the Dominion of Men. It is known that they dwindled further, but whether they still live within secret caverns of the World or have now gone to the Mansions of Aulë in the Undying Lands cannot be learned.

Dwimmerlaik

Middle-earth was a land that had seen many Ages of bloody war and strife. Multitudes had been laid to rest in its soil by sword, fire and pestilence. But then too there were those who, after death, by reason of some act of sorcery or broken oath, remained with unquiet spirits in the mortal World. Of these the 'Red Book of Westmarch' speaks of the Barrow-wights, the Dead Men of Dunharrow, the Phantoms of the Dead Marshes, and the terrible Ringwraiths who in Black Speech were named Nazgûl.

In the lands of Rohan in the time of the Riders of the Mark, all such haunting spirits were named Dwimmerlaik. Such were the superstitions of these Rohirrim horsemen that even the Elves of Lothlórien and the Ents of Fangorn were named Dwimmerlaik and were thought to be similar evil spirits.

Eä

After Ilúvatar, the Creator, emerged from the Void and built the Timeless Halls for his angelic host with a word and the power of the Flame Imperishable, He made Eä, the 'World That Is', that Elves and Men later named Arda, the Earth. Eä is all the created World of Arda: the continents, the great seas, the vaults of heaven, and all space and time within the created world.

Eagles

Noblest of the winged creatures of Arda were the Eagles, for they were brought forth by two mighty Valar: Manwë, Lord of the Air, and Yavanna, Queen of the Earth. The Eagles were numbered among the most ancient and wisest of races: they were made before the Stars were rekindled and the Elves awoke. In the Ages that followed, these birds were always messengers and servants of Manwë. On Taniquetil, the Great Mountain, the Eagles would rest. Over all the azure World they flew, for they were the eyes of Manwë and like thunderbolts fell on his foes. In the First Age of the Sun, a mighty breed of this race lived in Beleriand. They were called the Eagles of the Encircling Mountains and they lived in high eyries on the peaks called Crissaegrim. These Eagles were far-famed for their deeds in the War of the Jewels. Their lord was Thorondor and he was largest and most majestic of all Eagles. The full wing-spread of Thorondor was thirty fathoms and the speed of this great bird outstripped the fastest storming wind. Thorondor was strong and fearless and he perpetually fought the evil creatures of the Earth.

It was Thorondor who rescued Maedhros the Noldor lord from a pinnacle of Thangorodrim. He also brought the broken body of King Fingolfin back from Angband and scarred the face of Morgoth with his long talons. In the Quest of the Silmaril both Beren and Lúthien were rescued from Angband by Thorondor. And, though Gondolin finally fell through treachery, the Eagles guarded that hidden Noldor kingdom for many centuries.

Thorondor and his race earned their greatest glory in the War of Wrath. The 'Quenta Silmarillion' tells how the Eagles were victorious in the Great Battle against even that most terrible evil – the winged Fire-drakes of Angband.

In the Third Age of the Sun, Gwaihir, the Windlord, ruled over the Eagles of Middle-earth. Though he was not the size of even the least of the Eagles of the First Age, by the measure of the Third Age he was the greatest of his time. Gwaihir's people, the Eagles of the Misty Mountains, were fierce and much feared by the Dark Powers. The long tale of the Quest of the Ring and the War tells how Gwaihir, with his brother Landroval and one named Meneldor the Swift, often advanced in battle with the Eagle host. The Eagles of the Misty Mountains did many great deeds. They helped to achieve the death of the Dragon of Erebor and, later, the defeat of the Orcs in the Battle of Five Armies. They also rescued the Wizard Gandalf and the Hobbit Ringbearers and fought in the last battle of the Ring War before the Black Gate of Mordor.

Eärendil

Half-elven Dragon-slayer. Eärendil the Mariner was the son of the Edain lord, Tuor, and the Elven lady, Idril of Gondolin. Eärendil was born in the year 504 of the First Age in Gondolin, but grew up in the Elven haven of Arvernien. He became the Lord of Arvernien and married Elwing, the Elven daughter of King Dior and the inheritor of the Silmaril. They had two sons: Elrond and Elros. For Eärendil, whose name means 'sea

lover', Círdan built a miraculous ship called Vingilot. While he was at sea, Arvernien was attacked and Elwing was forced to flee. Seeing no means to escape she threw herself and the Silmaril into the sea. Ulmo, the Ocean Lord, saved her by transforming her into a sea bird and allowing her to fly to Eärendil. The couple used the power and light of the Silmaril to find their way to the Undying Lands, to ask the aid of the Valar. In response, the Valar and Maiar host, along with the Elves of Eldamar, came out of the Undying Lands in the War of Wrath. It ended in the Great Battle, in which Eärendil the Mariner also fought. With the Silmaril bound to his brow, and his magical ship given the power of flight, Eärendil slew Ancalagon the Black, the greatest Dragon the world has ever known. After the end of the First Age, Eärendil led the surviving Edain to the new island kingdom of Númenor. Ever after, Eärendil was destined to sail Vingilot through the firmament. Called the Evening Star and the 'flame of the west', the Silmaril on his brow shone down from the night sky forever after.

East Elves

At the time of the Rekindling of the Stars, all Elves lived in the East of Middle-earth. But in time the Lord of Forests, the huntsman Oromë of the Valarian race, came to the Elves and brought the summons to leave that land.

Many heeded Oromë's call and travelled to the West where they were variously called West Elves and Eldar. Those who remained were named East Elves or the Avari, the 'unwilling', who feared the Great Journey to the Undying Lands.

EAGLES The greatest Eagle of the Third Age was Gwaihir, the Windlord of the Misty Mountains. With his brother Landroval and Meneldor the Swift, he fought the Dark Lord in the War of the Ring.

Easterlings

In the First Age of the Sun, all Men arose first in the eastern lands of Middle-earth. Some went to the West, but those who remained in the East lived under the dark shadow of Melkor the Enemy and turned to evil ways. These people were called the Easterlings and their land was called Rhûn.

After a time, some of these Men left the East and went to the Elf-lands of Beleriand. These Easterlings were not a tall people, but broad, strong of limb, and swarthy-skinned with dark eyes and hair. They mostly proved untrustworthy and in war betrayed their allies the Elves to Morgoth. Few names of these Men were passed on in histories, but Ulfang the Black and his sons Ulfast, Ulworth and Uldor, earned fame by virtue of committing the greatest treachery. For in the Battle of Unnumbered Tears, Ulfang and his people turned upon their Elf allies in the midst of battle and slew them from behind; by this act the tide of battle was turned and the Elves were broken. However, not all Easterlings were unfaithful and one named Bór, and his sons Borlad, Borlach and Borthand, fought nobly to the death on behalf of Elves in that Age.

Yet, ever after, the Easterling people kept this alliance with Morgoth or his mighty servant Sauron, and came always in war against the noble descendants of the Edain. Through the Ages of the Sun the Easterlings became a confederacy of many kingdoms and races. In the Third Age many Easterling people came out of Rhûn. Among them were the fierce Balchoth and the chariot warriors called Wainriders. Then too, farther south in Harad, there lived many war-like Men who had come from the East of Middle-earth long before.

At Sauron's command the Easterlings sent warriors into the War of the Ring. Upon Pelennor Fields companies of armoured Easterlings, armed with great two-handed axes, battled fiercely and died. Others too met their end when the Black Gate was broken and Sauron's kingdom of Mordor was destroyed.

The War of the Ring broke the hold of the Dark Power over the Easterlings forever. So when King Elessar was crowned in Gondor, and in the Fourth Age came to Rhûn, the Easterlings sued for peace. This Elessar granted, and for long years after that treaty there was peace in the Westlands and in the lands of Harad and Rhûn.

Echoing Mountains

When the host of the Noldor King Fëanor returned to Middle-earth in their quest for the Silmarils, they first landed in a northern wasteland called Lammoth that was walled off from the rest of Beleriand by the Ered Lómin, the Echoing Mountains. Fortunately, the mountain range was cleft by the sea at the Firth of Drengist, and by this means the Noldor Elves made their way into Hithlum in northern Beleriand. The Echoing Mountains were called by that name because of their startling acoustic quality which resulted in the empty wastes of Lammoth being greatly amplified and echoed in the mountains above.

Edain

Of the Men of the First Age, those counted greatest were the Edain. They were the first Men to come out of the East into Beleriand, where the High Elves had made many kingdoms. Most were strong and brave Men, and the tales of that time tell of many great deeds.

These Men first entered Beleriand in three hosts led by the chieftains Bëor, Haldad and Marach, and these hosts became the Three Houses of Edain. Because the Elves were called the Firstborn Children of Ilúvatar, the Noldor

EASTERLINGS The barbarian Men who came out of the East of Middle-earth to make war on the Elf, Edain and Dúnedain kingdoms of the West. These savage tribesmen were the servants and soldiers of the Dark Lord.

in Beleriand called these Men the Atani, which means the 'Secondborn', and filled them with immense knowledge. Much that is counted great and noble in all Men had its beginning in the Noldor masters. In the space of quite a short time the common tongue of Beleriand became Sindarin, the language of the Grey-elves, and Quenya words were little used. This is why the Atani were most often called the Edain in all the written lore of Beleriand for such is the Sindarin form of Secondborn.

Of the Three Houses, the House of Bëor (which was later named the House of Húrin) was the first to meet the Noldorin Elves. Of all Men they were most like the Noldor, who loved them greatly. Their hair was dark and their bright eyes were grey. They were eager-minded, swift to learn and great in strength. Those of the Second House were named the Haladin and the People of Haleth; they were a forest-dwelling people, smallest in number and in stature of the Three Houses. The Third House was the House of Hador, whose people were golden-haired and blue-eyed and they were the most numerous of the Edain.

Many heroes arose among the Edain. Hador Lórindol, which is 'goldenhead', was named peer of Elf-lords and lord of Dor-lómin. Húrin the Steadfast was the mighty warrior who slew seventy Trolls in battle. As is told in the 'Narn i Hîn Húrin' Húrin's son was Túrin Turambar, who wore the heirloom of his people, the Dwarf-wrought Dragon-helm of Dor-lómin, and carried the Black Sword called Gurthang. With these weapons, and by strength and stealth, Túrin slew Glaurung, the Father of Dragons.

Of all the deeds of Men within the Spheres of the World, the greatest were those of Beren Erchamion, who was married to the Elven-princess Lúthien Tinúviel, the fairest daughter of the World. For Beren was the hero who, with the knife Angrist, cut a Silmaril from Morgoth's Iron Crown.

In the histories of Elves there were but two other unions of Edain and Elves. Tuor wed Idril, daughter of Turgon, Noldor lord of Gondolin. Because of this, it is claimed that Tuor is the only Man to have been taken into the Undying Lands and permitted to dwell there. The son of Tuor and Idril, Eärendil the Mariner, wed the Sindar princess Elwing. It was Eärendil who sailed the flying ship 'Vingilot' and carried the Silmaril, the flame of the blue star of twilight. In the Great Battle, Eärendil in his ship called 'Vingilot' also slew the winged Fire-drake Ancalagon the Black.

The remnant of the Edain were led out of Middle-earth by the guiding light of Eärendil in the Second Age, for the Edain were rewarded by the Valar for their suffering. Strengthened in body and mind and granted long life, they were led to the land of Númenór, which lay in the Western Sea between Middle-earth and the Undying Lands. At this time they were renamed the Dúnedain, the 'Edain of the West', and they lived there for the Second Age of the Sun and were counted the wisest and greatest of Men ever to walk the lands of Middle-earth.

Edhil

In the dialects of the Elven peoples, there arose various names by which they knew themselves. Among these was the term Edhil, by which the Sindar called all Elves.

Edoras

For the last five centuries of the Third Age of the Sun, the capital city of the Horsemen of Rohan was Edoras. It was built in the twenty-sixth century by the first two kings of the Rohirrim, Eorl and Brego, at the foot of the White Mountains. The name is a translation of the Rohirrim word for 'the courts' as this was the royal city, and contained the great feast-hall of Meduseld, the court of the king. From the high ground of Edoras, built as a hill-fort with a stockade and dyke, the kings looked out onto the great horse plains that made up the kingdom of Rohan.

Eglath

In the story of the Great Journey of the Elves in the Ages of Stars, there is the tale of how the Third Kindred, the Teleri, lost their king, Elwë Singollo. In the Forest of Nan Elmoth in the lands of Beleriand, he fell under an enchantment. And though they searched for the king for many years, the Teleri could not find him and finally they took Elwë's brother as king and went again westwards towards the Undying Lands. But many would not leave Nan Elmoth and stayed for the love of Elwë Singollo, though many more years passed. These were the Elves called the Eglath; they were divided from their kindred for ever and their name was Elvish for the 'forsaken'. In the end, their faithfulness had its reward, for their king did return. He was now called Elu Thingol or King Greymantle, and he was greatly changed. A great light shone about him, and with him he brought the source of his enchantment, his queen, Melian the Maia. With the return of the king and the blessing of the new queen a great destiny came to the Elgath. Ever afterwards they were named the Sindar, the Grey-elves, and in the years of Stars they were held to be mightiest of people in Middle-earth.

Ekkaia

From their beginning to the end of the Second Age of the Sun after the Change of the World that came with the sinking of Númenor, the continents of Arda were believed to have been encompassed by Ekkaia, the Encircling Sea. Ekkaia was a vast river-like ocean that flowed around the furthest limits of the Arda, from the Door of Night to the west of the Undying Lands, through the icy regions north of the great continents, on past the furthest eastern continent and the Gates of the Morning in the west, then southward through the uncharted regions of the south until it returned to where it began in the west. After the Change of the World and the removal of the Undying Lands from Arda, Ekkaia was reshaped and its waters intermingled with the other seas.

Elanor

In the Third Age of the Sun, there grew a fair winter flower in the land of Lothlórien. This flower was called Elanor, which means 'star-sun', and its bloom was Star-shaped and golden. The histories of Middle-earth link Elanor to the 'Tale of Aragorn and Arwen'. Both Elanor the Gold Star and Niphredil the White Star grew thickest on Cerin Amroth, the mound on which Aragorn, the mortal lord of the Dúnedain, and Arwen Undómiel, the daughter of Elrond Half-elven, plighted their troth. Arwen cast her lot with the race of mortal Men and, after the War of the Ring, Aragorn and Arwen were wed. Though her life was happy, soon after Aragorn died Arwen too perished, choosing the hill of Cerin Amroth as the place of her final rest.

Eldalië

After a time spent in the great Mere of the East called Cuiviénen in Middle-earth, the Elves were given a great choice. Either they must continue to abide in the East and know only starlight or they must make a Great Journey and come to the Land of Eternal Light in the Uttermost West. The Elves who in the First Age of Starlight chose the Great Journey out of Middle-earth to the Undying Lands were named the Eldalië, the people of the Eldar. They were of Three Kindred: the Vanyar, the Noldor and the Teleri, and much is told of them in song and tale.

Eldamar

The lands of the Eldar, or High Elves, in the Undying Lands were called Eldamar, the 'elvenhome'. Here the greatest of the Elves from among the three kindred of the Vanyar, Noldor and Teleri people lived with the mighty

Valarian powers. Eldamar was that part of the Undying Lands east of Valinor and west of the Great Sea. It was founded in the Second Age of the Trees of the Valar when the first Eldar arrived in the Undying Lands. Its territories were on both sides of the looming Pelóri Mountains and included vast fertile lands west of the mountains lit eternally by the Trees of Light, the Calacirya, or Pass of Light – the coastal lands west of the mountains lit only by starlight on the Bay of Eldamar – and the great island of Tol Eressëa. Here were a multitude of cities and settlements, but Tirion, built on the hill of Túna in the midst of the Pass of Light, was the first city of the Vanyar and Noldor, and the greatest. There was also the Noldor stronghold of Formenos in the land of light, and the Teleri cities of the Sea Elves of Alqualondë on the coast, and Avallónë on Tol Eressëa. The lands and cities of Eldamar were wealthy and beautiful beyond comparison. Their cities were built with precious stones and precious metals. Its crops of grain and fruits were bountiful and its people happy, resourceful and wise. It was claimed that even the shores of Eldamar were strewn with diamonds, opals and pale crystals. After the disaster of Númenor and the Change of the World at the end of the Second Age of the Sun, Eldamar, along with the rest of the Undying Lands, was taken out of the circles of the world, and beyond the understanding of mortals.

Eldar

According to the tales that have reached the ears of Men, and by what is written in the books that Men might read, the history of the Eldar is largely the history of the Elven race. In the First Age of Stars, when Oromë the Huntsman of the Valar discovered the Elves in the east lands of Middle-earth, he looked at them in wonder and named them the Eldar, the 'people of the Stars'. At this time all Elves were named Eldar, but later this name was taken only by those who had accepted the summons of the Valar to the West and undertook the Great Journey to the Undying Lands. Those who remained were named the Avari, the 'unwilling', and they stayed for love of Middle-earth, or because they distrusted the promise of the Land of Eternal Light.

So the Eldar were a chosen people and they were divided into Three Kindred: The Vanyar, the Noldor and the Teleri. The Journey was, however, long and perilous and many Eldar did not reach the Undying Lands; they were named the Umanyar, 'those not of Aman'. Among them were the Nandor, the Sindar, the Falathrim and the Laiquendi. But the greater number did reach the Journey's end and came to the Undying Lands in the days of the Trees of the Valar. There they took that land named Eldamar, which had been set apart for them, built fine cities and became a great people.

Even in the years of strife and darkness that came with their hopeless war against Morgoth the Enemy, the 'Quenta Silmarillion' tells of their great deeds, which blaze in that dark history, and for many Ages the kingdoms of the Eldar flourished in both Middle-earth and the Undying Lands. Much of this is told in the tale of the Elves, the histories of the many sundered Teleri, and in the 'Noldolantë' which Maglor sang.

Elendil

Dúnedain king of Arnor and Gondor. Elendil was a Númenórean prince of Andúnie. After the Downfall of Númenor in the year 3319 of the Second Age, Elendil and his sons, Isildur and Anárion, sailed their nine ships to Middle-earth and established the Dúnedain kingdoms of Middle-earth. Called Elendil the Tall, he chose to live in the north kingdom of Arnor, where he ruled as the first High King of Arnor and Gondor, while his sons lived in the south kingdom of Gondor. In 3429 of the Second Age, Sauron attacked the Dúnedain realms. The following year, the Last Alliance of Elves and Men was formed. Gil-galad, the last High King of Elves on Middle-earth, joined forces with Elendil's Dúnedain. At the Battle of Dagorlad in 3434, Sauron's army was defeated but the Ring Lord fled into Mordor. In the seven-year siege that followed, Anárion was killed. Although Elendil and Gil-galad finally managed to overthrow Sauron in a duel before the Dark Tower, they were also slain in the struggle. It was left to Isildur to take his father's broken sword, Narsil, and cut the One Ring from Sauron's hand.

Elendili

The 'Akallabêth' tells how when the Númenóreans foolishly went to war against the Powers of Arda in the Undying Lands, all their country was cast down and destroyed. However, before the Downfall, nine ships sailed away from that doomed land. These were the ships of the Elendili, the 'faithful', and the Elf-friends, who repudiated the ways of the Númenóreans and sailed to Middle-earth. There Elendil the Tall and his two sons made the kingdoms of the Dúnedain in the North in Arnor and in the South in Gondor.

Elladan and Elrohir

Elven princes of Rivendell. Elladan and Elrohir were the identical twin sons of Master Elrond of Rivendell and Princess Celebrían of Lothlórien. Born in the year 139 of the Third Age, the twin brothers were just a century older than their beautiful sister, Arwen. For most of their lives, they remained within the hidden Elven kingdoms of Rivendell and Lothlórien, but in the year 2509 their mother was attacked by Orcs. Although the brothers soon rescued her, Celebrían received a poison wound that none could cure, and finally had to set sail to the Undying Lands. For the rest of the Age, the brothers allied themselves with the Rangers of the Dúnedain and vengefully hunted Orcs wherever they could find them. During the War of the Ring, the twins rode with the Rangers of the North to join Aragorn in Rohan. They fought alongside Aragorn through all the major battles of the war, until the last confrontation before the Black Gate of Mordor. The brothers appear to have remained in Rivendell long after the departure of Elrond and other Elven nobles, and no tale survives which tells whether they chose to remain among mortals or make that final journey on the Elven ships to the Undying Lands.

Elrond and Elros

Half-elven princes of Beleriand. Born in Arvernien on the coast of Beleriand in 542 of the First Age of the Sun, Elrond and Elros were the twin sons of Eärendil and Elwing. After the War of Wrath, as the sons of a mortal hero and an Elven princess, the Valar allowed the brothers to choose their fates. Elros chose to be mortal, although he was granted a life span of five centuries.

At the beginning of the Second Age, Elros led the surviving Edain to Númenor and became their first king. Elros took the name of Tar-Minyatur and rule Númenor from the year 32 to 442. He built the royal palace and citadel of Armenelos. Elrond chose to be an immortal Elven prince and lived in Lindon at the beginning of the Second Age. In 1695, he was sent by High King Gil-galad to help defend Eregion during the War of Sauron and the Elves. However, when Eregion was overrun in 1697, Elrond led the survivors to the foothills of the Misty Mountains where he founded Rivendell, which was called 'Imladris' in Elvish. In the Last Alliance of Elves and Men at the end of the Second Age, Elrond was Gil-galad's herald. Before Gil-galad died, he gave Elrond the Ring Vilya, which was the 'ring of air' and the greatest of the Three Elven Rings.

In the year 100 of the Third Age, Elrond married Celebrían, the daughter of Galadriel,

ELROND AND ELROS Elrond and Elros were the twin sons of Eärendil and Elwing.

and the couple had three children: Elladan, Elrohir and Arwen. Through the Third Age, Master Elrond Half-Elven, as he was called, gave whatever help he could to the Dúnedain, and the heirs of Arnor were often raised under his protection in Rivendell. One such heir was Aragorn II, who was fostered by Elrond. In 2980, Aragorn met Arwen in Lothlórien. The couple fell in love, but Elrond forbade their marriage until Aragorn became High King of Arnor and Gondor. With Elrond's guidance, the Fellowship of the Ring was formed in 3018 in Rivendell, and the Quest of the Ring set. After the One Ring was destroyed and Aragorn assumed his kingship and married Arwen, the Third Age ended with Elrond sailing across the sea to the Undying Lands.

Elven-Smiths

In the Third and Fourth Ages of the Sun, legends of Men and Dwarves spoke widely of the Elven-smiths, a vanished race that once lived in Eregion, to the west of the Mountains of Mist. These were Noldorin Elves, who were more properly named the Gwaith-i-Mírdain. It was they who forged the great Rings of Power which for two Ages of the Sun loosed so much terror upon the lands of Middle-earth.

Elves

In the very hour that Varda, the Lady of the Heavens, rekindled the bright Stars above Middle-earth, the Children of Eru awoke by the Mere of Cuiviénen, the 'water of awakening'. These people were the Quendi, who are called Elves, and when they came into being the first thing they perceived was the light of new Stars. So it is that of all things, Elves love starlight best and worship Varda, whom they know as Elentári, Queen of the Stars, over all Valar. And further, when the new light entered the eyes of Elves in that awakening moment, it was held there, so that ever after it shone from those eyes.

Thus, Eru, the One, whom the Earthborn know as Ilúvatar, created the fairest race that ever was made and the wisest. Ilúvatar declared that Elves would have and make more beauty than any earthly creatures and they would possess the greatest happiness and deepest sorrow. They would be immortal and ageless, so they might live as long as the Earth lived. They would never know sickness and pestilence, but their bodies would be like the Earth in substance and could be destroyed. They could be slain with fire or steel in war, be murdered, and even die of great grief.

Their size would be the same as that of Men, who were still to be created, but Elves would be stronger in spirit and limb, and would not grow weak with age, but became only wiser and more fair.

Though far lesser beings in stature and might than the god-like Valar, Elves share the nature of those powers more than the Secondborn race of Men do. It is said that Elves always walk in a light that is like the glow of the Moon, just below the rim of the Earth. Their hair is like spun gold or woven silver or polished jet, and starlight glimmers all about them, on their hair, eyes, silken clothes and jewelled hands. There is always light on the Elven face, and the sound of their voices is various and beautiful and subtle as water. Of all their arts they excel best in speech, song and poetry. Elves were the first of all people on Earth to speak with voices and no earthly creatures before them sang. And justly they call themselves the Quendi, the 'speakers', for they taught the spoken arts to all races on Middle-earth.

In the First Age of Starlight, after the Fall of Utumno and the defeat of Melkor the Dark Enemy, the Valar called the Elves to the Undying Lands of the West. This was before

ELVES Stronger, nobler, wiser and more beautiful than humans, they did not grow weak with age or disease. If they were not slain in war or strife, they would never die, but would grow even wiser and more fair.

the Rising of the Sun and the Moon when only the Stars lit Middle-earth, and the Valar wished to protect the Elves from the darkness and the lurking evil that Melkor had left behind. And so, in the Undying Lands which lie beyond the seas of the West, the Valar prepared a place named Eldamar, meaning 'elven home', where it was foretold that in time the Elves would build cities with domes of silver, streets of gold and stairs of crystal.

In this way the Elves were first divided, for not all the Elven People wished to leave Middle-earth and enter the Eternal Light of the Undying Lands. At the bidding of the Valar a great number went to the West, and these were called the Eldar, the 'people of the Stars', but others stayed for love of starlight and were called Avari, the 'unwilling'. Though they were skilled in the ways of nature and, like their kindred, were immortal, they were a lesser people. They mostly remained in eastern lands where the power of Melkor was greatest and so they dwindled.

The Eldar were also known as the People of the Great Journey for they had travelled westwards across the pathless lands of Middle-earth towards the Great Sea for many years. Of these Elven people there were Three Kindred, ruled by three kings. The first was the Vanyar, and Ingwë was their king; the second the Noldor, with Finwë as their lord; and the third was the Teleri who were ruled by Elwë Singollo. The Vanyar and Noldor reached Belegaer, the Sea of the West, long before the Teleri, and Ulmo, Lord of the Waters, came to them and set them on an island that was like a vast ship. He then drew the two hosts over the sea to the Undying Lands, to Eldamar, the place that the Valar had prepared for them.

The fate of the Teleri was different from their kindred and they separated into various races. Because the Teleri were the most numerous of all the kindred, their passage was slowest. Many turned back from the Journey, and amongst these were the Nandor, the Laiquendi, the Sindar, and the Falathrim. Elwë, the High King, was himself lost and he remained in Middle-earth. However, most of the Teleri pushed westwards, taking Olwë, Elwë's brother, as their king, and they reached the Great Sea. There they awaited Ulmo, who at last took them to Eldamar.

In Eldamar, the Vanyar and Noldor built a great city named Tirion on the hill of Túna, while on the shore the Teleri built the Haven of Swans, which in their language was Alqualondë. These cities of the Elves of Eldamar were the fairest in all the World.

In Middle-earth, the Sindar (who were called Grey-elves), through the teachings and the light of Melian the Maia, grew mightier than all the other Elves in Mortal Lands. An enchanted kingdom with great power was made in the Wood of Doriath and it was the greatest kingdom amongst the Eldar who did not see the Trees of the Valar. With the help of the Dwarves of the Blue Mountains, the Sindar built Menegroth, called the Thousand Caves, for it was a city beneath a mountain. Yet it was like a forest hung with golden lanterns. Through its galleries could be heard bird song and the laughter of crustal water flowing in silver fountains.

These were the great Ages of the Eldar, both in Middle-earth and in the Undying Lands. It was during this time that the Noldor prince Fëanor wrought the Silmarils three jewels like diamonds that shone with a flame that was a form of life itself and shone too with the living Light of the Trees of the Valar.

At this time, the lies that Melkor had spread bore fruit, and there was strife and war. With the Great Spider, Ungoliant, Melkor came and destroyed the Trees, and Light went from the Undying Lands for ever. During the Long Night that followed, Melkor stole the Silmarils and with Ungoliant fled across Helcaraxë, the 'grinding ice', and returned to Middle-earth and the dark Pits of Angband, his great armoury.

Fëanor swore vengeance and the Noldor pursued Melkor to Middle-earth. In doing this they became a cursed people, for they captured the Swan ships of the Teleri of Alqualondë and slew their Elven brothers. This was the first Kinslaying among Elves. With the ships of the Teleri the Noldor crossed Belegaer, the Great Sea, while the Noldor led by Fingolfin, in an act of great courage, dared to cross Helcaraxë, on foot.

As the 'Quenta Silmarillion' tells, so began the War of the Jewels. The Noldor pursued Melkor and named him Morgoth, the 'Dark Enemy of the World'. The war was bitter and terrible and, of those Eldar who were in Middle-earth, few survived that struggle. Finally, the Valar and many Eldar in the Undying Lands came and, in the War of Wrath, crushed Morgoth the Enemy for ever. But in that war Beleriand was destroyed and was covered by the waves of the vast sea. The great kingdoms of that place disappeared for ever, as did the Elven cities of Menegroth, Nargothrond and Gondolin. Only one small part of Ossiriand, Lindon, survived the deluge. There the last Eldar kingdom in Middle-earth remained in the first years of the Second Age of the Sun. Most of the Eldar who survived the War of Wrath returned West and were brought by the white ships of the Teleri to Tol Eressëa in the Bay of Eldamar. There they built the haven of Avallónë. Meanwhile, those Men who had aided the Eldar against Morgoth went to an island named Númenórë.

Yet still, for a while, some Eldar remained in Mortal Lands. One such was Gil-galad and he was last of all the High Kings of the Eldar in Middle-earth. His reign lasted as long as the Second Age of the Sun and his kingdom of Lindon survived until the Fourth Age. Some Noldor and Sindar lords joined the Silvan Elves and made themselves kingdoms: Thranduil made Greenwood the Great his Woodland

Realm and Celeborn and Galadriel ruled Lothlórien, the Golden Wood. In that Age the greatest of the Eldarin colonies was Eregion, which Men named Hollin, where many great nobles of the Noldor went. They were named the Gwaith-i-Mírdain, but in later days they were called the Elven-smiths. And it was to them that Sauron the Maia, greatest servant of Morgoth, came in disguise. Celebrimbor, the greatest Elven-smith of Middle-earth and grandson of Fëanor, who made the Silmarils, lived in Hollin. At his order and with his skill the Rings of Power were made, and because of them and the One Ring that Sauron forged, the War of Sauron and the Elves was waged and many other wars.

The evil battles of Sauron's War were terrible. Celebrimbor perished and his land was ruined, and Gil-galad sent Elrond and many warriors from Lindon to the aid of the people of Eregion. Those Elves who survived the destruction of Eregion fled to Imladris (which in the Third Age was called Rivendell) and hid from the terror, and they took as their lord Elrond Half-elven. But, though the Elves were not strong enough to break the power of the Dark Lord as long as he held the One Ring, their allies, the Númenóreans, had grown mighty in the West. The Númenóreans came in their ships to Lindon and drove Sauron from the lands of the West. In a later time still, they came again, and captured the Dark Lord himself and in chains took him across the sea to their lands.

There Sauron remained until all the lands of Númenórë were swallowed up by the Sea of Belegaer, and there came the Change of the World when Undying Lands of Valinor and Eldamar were removed from the Circles of the World. Mortal Lands became closed in on themselves and the Undying Lands were set apart, unreachable except by the white Elven-ships.

But in that Second Age of the Sun there was still Sauron, Lord of the Rings, to deal with. For he had escaped the Downfall of Númenor and had returned to his kingdom of Mordor. Therefore, the Last Alliance of Elves and Men was made. They broke Mordor and Barad-dûr, his tower, and took his Ring from him. He and his servants perished and went into the shadows, but Gil-galad, the last High King of the Elves in Middle-earth, was also killed, as were nearly all the great lords of the Númenóreans.

There still remained a few Eldar to watch over the lands that the race of Men was slowly coming to possess. In the Third Age, the Eldar in Middle-earth were but a shadow of their former presence. Lindon remained but stood mostly apart from the strife of Middle-earth, and Círdan, lord of the Grey Havens, was held highest among them. The concerns of Elves seemed largely their own in all but one matter: that of the Lord of the Rings, who came to Mordor once again and sent his servants, the Nazgûl, out over the land. Then the Elves and the descendants of the Númenóreans once more fought in that which is called the War of the Ring. The One Ring in that time was destroyed. Mordor fell again, and finally, Sauron vanished for ever, as did his servants and his hold on all evil in the World was broken. In the Fourth Age, in the time of the dominion of Men, the last of the Eldar sailed the last white ship that Círdan of the Grey Havens made, out upon the Straight Road. And thus these People of the Stars passed away for ever to that place beyond the reach of mortals, save in ancient tale and perhaps in the dreams of children.

Elwë Singollo

Elven king of the Teleri. Elwë was one of the three kings of the Elves who led their people on the Great Journey to the Undying Lands. However, in Beleriand he abandoned the Journey and founded the realm of the Grey-elves. He was called King Thingol and his tale is told under that name.

Elwing

Elven princess of Doriath. Elwing the White was the beautiful daughter of King Dior and Queen Nimloth of Doriath. She was the only member of her family to survive the sacking of Menegroth by the Noldor in the year 509 of the First Age of the Sun. With her inheritance, the Silmaril, she found sanctuary in the harbour of Arvernien. There she met and married Eärendil the Mariner and gave birth to twin sons: Elrond and Elros. But when the Noldor learned where the Silmaril was hidden, they attacked again. Seeing no means of escape, Elwing threw herself and the Silmaril into the sea. At that moment, Ulmo, the Valarian Ocean Lord, intervened and transformed Elwing into a white sea bird. With the Silmaril in her beak she flew across the sea to find Eärendil. They managed to find their way through the Shadowy Seas to the Undying Lands, so that Eärendil might beg the Valar to intervene in the Wars of Beleriand. After the War of Wrath Eärendil, with the Silmaril bound to his brow, was placed in the firmament by the Valar. He sailed his ship across the sky and was known as the Morning Star. Thereafter, Elwing made her home in a tower on the northern coast of Eldamar, and each night as Eärendil's ship drew near the western horizon, Elwing – as a white bird – flew from her tower to join her husband.

Enchanted Isles

After Melkor the Vala and Ungoliant the Giant Spider extinguished the light of the world by destroying the Trees of the Valar, Manwë and the other Valar built many fortifications and defences in the Undying Lands for fear of the return of these evil beings and their legions. Among the most effective was the vast chain of islands along the eastern coast of the Undying Lands. These were the Enchanted Isles and the waters about them were called the Shadowy Seas. The islands were enchanted by the power of a mighty spell: its maze of waterways confounded all mariners' means of reckoning, and if sailors landed on the islands themselves, they immediately fell down into a deep and eternal sleep.

Engwar

At the time the race of Men first came into the World, the Elves were much amazed. Compared with Elves, Men were a frail race, unable to withstand the harsh elements, illness or old age. So the Avari, the Elves of the East, taught skills to many of these Men that they might live without deprivation and fear. However, the Elves still found that these people faded quickly, as they were mortal beings; the Elves could hardly learn the worth of a Man before he would be dead with the frost of age. Most terrible and mysterious to Elves were the sicknesses of the body that swept through the race of Men like flames in a wheat field. When these plagues came to Men they perished, while no Elf could ever know such evil. One of the names, therefore, that Elves called Men was given with great pity: the Engwar, which in the Elven tongue means the 'sickly'.

Ents

During the War of the Ring the strange forest giants called Ents came in battle against the Orcs and Men of Isengard. Half Men, half trees, they were fourteen feet tall, and the eldest had lived in Middle-earth for nine Ages of Stars and the Sun.

Lord of the Ents was Fangorn who in the common tongue was called Treebeard. He was huge and ancient, for he belonged to the tallest and strongest race born into the World. Like oak or beech was the huge rough-barked trunk of Treebeard, while his branch-like arms were smooth and his seven-fingered hands were gnarled. Treebeard's peculiar, almost neckless head was tall and thick as his trunk. His brown eyes were large and wise and seemed to glint with a green light. His wild grey beard was like a thatch of twigs and moss. He was made of the fibre of trees, yet he moved swiftly on unbending legs with feet like living roots, swaying and stretching like a long-legged wading bird.

Elvish histories tell how, when Varda, Queen of the Heavens, rekindled the Stars and the Elves awoke, the Ents also awoke in the Great Forests of Arda. They came from the thoughts of Yavanna, Queen of the Earth, and were her Shepherds of Trees. Shepherds and guardians they proved to be, for if roused to anger, Entish wrath was terrible and they could crush stone and steel with their hands alone. Justly they were feared, but they were also gentle and wise. They loved the trees and all the Olvar and guarded them from evil.

At the time of their awakening Ents could not speak, but the Elves taught them that art, and they loved it greatly. They delighted in learning many tongues, even the short chirping languages of Men. Dearest of all they loved the language they had devised themselves that none but Ents ever mastered. It rolled deep and full from their tongues as slow thunder or the timeless booming of waves on forgotten shores. In the slow passing of Entish time they formed their thoughts in unhurried meditation, and framed them into speech as undisturbed and rolling as the changing seasons.

Though Ents at times had great gatherings, called Entmoots, for the most part they were a solitary folk living apart from one another in isolated Ent houses in the great forests. Often these were mountain caverns plentifully supplied with spring water and surrounded by beautiful trees. In these places they took their meals, not solid food but clear liquid stored in great stone jars. These were Ent-draughts and the magical fluid glowed with gold and green light. And in the Ent houses they took their rest, often finding refreshment in standing beneath the crystal coolness of a waterfall cascading throughout the night.

So the Ents lived out their wise, almost immortal lives, and the many races of the Earth thrived and declined around them without troubling their greatness. Only when the foul Orcs came armed with weapons of steel were the Ents roused in wrath. The Dwarves too were not loved by Ents, for they were axe-bearers and hewers of wood. And it is said that in the First Age of the Sun the Dwarf-warriors of Nogrod, who had sacked the Grey-elven citadel of Menegroth, were caught by Ents and utterly destroyed.

Ents, in the years of Starlight, had been both male and female, yet in the Ages of the Sun the Entwives became enamoured of the open lands where they might tend the lesser Olvar – the fruit trees, shrubs, flowers, grasses and grain; whereas the male Ents loved the trees of the forests. So it was that the Entwives went to the open Brown Lands, where they were worshipped by the race of Men who learned from them the art of tending the fruits and the crops of the Earth.

Yet before the end of the Second Age of the Sun, the gardens of the Entwives were destroyed, and with the gardens went the Entwives. Among them was the spouse of Treebeard, Fimbrethil, who was called Wandlimb the Lightfooted. No tale tells of their fate. Perhaps the Entwives went to the South or East; but, wherever it was, it was beyond the knowledge of the Ents of the Forests, who wandered in search of them for many long years.

So, though Ents could not die in the manner of Men, through age, they became a dwindling race none the less. They were never numerous, and some were slain with steel and fire, and no new Entings came after the departure of the Entwives. As well, the vast forests of Eriador where many once roamed had, by the Third Age, been hewn down or burnt, so only the Old Forest, which bordered the Shire, and the great Entwood of Treebeard remained.

By the War of the Ring Treebeard was counted among the three eldest Ents who had come forth under the stars at the Time of Awakening. Besides Treebeard, there was Finglas, which means 'Leaflock', and Fladrif,

which means 'Skinbark', but the latter two had withdrawn even from the affairs of other Ents. Finglas had retreated in Ent fashion into the nature of his being and had become 'treeish'. He moved but little and few could tell him from the trees. Fladrif had battled alone against the Orcs, who had captured his birch groves, slain many of his Entings, and had wounded him with axes. He eventually fled to live along on high mountain slopes.

Though only Treebeard of the elders remained limb-lithe and active, there were many younger Ents. Throughout the Entwood there was discontent because the Ents were being harassed by the servants of Saruman who inhabited neighbouring Isengard. So they entered the War of the Ring, and this was the great March of the Ents. Rank upon rank of the Ents marched on the stronghold of Isengard. With them came the Huorns, the Tree-spirits whom the Ents commanded and whose strength was nearly as great as their own. The very walls of Isengard were torn down and destroyed by Entish wrath and the power of Saruman was shattered. The Huorns advanced into the Battle of the Hornburg like a marching forest, and the legions of Saruman were exterminated. After the War of the Ring, the Ents again lived on peacefully in the Entwood, yet they continued to wane and the Fourth Age was believed to be their last.

Entwood

The large and ancient forest at the southern end of the Misty Mountains in the vales of the Anduin River was known as Entwood because it was inhabited by those ancient and powerful creatures called Ents, the Tree-herds and forest guardians. At the time of the War of the Ring, this forest was most often called the Fanghorn Forest after Fanghorn (or 'Treebeard'), the oldest living Ent on Middle-earth and the master of the forest.

ENTS Guardians of the Forest and the Shepherds of Trees. They were powerful giants who were half men, half trees. In the War of the Ring, an army of Ents marched on Isengard and tore down its walls.

Éomer

Northman, prince of Rohan. Born in 2991 of the Third Age, Éomer was the nephew of King Théoden of Rohan, and like nearly all of his race was tall, strong and golden–haired. Before the War of the Ring, Éomer was a marshall of Riddermark, but through his friendship with Gandalf and his concern about the evil influence of the king's adviser, Gríma Wormtongue, he fell out of favour. During the War of the Ring he fought with distinction at the battles of Hornburg, Pelennor Fields and at the Black Gate of Mordor. When King Théoden received his mortal wounds on Pelennor Fields, he named Éomer his heir. He became the eighteenth king of Rohan and ruled until the year 63 of the Fourth Age. In 3020, he married Princess Lothíriel of Dol Amroth, who soon after bore his son and heir, Elfwine the Fair.

Eönwë

Maia herald of Manwë. Eönwë is mightiest of the Maiar and standard-bearer of Manwë, the King of the Valar. Eönwë's strength in battle rivals that of even the Valar. His trumpet announced the coming of the Valar, Maiar and Eldar into the War of Wrath that destroyed Angband and ended Morgoth's reign forever. After the Great Battle, it was Eönwë who judged the Elves and gave the Edain their great wisdom and knowledge.

Eorl

Northman, king of Rohan. Eorl succeeded his father, Léod, as Lord of the Éothéod while still a youth. For this reason he was called Eorl the Young. Eorl gained fame for taming Felaróf, the sire of the legendary Mearas, the white 'horse princes' of Rohan. In the year 2510, Eorl's cavalry rescued the Men of Gondor from certain defeat at the Battle of Celebrant. In gratitude, the Steward of Gondor gave his allies the province of Calenardhon which was renamed Rohan, meaning 'horse land'. Eorl ruled as the King of Rohan from 2410 until 2545, when, at the age of sixty years, he was slain battling against the Easterlings in the Wold.

Eorlingas

In the fair and rolling grasslands that, in the Third Age of the Sun, lay north of the White Mountains, there lived a race of Men who were named the Rohirrim, the 'horse-lords'. They often called themselves the Eorlingas, in honour of Eorl the Young, the first in their line of kings. It was he who first tamed the Mearas, the 'horse-princes', and led his people in victory against the Easterlings. Five centuries of rulers of Rohan descended from this one great king.

Éothéod

Among those Northmen who lived east of the Mountains of Mist there arose a strong and fair race that entered the histories of the Westlands in the twentieth century of the Third Age of the Sun. They were led into the Vales of Anduin, between the Carrock and Gladden, by a chieftain named Frumgar. These people were named the Éothéod and they were great horsemen and men-at-arms. The son of Frumgar was named Fram and he slew Scatha the Worm, a Dragon of the Grey Mountains. Of Frumgar's line was Léod and his son, Eorl the Young, who first tamed the Horse Felaróf, sire of the Mearas, the princes of Horses. Eorl led the Éothéod cavalry into the Battle of the Field of Celebrant and crushed the Balchoth and the Orcs who had broken the shield-wall of Gondor's army. For that rescue Cirion, Ruling Steward of Gondor, made a gift of the southern province of Calenardhon (which was called the Mark) to the Éothéod, who came south willingly and afterwards were known as the Rohirrim, the 'horse-lords'. Eorl became the first in the line of Kings of the Mark, who were rulers of that rich and rolling grassland for five hundred years and more.

Éowyn

Northwoman, shield-maiden of Rohan. At the time of the War of the Ring, Éowyn was the beautiful, golden-haired niece of King Théoden of Rohan and sister of Prince Éomer. During the War of the Ring, Éowyn fell in love with Aragorn. Despairing at his assumed death, and frustrated by her inability to fight for her people, Éowyn disguised herself as a warrior called Dernhelm, and rode with the Rohirrim in the Battle of the Pelennor Fields. There she won the greatest fame of any warrior by standing over the mortally wounded King Théoden and fighting the Witch-king, the lord of the Ringwraiths. Protected by the prophecy that he could not be slain by the hand of Man, Éowyn revealed that she was a shield-maiden, and with her sword killed the Winged Beast on which he rode. Then – with the help of the Hobbit, Meriadoc Brandybuck – she slew the Witch-king himself. In that struggle, however, Éowyn was overcome by the poison 'Black Breath' of the Ringwraith and fell into a death-like sleep. She was eventually brought out of this coma by Aragorn, using the magical herb called Athelas.

After the War of the Ring, Éowyn recovered from both the evil spell of the Witch-king and her infatuation with Aragorn. She then married Faramir, the Steward of Gondor and Prince of Ithilien.

Erebor

In the Third Age of the Sun, Erebor the 'Lonely Mountain' could be found in Rhovanion, south of the Grey Mountains and between Mirkwood and the Iron Hills. In the year 1999 it was settled by the Dwarf King

ÉOWYN Éowyn disguised herself as a warrior called Dernhelm, and rode with the Rohirrim in the Battle of the Pelennor Fields.

Thrain I and became known as the Kingdom under the Mountain.

For over seven centuries the Dwarf-kingdom of Erebor grew wealthy and powerful, but in the year 2770 the winged, fire-breathing dragon called Smaug the Golden destroyed the realm, and drove out the Dwarves. For nearly two hundred years Smaug lived in Erebor and slept upon a vast treasure hoard in a great lair within its chambers. In the year 2941, the Hobbit Bilbo Baggins and the Dwarves of Thorin and Company disturbed the Dragon, but when Smaug came out in vengeful wrath, he was slain by Bard the Bowman. The Dwarves returned to Erebor, and King Dáin II re-established the wealth and fame of the Kingdom under the Mountain. During the War of the Ring, the forces of Sauron attacked and besieged Erebor. However, once the One Ring was destroyed, the forces of darkness melted away and the Dwarves and their allies the Men of Dale drove off the Orc and Easterling army that had besieged them. In the Fourth Age, Erebor retained its wealth and independence, but became closely allied to the Reunited Kingdom of Arnor and Gondor under King Elessar.

Eregion

West of the Misty Mountains in the woodland below the Dwarf-kingdom of Khazad-dûm during the Second Age of the Sun was the realm of Eregion. Called Hollin by Men, Eregion is Elvish for 'land of holly'. It was first settled in the year 750 of the Second Age by the Gwaith-i-Mírdain, the Elven Smiths who with Sauron forged the Rings of Power. Its primary city was Ost-in-Edhil, but the city and the realm were entirely destroyed by 1697 of the Second Age during the War of Sauron and the Elves. By the end of the Third Age and the passage of the Fellowship of the Ring there were few who knew anything of the history of this empty forest realm.

Eriador

The vast tract of land between the Blue Mountains and the Misty Mountains was called Eriador. During the First Age of the Sun Eriador was inhabited by Men who were under the evil influence of Morgoth the Dark Enemy. In the Second Age, it was largely Sauron's power that held sway, and many of the dark-haired Men of Eriador, who were ancestors of the Dunlendings, made alliances with the Dark Lord. It was not until the coming of the Dúnedain and the founding of the Kingdom of the North in the year 3320 that Sauron's influence diminished. During the first half of the Third Age, the whole of this land was the Kingdom of the North, the realm of Arnor. But by the time of the War of the Ring, plagues, floods and wars with the Witch-kingdom of Angmar had wiped out this once wealthy and highly populated land. There was only a handful of settlements remaining: the Hobbitland of the Shire, the Men of Bree and the Elves of Rivendell.

Eruhíni

The 'Ainulindalë' tells that in the time of the Ordering of the World, it was Eru, who is called Ilúvatar, who brought into being the races of Elves and Men. So it is that these races were in the Elvish tongue called the Eruhíni, which in Westron would be the 'children of Ilúvatar'.

Erusën

The races of Elves and Men were made by Eru and were given life with the Flame Imperishable. The Elves therefore called these races His children and named them Erusën, the 'children of Eru'.

Esgaroth

There was a city of Men during the Third Age, just to the northeast of Mirkwood and south of Erebor, the Lonely Mountain. This was Esgaroth, the city of the Men of the Long Lake. The city was built upon pylons driven into the Long Lake and connected to the land by a wooden bridge. Because Esgaroth was just south of the Dwarf-kingdom of Erebor and downriver from the Woodland Elves, the Lake Men had become wealthy traders. It was ruled by a Master elected from among its people. In the year 2270, their trade with the Dwarves of Erebor ceased when Smaug the Golden Dragon took possession of the mountain. Still Esgaroth survived, although its neighbouring city of Dale was utterly destroyed. In the year 2941, Smaug the Golden came in a fiery wrath and attacked Esgaroth itself. Although the Dragon was killed, Esgaroth was burned down. Yet all was not lost, for with the vast wealth of the Dragon hoard, the city was rebuilt and its prosperity restored.

Estë

Valar called 'the Healer'. In the gardens of Lórien in Valinor is the Isle of Estë in the midst of Lake Lórellin, the home of the Dream Master's wife, Estë the healer, whose name means 'rest'. Estë is one of the seven queens of the Valar and she is called the 'gentle one'. Her robes are grey and healing sleep is her gift to the world.

Evermind

The fair white flowers that in the Westron tongue of common Men were called Evermind grew over the grave barrows of the kings of the Mark near Edoras in the land of Rohan. These flowers, which were called Simbelmynë in the Rohirrim tongue, were like glittering crystals of snow that blossomed in all seasons, glinting always with starlight on the tombs of these kings. And to the Rohirrim and common Men alike these white flowers on the green swards were always a reminder of the power of the strong kings of the Mark.

Fair Elves

Of all the Elvish race, those most favoured and loved are the First Kindred of the Vanyar, for they are the wisest Elves and they always sit at the feet of Manwë, High Lord of all the Powers of Arda. They are called Fair Elves and have resided longest in the bright Light of the Trees of the Valar, and their eyes burn most brilliantly of all Elves with that Light. Furthermore, they are a blonde race, and their hair and skin is fairest of the Eldar. They seem golden and powerful, and their king, who is named Ingwë, has always been High King of all the Elves of the World.

Fair Folk

From the beginning, before the making of Arda and the Count of Time, Ilúvatar planned to bring the race of Elves into the World. In his grand plan these were to be the first people to be born and the fairest of all races to come into being. And so ever afterwards, by all but their evil enemies, the Elves were usually called the Fair Folk.

Falas

Among the Grey-Elf kingdoms of Beleriand was the coastal realm of West Beleriand, called the Falas. This was the home of the Falathrim, the sea-loving Elves who were ruled by Lord Círdan, later called Círdan the Shipwright, for his people were the first on Middle-earth to master the art of ship building. The chief ports of the Falas (the Elvish name for 'coast') were Brithombar and Egla-rest, and though they long resisted, during the War of Jewels these cities were destroyed by the might of Morgoth the Enemy. And though the Falas were taken, the Falathrim themselves did not perish for Círdan took his people in their white ships to the safety of the Isle of Balar. Later when all the lands of Beleriand sank into the sea, Círdan's people survived by sailing once again to the Gulf of Lune and founding a new port in the land of Lindon known as the Grey Havens.

Falathrim

The Falathrim, the Elves of the Falas, lived on the coast lands of Beleriand in the years of Starlight and the First Age of the Sun, ruled by the lord Círdan. They were of the Teleri kindred, but, when Ulmo the Ocean Lord came to the Teleri, Círdan and his people refused the final journey to the Undying Lands and so were divided from their kindred. The Falathrim lived by the sea for a long time and they were wisest of the sea-folk on Middle-earth. They were the first to build ships in Mortal Lands. The ships of Círdan were magical and they were able to make that far journey into the Undying Lands, even after the Change of the World, when Middle-earth and the Undying Lands were drawn apart for ever. Then only the Elven-ships of the Falathrim could make that lonely journey.

For a time after the departure of the Teleri to the Undying Lands, the Falathrim lived alone on the shores of Beleriand, and they built there two great havens named Eglarest and Brithombar. But after a period of peace under starlight, they discovered that another part of the Umanyar had become powerful in the Wood of Doriath just east of the Falas. The king of these Elves was Elwë Singollo, who had been lost, and with him was Melian the Maia, who was his queen. At this time Círdan and the Falathrim came to know these brethren, the Grey-elves, once again and after a while they became allied with these people, for they spoke the tongue of the Grey-elves and took all their causes to their hearts. In the years of strife that came with the Rising of the Sun, the Falathrim fought for them against Morgoth the Enemy, who arose in the North.

In that First Age of the Sun, the Falathrim were besieged by Orcs for a time, and later still their havens fell to Morgoth, but they took their ships and sailed to the Isle of Balar, and no power of Morgoth was able to come on the sea, for he greatly feared the Ocean Lord, Ulmo. There the Falathrim remained safe until the War of Wrath, when Beleriand itself was thrown down into the sea with the destruction of Angband. Again the ships of the Falathrim sailed and went south to the Gulf of Lune in the land of Lindon, the last of the Elf-realms of Beleriand to survive the holocaust of that Great Battle. Here Círdan built the last haven of the Elves on Middle-earth. This was called the Grey Havens and from this place the last Elven-ship sailed for ever from Mortal Lands.

Fallohides

Of the Halfling people called Hobbits there were said to be three strains: the Fallohides, the Stoors and the Harfoots.

The Fallohides were a woodland folk and were wisest in the arts of song and poetry. By Hobbit standards they were tall, fair-haired and fair-skinned. They numbered fewer than either of the other Hobbit strains but were more adventurous and inclined to commit acts of daring. Because of this, Fallohides often became leaders of their people and were known to seek the company and advice of Elves. The Fallohide brothers, Marcho and Blanco, founded the Shire in the year 1601 of the Third Age. And those of the families of Tooks, Brandybucks and Baggins who contributed famous heroes to the great conflict of the War of the Ring, all had strong blood ties to the Fallohide strain.

FALATHRIM Sea Elves of the coast lands of Beleriand, ruled by Círdan the Shipwright. In the Third Age they inhabited the Grey Havens and built the magical Elven-ships that alone could sail to the Undying Lands.

Falmari

Of all Elves, the Third Kindred, the Teleri, lived longest on the shores of Belegaer, the Great Sea of the West. These people were wisest in the ways of the sea and so they were named the Falmari and the Sea-elves. Their knowledge of the ways of Ulmo the Ocean Lord and his minions Ossë of the Waves and Uinen of the Calms perpetually increases. In the days when the Falmari travelled to the Bay of Eldamar on the Lonely Isle, Ossë came among them and because of his teaching they were the first people to know the skills of shipbuilding. The fleets of the Teleri were made, and the Falmari came in these ships to Eldamar, where they built Alqualondë, the 'haven of Swans', and lived in mansions of pearl. In their ships the Falmari are always sailing in and out of the sea-sculpted archway of stone that is its gate on the Bay of Eldamar.

All races later came to know the arts of building ships and sailing from the Falmari, but they only learned a little of the Falmari's knowledge of the sea, for other peoples did not have the skill of language nor the subtlety of voice and ear to know the ways of the seas as well as the Falmari did.

FANGORN Large though the forest was, it was a mere remnant of the vast forest that once stretched northward covering all of Eriador.

Fangorn

Ent of Fangorn Forest. At the time of the War of the Ring, Fangorn was the oldest Ent on Middle-earth. His name in the Westron tongue of Men was 'Treebeard', and under that name his life story is told.

Fangorn Forest

One of the most ancient forests on Middle-earth, at the time of the War of the Ring, Fangorn Forest was on the southeastern end of the Misty Mountains. Large though the forest was, it was a mere remnant of the vast forest that once stretched northward covering all of Eriador and huge tracts of the lost lands of Beleriand. Called the Entwood by the Rohirrim because it was the last refuge of those giant forest guardians called the Ents, it was a haunted and frighteningly old forest filled with many strange and often bad-tempered spirits. The forest was named after its chief guardian, Fangorn, the oldest surviving Ent upon Middle-earth. Fangorn's name meant 'Treebeard', and it was by this name that he was known to the Companions of the Ring.

Angered by the wanton destruction of the forests carried out by Orcs and other servants of the evil wizard Saruman, Treebeard led an army of Ents and Huorn Tree-spirits out of Fangorn Forest and with their terrific strength they ripped down the walls of Saruman's great fortress of Isengard with their bare hands.

Faramir

Dúnedain lord of Gondor. Born in the year 2983 of the Third Age. Faramir was the second son of Denethor II, the last Ruling Steward of Gondor. As the Captain of the Rangers of Ithilien, Faramir led the retreat from Osgiliath to Minas Tirith before the Siege of Gondor. After his brother Boromir had been slain, Faramir was struck down by the Witch-king. Denethor went mad and he was only narrowly prevented by Gandalf from cremating the comatose Faramir. It took the healing hands

TURTLE-FISH A giant sea creature, known as the Fastitocalon in Hobbit lore, which was mistaken for an island by passing sailors. When they attempted to light a camp fire, it dived to the bottom of the sea.

of Aragorn to bring Faramir out of the death-like sleep brought on by the 'Black Breath' of the Witch-king. Once recovered, he fell in love with Éowyn, the Shieldmaiden of Rohan. After the war, the couple married and Faramir became Steward of Gondor and Prince of Ithilien until his death, in the year 82 of the Fourth Age.

Fastitocalon

In the fanciful lore of the Hobbits is the tale of a vast Turtle-fish that Men thought was an island in the seas. All seemed well when Men made a dwelling place on the beast's back until they lit their fires and in alarm the beast dived deep beneath the sea, drowning the encampment.

By Hobbits the beast was named the Fastitocalon, but whether the tale, like that of the Oliphaunt was based on fact cannot be discovered from the histories that have passed on to Men. For though the creatures of Middle-earth were many, no leviathans are mentioned in the tales of other races.

It is likely that the story is in fact an allegory of the Downfall of the Númenóreans, as told in the 'Akallabêth'. For in the Second Age of the Sun these most gifted of Men rose to the greatest power that was allowed them within the Spheres of the World, and the flame of passion and ambition overwhelmed them, and their great island, like the Fastitocalon, sank beneath the wide ocean and most of the Númenóreans perished in that terrible Downfall.

Fëanor

Elven prince of Eldamar. The creator of the Silmarils, Fëanor was the son of the Noldor High King Finwë and Queen Míriel. Called Curufinwe at birth, he was later named Fëanor, meaning 'spirit of fire'. In Eldamar he married Nerdanel, and by her sired seven sons. Fëanor was the genius who first created Elven-gems, those magical crystals filled with starlight. He also made the Palantíri, the 'seeing stone'. But Fëanor's greatest deed was the forging of the Silmarils: the three gems filled with the living light of the Trees of the Valar. The most beautiful gems in the world, they became a curse upon Fëanor and his race. For after Melkor destroyed the Trees of Light he murdered Fëanor's father, took the Silmarils and fled to Middle-earth. Fëanor led the Noldor to Middle-earth in pursuit of Melkor, who he renamed Morgoth, meaning 'the Dark Enemy'. When Fëanor's Noldor entered into Beleriand, they met Morgoth's challenge in the ten-day Battle Under the Stars, and slaughtered his huge Orkish army. However, Fëanor recklessly rode ahead of his army in pursuit of the Orcs. Separated from his bodyguard, Fëanor was surrounded by Balrogs, and was slain by their lord, Gothmog, the High Captain of Angband.

Felaróf

Mearas, Horse of Rohan. In the twenty-sixth century of the Third Age of the Sun, Lord Léod of the Éothéod was killed trying to tame a wild Horse called 'Mansbane'. It was left to Léod's son, Eorl the Young, to tame it, but there was no need, for the Horse surrendered in atonement for the slaying. Eorl renamed him Felaróf, meaning 'father of Horses', for from him were descended the Mearas, who were that magical, silver-grey race. The Éothéod thereafter were called the Rohirrim, the 'horse lords', and the banner of Rohan is the white image of Felaróf running on a green field. Felaróf and his heirs could not speak, but understood the speech of Men, and could be ridden without saddle or bridle. Felaróf carried Eorl victoriously into many conflicts, but in 2545, both were slain in battle with the Easterlings. They were buried together in honour beneath a mound in the Wold.

Fíli

Dwarf of Thorin and Company. In the year 2941 of the Third Age, Fíli joined the Quest of the Lonely Mountain which eventually resulted in the slaying of Smaug the Dragon and the reclamation of the Dwarf-kingdom under the Mountain at Erebor. Fíli was born in the year 2859, the son of Thorin Oakenshield's sister, Dís. Fíli and his brother, Kíli, were so fiercely loyal to their uncle that both were slain while defending the dying Thorin in the Battle of the Five Armies.

Finarfin

Elven king of Eldamar. Finarfin was the third son of High King Finwë of the Noldor. Finarfin and his brother Fingolfin were born after Finwë's second marriage to Queen Indis. Fëanor was their older half-brother. Finarfin married the Teleri princess Eärwen of Alqualondë, and the couple had five children: Finrod, Orodreth, Angrod, Aegnor and Galadriel. After the theft of the Silmarils and the slaying of his father by Morgoth, Finarfin joined his brothers, swearing vengeance. However, when Fëanor raided Alqualondë and slew many Teleri Elves in order to use their ships to sail to Middle-earth, Finarfin refused to continue. He returned to Tirion and ruled as High King of the Noldor who remained in Eldamar. At the end of the First Age of the Sun, Finarfin led the Noldor to Middle-earth with the Valarian Host in the War of Wrath. Afterward, Finarfin returned to Eldamar and continued to rule his people wisely and well.

Finduilas

Dúnedain princess of Dol Amroth. Finduilas was the wife of Denethor II, Ruling Steward of Gondor. Born in 2950 of the Third Age, the daughter of Prince Adrahil of Dol Amroth, Finduilas was the beautiful and devoted mother of Boromir and Faramir. However, during twelve years of marriage, she found that she was increasingly isolated from her brooding husband. Finduilas also appeared to miss her childhood home by the sea. Wasting away, she died in 2988. Finduilas of Dol Amroth was undoubtedly named after the Elven princess Finduilas of the First Age of the Sun. The earlier Finduilas loved first Gwindor, an Elven lord of Nargothrond, and then Túrin, hero of the Edain. After Gwindor's death and the destruction of Nargothrond, in 496 of the First Age, Finduilas was captured and carried off by Orcs. Just at the point at which it appeared she may have been rescued, when the Haladin ambushed the Orc horde at the Teiglin Crossings, her evil captives slew her.

Fingolfin

Elven king of Beleriand. Fingolfin was the second son of Finwë, the Noldor High King of Eldamar. His brothers were Fëanor and Finarfin. Fingolfin's children were Fingon, Turgon and Aredhel. Although initially reluctant to do so, he joined Fëanor in the pursuit of Morgoth to Middle-earth. However, when Fëanor took the Elven ships of Alqualondë, Fingolfin was forced to lead his people northward across the Helcaraxë, the 'grinding-ice' bridge to Middle-earth. As Fingolfin set foot on Middle-earth, the first Moon rose and Morgoth's hordes retreated before them. After Fëanor's death after the Battle Under Stars, Fingolfin became the High King of the Noldor on Middle-earth. Establishing himself in Hithlum, Fingolfin kept Morgoth's forces shut up in Angband until the devastating Battle of Sudden Flame in 455 of the First Age. Seeing destruction all about him, Fingolfin was filled with such anger and despair that he rode to the gate of Angband to challenge Morgoth. In the ensuing duel, Fingolfin managed to give Morgoth seven great wounds with his sword, Ringil, before Morgoth slew him. His body was rescued by Thorondor, the eagle, and buried in the Encircling Mountains.

Fingon

Elven king of Beleriand. Born in Eldamar, Fingon was the son of Fingolfin, and was among the Noldor who pursued Morgoth to Middle-earth. There, he claimed Dor-lómin in Beleriand, and fought bravely throughout the War of the Jewels. With the help of Thorondor the Eagle, Fingon rescued Fëanor's son, Maedhros, from his chains high on the mountain of Angband. He also was the first to fight and drive off Glaurung the Dragon. After the death of his father in 455 of the First Age, Fingon became High King of Noldor. His reign, however, lasted only 18 years, for he was slain by Balrogs in the cataclysmic Battle of Unnumbered Tears in 473. He was succeeded by his brother Turgon, and finally by his son, Gil-galad.

Finrod Felagund

Elven king of Nargothrond. Born during the Ages of Starlight in Eldamar, Finrod was the son of the Noldor prince Finarfin, and husband of the Vanyar princess Amarië. Although initially reluctant, Finrod was among those Noldor who pursued Morgoth to Middle-earth. In Beleriand, Finrod first built an Elven tower on Tol Sirion, but later discovered a network of wonderful hidden caverns on the Narog River, and built the mansions of Nargothrond. Forever after he was called Finrod Felagund, the 'master of caves'. Ruler of the largest Noldor kingdom upon Middle-earth, Finrod was the first of his race to befriend mortal Men. In the terrible Battle of Sudden Flame in 455 of the First Age, Finrod was rescued from certain death by Barahir of the Edain. Consequently, when Barahir's son, Beren, came to Nargothrond for help in his Quest of the Silmaril in 466, Finrod felt bound to aid him. Attempting to overcome Sauron and the army of Werewolves who occupied the Elven tower Finrod himself had built on Tol Sirion, the Elf-king engaged Sauron in a sorcerer's duel of songs of power. Tragically, he was defeated and captured. Held in the dungeons of the tower, Finrod was finally slain by a Werewolf while attempting to defend Beren.

Finwë

Elven king of Eldamar. Finwë was the First High King of the Noldor Elves. He was chosen by the Valar to lead his people in the Great Journey out of Middle-earth into the Undying Lands. In Eldamar, Finwë ruled as High King from the city of Tirion. Finwë was twice married. His first queen was Míriel who gave birth to Fëanor, the maker of the Silmarils. His second queen was Indis, by whom he sired Fingolfin and Finarfin. After the Darkening of Valinor, Finwë was slain by Melkor while defending the Silmarils.

Fire-Drakes

Of all the creatures bred by Morgoth the Dark Enemy in all the ages of his power, the evil reptiles that were called Dragons were feared most. There were many breeds of these beings; the most deadly were those that vomited leaping flames from their foul bellies. These were called Fire-drakes, and among them were numbered the mightiest of Dragons. Glaurung, Father of Dragons, was the first of the Urulokí Fire-drakes, and he had many offspring. The evil work of these Dragons on the kingdoms of Elves, Men and Dwarves in the First Age of the Sun was terrible.

In the last days of that Age, when most of the Earth-bound brood of Glaurung had been put to death in the War of Wrath, the winged Fire-drakes appeared out of Angband. They are said to have been among the greatest terrors of the World, and Ancalagon the Black, who was of this breed, and whose name means 'rushing jaws', was said to have been the mightiest Dragon of all time.

In later Ages, the histories of Middle-earth tell of one last mighty winged golden-red Fire-drake that was almost as fearsome as

Ancalagon. This was the Dragon of Erebor, which drove the Dwarves of Durin's Line from the kingdom under the Mountain. He was called Smaug the Golden, and in the year 2941 of the Third Age he was killed by a deadly black arrow shot by Bard the Bowman of Dale.

Fírimar

In the First Age of the Sun, the Elves of Middle-earth found a new race had arisen in the land of Hildórien far to the East. This was the race of Men, whom Elves named Fírimar, which is the 'mortal people'. To the minds of the immortal Elves, it was a frail race with little wisdom, for Men could at best but briefly learn the least murmur of knowledge before death took them.

First born

As the 'Ainulindalë' relates, in the Timeless Halls before the World was made, there was Music, and in it the Ordering of all things. In that Music came a theme that was made by Ilúvatar alone. This was the coming of the first race to awaken in Arda, an immortal race that was to last as long as the World itself. This is the race of Elves, who awoke in the East when only starlight shone upon Middle-earth and thereafter in honour were called the Firstborn. Many ages passed before the coming of the Sun heralded the time of the Secondborn, when that lesser race called Men arose, as had the Elves, in the eastern lands.

Flies of Mordor

In the Black Realm of Mordor it was said there lived only Orcs, Trolls and Men, who were thralls of Sauron the Dark Lord. The only beasts in Mordor were the evil swarms of bloodsucking flies. These were grey, brown and black insects; they were loud, hateful and hungry, and they were all marked, as Orcs of that land were marked, with a red eye-shape upon their backs. So the Dark Lord's power had spread to the smallest evil in his land.

Forgoil

Among the Northmen who resided east of the Mountains of Mist in the Third Age of the Sun were the Rohirrim. These were a golden-haired people who boasted the fiercest cavalry of the Westlands. They were greatly feared and hated by their barbarous neighbours, the Dunlendings, who in their contempt called them Forgoil, which in that tongue means the 'strawheads'.

FLIES OF MORDOR The only beasts in Mordor were the evil swarms of bloodsucking flies.

Formenos

After the Noldor prince Fëanor created those great jewels the Silmarils, he built a fortress and treasury in the north of Valinor in the Undying Lands. This stronghold was built upon a fortified hill and was named Formenos which in the High Elven tongue means 'north citadel'. Formenos was home to Fëanor's clan during his years of exile from Tirion. After the destruction of the Trees of the Valar, Morgoth came to the doors of Formenos and slew Fëanor's father, Finwë the High King of the Noldor, then broke into the treasury and stole the Silmarils.

Fornost

From the fourth or fifth centuries of the Third Age, the first city and capital of the Dúnedain kingdom of Arnor was Fornost, the 'north fortress'. It was a powerful and prosperous city until the wars with the Witch-king of Angmar began to take their toll. Finally in 1974, the Witch-king's army took and destroyed much of Fornost and its royal court. Although Fornost was taken back the following year at the Battle of Fornost, the ruined city was deserted and its people scattered. It was called Norbury in the language of Men, although it was also known as Deadman's Dike after its destruction.

At the time of the War of the Rings, it was primarily noteworthy as a ruin north of Bree on the Great North–South Road which, in its years of prosperity had been the great highway between the capital of Arnor and Minas Tirith, the capital of Gondor.

Forochel

The cold land of snow and ice to the north of the Dúnedain kingdom of Arnor was called Forochel. Its people were the Lossoth or Snowmen of Forochel; they were a tribal folk who built no cities and had no kings. They were said to be descended from the Forodwaith of the northern wastelands, but they became a wandering people, building their homes from snow and hunting the wild beasts of the north. Beyond the charts and maps of Middle-earth that mark the Cape and Ice Bay of Forochel, little is known of the land or its people.

Forodwaith

The 'Annals of the Kings and Rulers' relate how after the Fall of Angband, the fortress of Melkor, a bitter cold descended on the northern desert land of Forochel. For a long time afterwards a people named the Forodwaith lived in that land. Little is told of these people except that they endured the icy colds of the North, and from them were descended the Lossoth, who in the Third Age of the Sun, were called the Snowmen of Forochel by the Men of the West.

Frodo Baggins

Hobbit of the Shire and Ring-bearer. Frodo was born in 2968 of the Third Age, the son of Drogo Baggins and Primula Brandybuck. Orphaned in childhood, he was adopted by his cousin, Bilbo Baggins of Bag End. Frodo was extremely adventurous for a Hobbit, and remarkably learned, being a song-writer and something of a scholar of Elvish lore and language. In 3001, when Bilbo mysteriously left the Shire, Frodo inherited Bag End and the One Ring. In 3018, Gandalf the Wizard reappeared and set Frodo on the Quest of the Ring to Rivendell where the Fellowship of the Ring was formed. Frodo just survived the many adventures and perils of the journey, but succeeded in delivering the One Ring to the fires of Mount Doom. Thus, Frodo brought about the end of the War of the Ring. After the war, he returned to Bag End, but the poison wounds and the mental trauma he experienced during the Quest began to tell. In 3021, Frodo embarked on the Last Riding of the Keepers of the Rings, and boarded an Elven ship and sailed to the Undying Lands.

G

Galadhrim

The forest that in the Second Age of the Sun was first named Laurelindórenan, 'land of the valley of singing gold', and later Lothlórien, 'land of blossoms dreaming', and even by some Lórien, 'dreamland', was east of the Misty Mountains by the Silverlode, which flows into the Great River Anduin. It was the Golden Wood, where the tallest trees on Middle-earth grew. They were called the Mallorn trees and were the most beautiful trees in Mortal Lands. Their bark was silver and grey, their blossoms golden and their leaves green and gold.

Within the forest was the concealed Elven kingdom of the Galadhrim, the 'tree-people', who made their homes on platforms called telain, or flets, high in the branches of the sheltering Mallorn.

The Galadhrim did not build mighty towers of stone. Indeed, to most people, the Galadhrim lived invisibly in their forest kingdom, where they wore Grey-elven cloaks that were like a chameleon's coat. By use of ropes and woodlore they needed no bridges or roads. Deep within the Golden Wood they did have one great city, which was named Caras Galadhon, the 'city of the trees'. There grew the greatest Mallorn on Middle-earth, and the king and queen resided in a great hall in that tallest of trees, on the crest of a high green hill. It was walled and gated and encircled with other great trees like towers. At the very heart of the forest there was a magical hill called Cerin Amroth where once the house of an Elven-king stood. And from this place came a power and light that were like those in the Undying Lands in the Ages of the Trees.

The Galadhrim were mostly Silvan Elves, but their lords were Sindar and Noldor nobles. Their king was Celeborn, kinsman of Thingol ('grey-cloak'), and he was the greatest lord of the Sindar on Middle-earth. Their queen was the sister of Finrod and daughter of Finarfin, High King of the Noldor, who had remained in Eldamar after the Trees of the Valar were destroyed. By the Third Age of the Sun she was the highest noble of all the Elves in Mortal Lands. And though her Quenya name was Altárial, in Middle-earth she was called Galadriel, the 'lady of light'.

The power of the Galadhrim under such rulers was very great, for their king and queen had lived in the first kingdom of the Sindar in the days of Thingol and Melian the Maia and had learned much concerning their powers. Their queen had lived in the Undying Lands in the days of the Trees of the Valar and had visited the Valarian Garden of Lórien, the most beautiful in all Arda. Some part of these magical places came with these nobles to the Golden Wood of Lothlórien. A golden light was there, though it was but an ember of the glory of the Valarian Garden, the Golden Wood was brilliant and precious to the peoples of Middle-earth. This place was protected from evil powers by a force that was like the Girdle of Melian that once protected Doriath, the Sindarin kingdom. For Galadriel was bearer of the second of the three Elf Rings – Nenya, the Ring of Adamant and the Ring of Water – and her power held off the ravages of Time and made her aware of Sauron's moves and caused her people to be invisible to Sauron's eye. She commanded the Mirror of Galadriel, a silver basin that she could fill with fountain waters and by the power of her Ring could cast the image of future events on its dark, still surface.

The kingdom of the Galadhrim had been founded in a time of peace when Sauron had been taken captive by the Númenórean king before the Change of the World, in the third millennium of the Second Age of the Sun. It was ruled first by the Sindar King Amdír, and then his son Amroth before Celeborn and Galadriel came to power. Since the first fall of Mordor, it had remained a land apart and, throughout the Third Age, the Golden Wood of Lothlórien was protected and sustained by the power of the Elf Ring Nenya. With the destruction of the One Ring, its power faded, and the queen went to the Undying Lands; the great light of Lothlórien faded as well, and Time re-found it. The Galadhrim again became a wandering folk and dwindled with their Silvan brethren of the East.

Galadriel

Elven queen of Lothlórien. Galadriel was a Noldor princess who was born in Eldamar during the Ages of Starlight. Galadriel and her brothers joined the Noldor who pursued Morgoth and the Silmarils to Middle-earth. Tall and beautiful, with the golden hair of her Teleri mother, Eärwen, she was called Altariel in Eldamar. This was translated as Galadriel, meaning 'lady of light', in Sindarin. During the First Age of the Sun in Beleriand, Galadriel lived with her brother Finrod, in Nargothrond, before entering the Sindar realm of Doriath where she was befriended by Queen Melian and married the Grey-elf prince, Celeborn. From the beginning of the Second Age, the couple and their only child Celebrían, lived in Lindon; then in the eighth century they moved to Eregion, the realm of the Elven-smiths. Later Galadriel and Celeborn crossed the Misty Mountains and came to rule over their own kingdom in the Golden Wood of Lothlórien. Commanding one of the Three Elven Rings of Power, Galadriel used her powers to weave a ring of enchantment and protection around Lothlórien. During the time of the War of the Ring, Galadriel gave shelter and magical gifts to the Fellowship of the Ring. During the War itself, Galadriel repelled three attempts at invasion, and used her powers to bring down the walls of Dol Guldur and cleanse Mirkwood. Then, as the Third Age ended, she sailed westward to the Undying Lands.

GALADRIEL The Elven Queen of the Galadhrim Elves of Lothlórien, and by the Third Age, highest ranking Elf noble on Middle-earth. She possessed the power of prophecy by commanding the watery Mirror of Galadriel.

Galenas

In the land of Númenor grew the broad-leafed herb Galenas, which was prized for the fragrance of its flowers. Before that land was swallowed by the Western Sea, mariners of Númenor brought it to Middle-earth, where it grew in abundance about the settlements of the Númenóreans' descendants.

However, it was not until such an unlikely people as the Hobbits discovered Galenas in their own land that the special properties of this plant were revealed. The Hobbits took the broad leaves of Galenas, dried them and shredded them. Then they put fire to them in long-stemmed pipes. This was the herb nicotiana, afterwards known on Middle-earth as Pipe-weed after the habit of the Hobbits. It was commonly smoked by Hobbits, Men and Dwarves and they derived much comfort from it.

Gallows-weed

In the swamplands of Middle-earth where the evil phantoms called Mewlips lurked and the birds called Gorcrows flew, there also grew the Gallows-weed. In the lore of Hobbits this tree-hanging weed is known by name but its properties are not spoken of; for few who entered those unhappy and haunted marshes ever returned.

Gandalf

Istari, Wizard of Middle-earth. In the Undying Lands, Gandalf was a Maia spirit, Olórin, who lived in the gardens of Lórien, the Dream Master, and often visited Nienna the Compassionate. About the year 1000 of the Third Age of the Sun, he was chosen as one of the Istari or Wizards that were sent to Middle-earth. Called Gandalf the Grey in Westron, he was Mithrandir, 'grey pilgrim', to the Elves, Tharkûn to the Dwarves and Incánus to the Haradrim. His outward form was that of a bearded old man dressed in a great cloak with a tall pointed hat and a long staff. Upon his arrival in the Grey Havens, Círdan gave him Narya, the 'ring of fire'. For over two thousand years, Gandalf worked against the rising evil powers on Middle-earth. In 2941, Gandalf inspired the Quest of the Lonely Mountain that resulted in the slaying of Smaug the Dragon. During this quest, Gandalf acquired the sword Glamdring, and Bilbo Baggins acquired the

PIPE-WEED The Hobbit name for the herb, nicotiana, which the Elves called Galenas. The herb originated in Númenor where it was grown for its scented flower. The Hobbits first cultivated it for smoking in pipes.

One Ring. It was Gandalf who recognized the power of the One Ring and learned how it might be destroyed. In 3018, Gandalf came to Frodo Baggins in the Shire and initiated the Quest of the Ring. In Rivendell, he became one of the Fellowship of the Ring, and led them through many perils. Then, upon the bridge of Khazad-dûm, Gandalf fell into mortal conflict with the Balrog of Moria. However, the Wizard's spirit was resurrected as Gandalf the White, a radiant being that no weapon could harm. During the War of the Ring, Gandalf the White on his horse Shadowfax was everywhere: inspiring King Théoden in Rohan, vanquishing Saruman in Isengard, and holding back the Witch-king at the gates of Minas Tirith. He fought with the captains of the Army of the West before the Black Gates of Mordor, while the Ring-bearer destroyed the One Ring. After the war, Gandalf oversaw the reuniting of Gondor and Arnor, then in 3021 embarked on the Last Sailing of the Keepers of the Rings to the Undying Lands.

Gaurhoth

In the First Age of the Sun, in the time of the Wars of Beleriand, many evil spirits in Wolf form came to Sauron the Maia. The Elves called them Gaurhoth, or the 'Werewolf host'. From these creatures Sauron forged a mighty army that went to battle with Elves and killed many of the strongest amongst them. Sauron captured and held for a time an Elvish tower upon the River Sirion by the power of the Werewolves; hence the name of that place: Tol-in-Gaurhoth, the 'isle of Werewolves'.

Gelion River

One of the two great rivers of Beleriand, the Gelion was twice the length of its rival – the Sirion – although not so broad or deep. It drained the lands of East Beleriand, particularly Thargelion and the woodlands of Ossiriand. Among its many tributaries were the rivers Adurant, Duilwen, Brilthor, Legolin, Thalos, Ascar, and the Greater and Little Gelion. Its source and that of nearly all its tributaries was the Blue Mountain range to the east.

Ghân-buri-Ghân

Wose chieftain of Druadan. During the War of the Ring, Ghân-buri-Ghân was the leader of the white-skinned, pygmy-like race called the Woses that inhabited the Druadan Forest, and helped the Rohirrim and Dúnedain in breaking the siege of Gondor. Ghân led the Rohirrim through the secret trails of the forest so they might have the advantage of surprise in the Battle of Pelennor Fields. Also in the ensuing battle, Ghân's people slaughtered many Orcs who attempted to flee into the woodlands. After the war, Ghân and his people were granted legal title to their forest land.

Giants

Many beings of Giant size, both good and evil in nature, lived in Middle-earth. In the First Age of Stars there were the Ents, the Tree-herds, who measured fourteen feet in height and were of immense strength and great wisdom. Later came Giants filled with evil; those named Trolls and Olog-hai served the Dark Power and made the wild lands of the World perilous for travellers. Also, in the tales of Hobbits, there were rumours of great Giants who, in league with Orcs, guarded the High Passes in Rhovanion.

Gil-galad

Elf King of Lindon. Gil-galad was born during the First Age of the Sun in Hithlum in Beleriand, the son of High King Fingon. Forced to flee to the Isle of Balar after the death of his father in 473, Gil-galad – whose name means 'radiant star' – was made High King after the fall of Gondolin and the death of Turgon, his uncle, in 511. After the sinking of Beleriand,

Gil-galad ruled over the surviving Noldor Elves in Lindon. During the Second Age, Gil-galad sent his forces into the War of Sauron and the Elves, and later joined the Dúnedain in the Last Alliance of Men and Elves. In 3434 Gil-galad, armed with his dreaded spear Aeglos, led the Alliance into the Battle of Dagorlad. Sauron's forces were crushed, and for seven years the Alliance laid siege to Mordor. Sauron was forced into the open and overthrown, but in that last duel, both the Dúnedain king and Gil-galad were also slain.

Gimli

Dwarf of Erebor. Born in 2879 of the Third Age in the Blue Mountains, Gimli went to live in Erebor in 2941 after the death of Smaug the Dragon. Gimli's father was Glóin, a Dwarf of Thorin and Company. In 3018, Gimli went with his father to Rivendell where he was chosen for the Fellowship of the Ring. Gimli was one of the few Dwarves to become friendly with Elves. Indeed, after his entry into Lothlórien, he became devoted to the memory of Galadriel, the Elf Queen, and carried a lock of her hair with him always. His closest friend was Legolas, the Sindar Elf.

Gimli fought bravely at the Battles of Hornburg, Pelennor Fields, and the Black Gates of Mordor. After the war, Gimli became the Lord of the Glittering Caves, the caverns beneath Helm's Deep. He remained Lord of the Caves until after the death of Aragorn in 120 of the Fourth Age, when, joined by his friend Legolas, he sailed on an Elven ship into the Undying Lands.

GIL-GALAD In 3434 Gil-galad, armed with his dreaded spear Aeglos, led the Alliance into the Battle of Dagorlad.

Gladden Fields

From its headwaters in the Misty Mountains just north of Moria and Lothlórien, the Gladden River flows eastwards until it reaches the Great River Anduin. It is here in the vales of Anduin that the tributary floods a marshland known as the Gladden Fields. In the second year of the Third Age a fateful event in the history of Middle-earth was enacted here for this was the site of the Battle of Gladden Fields when the Dúnedain King Isildur was killed and the One Ring was lost in the river. The One Ring remained hidden here until the year 2463 when it was found by two Stoor Hobbits named Déagol and Sméagol. Sméagol killed Déagol for possession of the Ring and eventually degenerated into the evil being known as Gollum.

Glamhoth

When the evil race of Orcs first entered the Grey-elven lands of Beleriand in the Ages of Starlight, the Sindar did not know what manner of being they were. Though none doubted that they were a vile and evil race, at that time they had no name. So the Grey-elves called them the Glamhoth, the 'din-horde', for their cries in battle and the noise of their iron shoes and battle-gear were loud and evil.

Glaurung

Dragon of Angband. Glaurung the Golden was the first and greatest of the Urulóki or Fire-breathing Dragons. Called the Father of Dragons, he emerged from the pits of Angband in the year 260 of the First Age of the Sun, but was driven back. In Angband he grew for two more centuries before being released in the terrible Battle of Sudden Flame, which broke the Siege of Angband. This was followed by the Battle of Unnumbered Tears, in which Glaurung was followed into battle by a legion of lesser Fire-drakes. Against them only the Dwarves of Belgost could stand.

Although it cost him his life, the Dwarf King Azaghâl wounded Glaurung and forced him to withdraw from the field. In 496, Glaurung destroyed the armies of Nargothrond at Tumhalad and took possession of the great hall. He gathered his treasure hoard and lay down on it. While guarding this hoard, he used his hypnotic Dragon-spells to destroy or blight the lives of Túrin, Nienor and Finduilas. However, in the year 501, it was the hero Túrin Turambar who by stealth managed to drive his sword deep into Glaurung's belly and slay the beast.

Glóin

Dwarf of Thorin and Company. Glóin, son of Gróin, was born in the year 2783 of the Third Age. He fought in the Battle of Azanulbizar and was a companion of King Thrain II, and his son, Thorin Oakenshield. With Thorin and Company he went on the Quest of Erebor which resulted in the death of Smaug the Dragon, and the re-establishment of the Dwarf Kingdom under the Mountain, where he became a wealthy and important lord. In the year 3018, he travelled with his son to Rivendell. His son, Gimli, was chosen as one of the Fellowship of the Ring, and Glóin returned to Erebor. During the War of the Ring, he fought in defence of Erebor. He died in the year 15 of the Fourth Age.

Glorfindel

Elf lord of Rivendell. During the time of the War of the Ring, Glorfindel appears to have been second only to Elrond Half-Elven in rank in Rivendell. In 3018 of the Third Age, he met Frodo the Ringbearer on his way to Rivendell and, mounted on his white horse Asfaloth, he dared to stand and fight the Ringwraiths at the Ford of Bruinen. Glorfindel also led Elvish warriors into the Battle of Fornost which, in 1975 of the Third Age, resulted in the destruction of the realm of the Witch-king of Angmar. However, this Third Age hero was actually a reincarnation of the legendary Glorfidel of Gondolin who was slain in the First Age, but by the command of Manwë was re-embodied and allowed to return to Middle-earth. In the First Age, Glorfindel was a commander in King Turgon's forces who fought in the Battle of Unnumbered Tears, but he won greatest fame after the fall of Gondolin in 511 of the First Age. Ambushed by Morgoth's forces, Glorfindel fought a mighty Balrog and both toppled from a cliff to their deaths.

Goblins

Those creatures that Men now name Goblins are dwellers in darkness who were spawned for evil purposes. In earlier days they were called Orcs. Black-blooded, red-eyed and hateful in nature are these Goblin people, and though they are now reduced to beings committed to minor deeds of mischief, they were once a race bent on vast plans of terrible tyranny.

Goldberry

River-daughter of Old Forest. Goldberry was the daughter of the River-woman of the Withywindle River, and the spouse of Tom Bombadil. She was a golden-haired and beautiful nature spirit who may have been a Maia. Whatever her origin, like Tom Bombadil, her concerns were with the natural world of forest and stream. During the Quest of the Ring, the Hobbits were rescued and sheltered by Bombadil and Goldberry. Compared to an Elf-queen in her radiance, Goldberry wore flowers in her hair and belt. She wore garments of silver and gold, and shoes that shimmered like fish-mail. The sound of her singing was said to resemble a bird song.

Gollum

Ghoul and former Hobbit. Gollum was once a Hobbit of the Stoor strain called Sméagol, who was born not far from Gladden Fields

in the Vales of Anduin. In 2463 of the Third Age, Sméagol's cousin Déagol found the One Ring while fishing and Sméagol immediately murdered him for it. The power of the Ring lengthened Sméagol's life, yet it warped him beyond recognition. Thereafter, he was called Gollum because of the nasty, guttural sounds he made when trying to speak. He became a ghoulish being who shunned light and lived by foul murder and eating unclean meat. He found comfort in dark pools in deep caverns. His skin became hairless, black and clammy, and his body thin and gaunt. His head was like a skull and his eyes bulged like those of a fish. His teeth grew long like Orc fangs, and his Hobbit feet grew flat and webbed. For nearly five centuries, Gollum lived hidden in caverns beneath the Misty Mountains.

Then, in 2941, the Hobbit Bilbo Baggins made a fateful visit to his cavern and took the One Ring from Gollum. In 3019, Gollum at last hunted down Frodo Baggins, the new Ringbearer, but try as he might, he could not overcome him. For a time Frodo almost seemed able to tame Gollum, but Gollum lived by treachery. So it was at the final moment, when the power of the Ring overcame even the good Frodo upon Mount Doom, Gollum attacked the Ringbearer on the edge of the Cracks of Doom. Summoning all his evil strength, Gollum won the Ring by biting off Frodo's finger, but at that moment of victory, he toppled backwards with his precious prize down into the fiery bowels of the Earth.

GOLLUM The power of the Ring lengthened Sméagol's life, yet it warped him beyond recognition.

Golodhrim

In the First Age of the Sun, the Noldor came out of the Undying Lands and entered Beleriand. There they were greeted by the Grey-elves, who, in the Sindar tongue, called the Noldor the Golodhrim.

Gondolin

When the Noldor Elves of Eldamar returned to Middle-earth and entered Beleriand in the year 52 of the First Age of the Sun, Prince Turgon found a stronghold and a secret valley in which to build an Elven city safe from the evil forces of Morgoth. This city was Gondolin, the 'Hidden Kingdom', in the valley of Tumladen within Echarioth, the Encircling Mountains, to the north of the forests of Doriath, the realm of the Grey Elves. Within the natural barriers of the Encircling Mountains, Gondolin was also protected by the vigilance of the Great Eagles who destroyed or drove off all spies and servants of Morgoth. So defended, for over fifty years the Noldor secretly built the white stone city of Gondolin, meaning 'hidden stone', on the hill of Amon Gwareth. Gondolin's name in the High Elven tongue was Ondolindë, meaning 'stone song', and being modelled on Tirion, the first city of Eldamar, it was the most beautiful city of the Noldor on Middle-earth. For five centuries Gondolin prospered while one by one the other Elven kingdoms of Beleriand were destroyed. Then, in the year 511 Gondolin was betrayed and its secret passes were revealed to Morgoth. The Dark Enemy sent a huge force of Orcs, Trolls, Dragons and Balrogs into the Hidden Kingdom. Terrible were the battles beneath its walls, but finally Gondolin was overrun and its people slaughtered. The last of the High Elf kingdoms of Beleriand, the towers of Gondolin were torn down and the ruined walls and foundations scorched black with Dragon fire.

Gondor

Founded in the year 3320 of the Second Age by Elendil the Númenórean, Gondor was the South Kingdom of the Dúnedain of Middle-earth. Elendil ruled as High King from the North Kingdom of Arnor while his two sons, Isildur and Anárion, ruled jointly in Gondor. However, after Elendil's death in 3441, Isildur and his heirs became the kings of Arnor, while Anárion's heirs ruled as the kings of Gondor until the year 2050 of the Third Age when the line failed. For over nine centuries after this time, Gondor was governed by the Ruling Stewards. Gondor's chief cities were Minas Anor, Minas Ithil, Osgiliath, and the ports of Pelargir and Dol Amroth. By the first millennium of the Third Age Gondor's realm included the fiefs of Anórien, Ithilien, Lebennin, Anfalas, Belfalas, Calenardhon, Enedwaith, South Gondor, and most of Rhovanion as far east as the Sea of Rhûn. From its beginning Gondor (and Arnor) were rivals of Sauron the Ring Lord of Mordor and his many allies. Because of this, Gondor was invaded many times by Easterling armies out of Rhûn and Southron armies from Harad. During the first two millennia the worst blows to Gondor's power were caused by the civil war of 1432 and the Great Plague of 1636. These were followed by the bloody Wainrider Invasions of 1851 and 1954. So weakened was Gondor that in the year 2002 Sauron's servants, the Nazgûl Ring Wraiths, took the city of Minas Ithil in Gondor's heartland. For over a thousand years it was held by dark powers and was renamed Minas Morgul. At the time of the War of the Ring, exhausted by centuries of conflict though it was, Gondor was the last hope for the Free Peoples of Middle-earth in resisting total dominion by Sauron. At the end of the war, Mordor was destroyed and the kingship of the Reunited Kingdom of Gondor and Arnor restored by Aragorn, the true heir of Isildur. As King Elessar, he ruled well into the Fourth Age, restoring Gondor to its former glory.

Gondor Men

Of the Dúnedain who made kingdoms upon Middle-earth, the most famous were the Gondor Men of the South Kingdom. Isildur and Anárion raised the white towers of Gondor in the year 3320 of the Second Age of the Sun, after fleeing from the destruction of

Númenor with their father Elendil, who then built the North Kingdom of Arnor.

The tale of Gondor is long and glorious. The 'Annals of Kings and Rulers' tell how, at the height of their power, the Gondor kings ruled all the lands of Middle-earth west of the Sea of Rhûn, between the rivers Celebrant and Harnen. Even when the kingdom of Gondor was in decline, its rulers held all the fiefs and territories of Anórien, Ithilien, Lebennin, Lossarnach, Lamedon, Anfalas, Tolfalas, Belfalas and Calenardhon.

Within Gondor there were five cities of the first rank, two of which were great ports: ancient Pelargir, upon the delta of the Great River Anduin, and Dol Amroth, the citadel that ruled the coastal fiefs upon the Bay of Belfalas. There were three great cities in the centre of Gondor. They stood upon a vast plain between the White Mountains in the west and the Mountains of Mordor in the East. The eastern city was Minas Ithil, the 'tower of the Moon', the city of the west was Minas Anor, the 'tower of the Sun', and the greatest city of them all was Osgiliath, the 'citadel of the Stars'. Osgiliath was the capital of Gondor and was built upon both banks of the Great River Anduin; the city's two parts were joined by the wide white stone bridge.

The kingdom of Gondor was often attacked in the Third Age and it suffered a great many troubles. In the year 1432 a long civil war began; in 1636 a Great Plague struck; and between 1851 and 1954 the Wainriders invaded. In 2002, Minas Ithil fell to the Nazgûl and the Orcs. Thereafter, it was always an evil place and was renamed Minas Morgul. In 2475, the great Orcs, the Uruk-hai, came out of Mordor and in vast legions overpowered a weakened Osgiliath, setting fire to much of it and demolishing its great stone bridge over the Anduin.

In this way the realm of Gondor had been much diminished in the years before the War of the Ring. Of the three great cities at its centre, only Minas Anor remained unbroken. The Tower of the Sun stood against the gathering darkness in Mordor, Morgul, Rhûn and Harad for many centuries. It seemed that this last city of Gondor was the only power that withstood a vast conspiracy of evil, for the Dúnedain Kingdom of the North had fallen and the Elves seemed little concerned with the affairs of Middle-earth. Yet in this grim time, when little hope remained and the might of Sauron had no bounds, Gondor's Men won their greatest fame.

For within the kingdom of Gondor there stood knights who were like the great warriors of old and in Minas Anor they still wore the high crowned helms of silver and mithril fitted with the wide white wings of seabirds. Their robes and mail were black, their armour and arms were silver; on their sable surcoats was the emblem of Gondor: a white blossoming tree under seven stars and a silver crown. In the days of the War of the Ring, though these knights were fewer than were wished for, they were of great valour, and allies came from unexpected places in the moment of need.

According to the 'Red Book of Westmarch', at the time of the War of the Ring, Gondor was ruled by the Steward Denethor II, for the line of kings had failed long ago. Though a strong and able Man, Denethor foolishly sought to fight Sauron with sorcerous weapons. Therefore, he sent his elder son, Boromir, in search of the One Ring, and, though Boromir was one of the Nine who went on the Quest of the Ring, he failed in his mission and perished. Denethor was afterwards without hope, the more so when his second son, Faramir, was given an apparently deadly wound by the Nazgûl. Deluded by Sauron and in despair for the kingdom of Gondor, Denethor ended his own life. Yet Faramir recovered and when the Dúnedain chieftain of the North, called Aragorn, came to Gondor, Faramir recognized him as the rightful king of all the Dúnedain. So, in its time of greatest peril, the king returned, and with him came such allies that, in the Battle of Pelennor Fields, the forces of Morgul, Harad and Rhûn were crushed, and before the Black Gate of Mordor, the hand of Sauron was forced in a gambit whereby his power was ended for ever.

Gonnhirrim

Dwarves were wondrous stonemasons and quarries. Long and deep they worked within mountains to unlock treasure hoards of metals, both precious and base, and jewels of great beauty. Their vast kingdoms of Belegost, Nogrod and Khazad-dûm, which were built in Middle-earth in the Ages of Starlight, were famous, but most renowned among Elves was the Dwarves' work on the hidden Kingdom of the Grey-elves, which was named Menegroth, the Thousand Caves. Dwarf craftsmen carved a place there which was like a forest grotto of glittering beauty, with many fountains and streams and lights of crystal. For this deed Grey-elves named them Gonnhirrim, 'masters of stone'.

Gorbag

Uruk-hai of Minas Morgul. During the War of the Ring, Gorbag was a captain of a company of Morgul Orcs who became involved in a fight with another company of Orcs over possession of Frodo Baggins' mithril coat. The Tower Orcs led by the Uruk-hai, Shagrat, were victorious and Gorbag was killed.

Gorcrows

Ancient Hobbit folklore spoke of the swamplands where evil phantoms called Mewlips dwelt. In these haunted marshes there was also an evil breed of blackbird, the Gorcrow. Gorcrows were carrion birds and lived close alongside the Mewlips, the remains of whose prey they devoured.

Gorgoroth

The mountains and cliffs of northern Beleriand above the vales of the Sirion River and the Grey-Elf kingdom of Doriath were called the Gorgoroth or the 'Mountains of Terror'. These precipices – running east and west – dropped from the high plateau of Dorthonion, the 'land of pines', which lay to the north. Gorgoroth gained its name because that monstrous evil being called Ungoliant with her terrible brood of Giant Spiders made their home in the valley at the base of these mountains. The histories of Beleriand tell us that the Edain hero Beren was the only person to attempt a crossing of the Gorgoroth and survive. Long after Beleriand had sunk into the sea, when Sauron the Ring Lord founded his evil kingdom of Mordor, he called that part of his realm around Barad-dûr, the Dark Tower, upon which rained the volcanic ash of Mount Doom, the Plateau of Gorgoroth. It was a large and desolate plateau blighted with many Orc pits where none but the blackest and most vile thorns and brambles grew beneath the grey skies. It was across this dreadful land that Frodo Baggins the Ringbearer made his weary way to reach the fires of Mount Doom, where alone he might unmake the One Ring.

Gorgûn

The tales of Elves relate how the evil race of Orcs came into the forests of Middle-earth. These creatures were known as the Gorgûn to the ancient primitive Men called the Woses, who inhabited the Forest of Druadan, which lies in the shadow of the White Mountains.

Gothmog

Balrog of Angband. Mightiest of Morgoth's lieutenants, Gothmog, the Lord of Balrogs, was a Maia spirit of fire in his origin. Along with the other Balrogs, he revolted with Morgoth against the Valar and made war on them and the Elves. At his master's bidding he slew High King Fëanor before the gates of Angband. Throughout the Wars of Beleriand, Gothmog wreaked terrible vengeance with his whips of fire and his black axe. During the Battle of Unnumbered Tears he slew Fingon and captured Húrin. In the year 511 of the First Age he successfully led the forces of darkness against Gondolin. Leading the Balrog host, the Orc and Dragon legions, and surrounded by his body-guard of Trolls, Gothmog overwhelmed the defenders of the last Noldor kingdom. During the sack of the city itself, Gothmog slew and was slain by the Noldor Elf Ecthelion, the high-captain of Gondolin.

Green-elves

In Ossiriand, in the lost realm of Beleriand, lived the Green-elves in the last Age of Starlight and the First Age of the Sun. These Elves wore garments of forest green so that they might be invisible to their foes in the woodland. In the High Elven tongue they were named the Laiquendi. They were not a great or powerful people, but by their knowledge of the land they survived while the mightiest Eldar fell to Melkor and his servants.

Greenwood the Great

The greatest forest of Rhovanion and the vales of the Great River Anduin were known as Greenwood the Great. The Woodland Realm of the Elf King Thranduil was to be found in the northeast of the forest, but in the year 1050 of the Third Age another power entered the southmost part of Greenwood and built a citadel called Dol Guldur. This was Sauron the Ring Lord and the Nazgûl who came in secret and rapidly corrupted this once beautiful forest which became infested with evil magic, Orcs, Wargs and huge Spiders. So great was Sauron's influence that for two thousand years Greenwood was called Mirkwood because of the shadow of evil which so darkened the place. Fortunately, by the end of the War of the Ring, the evil of Dol Guldur was eliminated by an army of Elves from the Woodland Realm in the north and another army out of Lothlórien in the south. Thereafter, this place was renamed Eryn Lasgalen, the 'Forest of Green Leaves'.

Grey-elves

Of all the Úmanyar, the Elves of the Journey who never saw the Light of the Trees, the mightiest were the Sindar, or 'Grey-elves'. These people were ruled by one who had seen the Light and they were protected by one who was handmaid to the Powers that made the Trees. The king of the Grey-elves was Elwë Singollo, which in the tongue of the Grey-elves was Elu Thingol, 'King Greymantle'. Thingol was the tallest of all the Elves and his hair was silver. His queen was Melian the Maia, and Ages before the coming of the Sun these two made a kingdom in the Wood of Doriath, and therein built a great city named Menegroth. So long as Melian was queen and Thingol lived, the Sindar were a prosperous and happy people. But when Thingol was drawn into the War of the Jewels and lost his life and his queen went away, the enchantment was broken, as were the people.

Grey Havens

Last of the havens of the Elves on Middle-earth was the town and harbour known as the Grey Havens, the domain of the Falathrim of Lord Círdan. Called Mithlond in Elvish, the Grey Havens were settled and built at the beginning of the Second Age of the Sun on the upper reaches of the Gulf of Lune and at the mouth of the Lune River. For two ages it was the chief port of the Elves of Middle-earth, and from this haven all the great and good of that race who survived the conflicts of Middle-earth sailed out on Círdan's magical white ships to the Undying Lands. In the Fourth Age, many of those who were numbered among the heroes of the War of the Ring also made this vast westward journey, until finally Círdan himself, with the last of the Eldar of Middle-earth, took the last Elven ship out of the Grey Havens beyond the circles of the word to the Undying Lands of the immortals.

Grey Mountains

Just to the north of the great forest of Mirkwood there is a chain of mountains which runs east-west and marks the northern limit of Rhovanion. The most northerly source of Anduin, the Great River, these are the Grey Mountains, which are called Ered Mithrin in Elvish. From the year 2000 in the Third Age, this was a refuge and home to the Dwarves of Durin's Line. Here they became immensely wealthy because of the enormous quantities of gold they found and for five centuries they prospered. During the twenty-sixth century, the fame of wealth to be found in the Grey Mountains reached the ears of the Cold-drakes, who attacked mercilessly. Though the Dwarves' defence was valiant, they were overwhelmed and the gold-rich mountains were left entirely to the Cold-drakes.

Grishnákh

Orc of Mordor. During the War of the Ring, Grishnákh was the captain of the horde that attacked the Fellowship of the Ring, and slew Boromir. Grishnákh and his band then took captive Meriadoc Brandybuck and Peregrin Took, who he believed could lead him to the One Ring. As treacherous as he was evil, Grishnákh wished to possess the One Ring himself, and so snatched the captive Hobbits from the Isengard Orcs who guarded them. For the Hobbits it was a blessing in disguise. That evening the Orc camp was wiped out by the Horsemen of Rohan, who then killed Grishnákh, and allowed the Hobbits to escape.

Gwaihir the Windlord

Eagle of the Misty Mountains. At the end of the Third Age of the Sun, Gwaihir was the largest and most powerful Eagle of his day. He was the King of All Birds and a special friend to the Wizards and Elves, particularly after Gandalf healed him after he received a poisoned wound. During the Quest of Erebor in 2941, Gwaihir and his Eagles rescued Thorin and Company from Orc attack. During the Battle of Five Armies before Erebor, Gwaihir and his Eagles played a critical role in turning the tide of the battle. During the War of the Ring, Gwaihir freed Gandalf from Isengard, and later carried him down from the peak of Zirak-zigil after his battle with the mighty Balrog of Moria.

During the last battle of the war, before the Black Gate of Mordor, Gwaihir and his brother Landroval led all the Eagles of the North against the Ringwraiths, just as the One Ring was being destroyed. Then Gwaihir and his brother, Landroval, flew to the slopes of Mount Doom where they rescued Frodo Baggins and Samwise Gamgee.

Gwaith-i-Mírdain

In the year 750 of the Second Age of the Sun, many Noldor left Lindon and went to Eriador. Their lord was Celebrimbor, the greatest Elven-smith in Mortal Lands; he was the grandson of Fëanor, who made the Great Jewels, the Silmarils. In the Sindarin tongue the people of Celebrimbor were named the Gwaith-i-Mírdain, the 'people of the jewel-smiths'.

When the magical metal, mithril, otherwise known as true silver, was discovered in the Misty Mountains, Celebrimbor and his people were overcome by a desire to possess it. So they travelled to Eregion, which was named Hollin by Men, and lived at the foot of the Misty Mountains in the city of Ost-in-Edhil, near the West Door of Khazad-dûm, the mightiest city of Dwarves. The Dwarves and the Gwaith-i-Mírdain made a pact between themselves whereby both races chose to put all their past

quarrels to rest, and in fact they managed to keep that peace for a thousand years. For many years the trade between Dwarves of Khazad-dûm and Elves of Eregion brought prosperity to both races.

However, in the year 1200 one named Annatar came among them. None knew him, but his knowledge was great and he freely gave what aid he could to the Gwaith-i-Mírdain, as well as gifts that he made himself. By 1500 they had come to trust him fully and planned to make many magical things with his aid. So it was that the Rings of Power were made by the Gwaith-i-Mírdain. For a full century Celebrimbor and his people laboured on this great work. However, Annatar was in fact Sauron the Dark Lord disguised, and in that time among the Dwarves and the Gwaith-i-Mírdain, in secret, he made the One Ring, the Ruling Ring that would wield power over all the others. With this One Ring, the Dark Lord hoped to rule the World.

GWAITH-I-MÍRDAIN The Elven-smiths of Eregion who forged the Rings of Power. A wise and prosperous folk until the disastrous War of Sauron and the Elves, which destroyed Eregion and scattered its people.

Yet once Sauron placed the Ring on his finger, the Elves knew him for the Dark Lord, and they removed their Rings and hid them from him. The War of Sauron and the Elves followed; Eregion was destroyed and Celebrimbor was slain with the greater part of his people. In that year of 1697 of the Second Age, the few Gwaith-i-Mírdain who remained were given aid by Elrond Half-elven. At the command of Gil-galad, Elrond came out of Lindon with a guard of warriors and took the survivors to a place of refuge – a deep, narrow valley in Rhudaur – which they named Imladris but which Men called Rivendell. Thereafter, this refuge of the Gwaith-i-Mírdain was the last surviving Elf-kingdom between the Misty Mountains and the Blue Mountains.

Haladin

In the First Age of the Sun, three hosts of Men first came to the Elf-realms of Beleriand and allied with the Noldorin Elves. The hosts were the Three Houses of Elf-friends, the Edain; of the Three Houses the Second was named Haladin. A forest-loving people, the Haladin were less numerous and smaller than those of the other Houses. Their first chieftain was Haldad who, along with many of his people, was slain by Orcs. His daughter Haleth then led the Haladin to the Forest of Brethil, where they grew wiser in the ways of the woodlands. There, like the wise Green-elves of Ossiriand, they fought against the minions of Melkor. But, as the tide of the Wars of Beleriand turned against all the Edain, and though such a great hero as Túrin Turambar came to fight with them, the Haladin also suffered loss and dwindled before the evil onslaught of Orc legions.

Half-Orcs

Among the Dunlendings who, in the Third Age of the Sun, came to Saruman's banner of the White Hand in Isengard, were some whose blood, by the sorcery of Saruman, became mixed with that of the Orcs and Uruk-hai. These were large Men, lynx-eyed and evil, who were called Half-orcs. Many were among the strongest servants of Saruman. They mostly perished at the Battle of Hornburg, either before the fortress walls or in the Huorn forest. Yet some lived beyond that day of doom and followed Saruman into exile, even to the Shire, where they served the fallen Wizard until his last breath.

Halflings

No history tells how or when the Hobbits, the smallest of the peoples of Middle-earth, entered the World, but it is thought that perhaps it was in the First Age of the Sun, as they are near relatives of Men. However, in the time that Men arose, there were many wars and great deeds wherein powerful races and forces fought for supremacy. In the struggle for dominion, little heed was taken of such a diminutive people, who, being half the height of Men were by Men most often called Halflings.

Harad

South of the realms of Gondor and Mordor were the wild barbarian lands of Harad. During Sauron's many wars, the brown-skinned men of Near Harad and the black-skinned men of Far Harad often came to fight for the Ring Lord against the Dúnedain. Harad, meaning 'south' in Elvish, was also called the Sunlands, Sutherland and Haradwaith. Its people were called the Haradrim or the Southrons. The land itself was vast and hot with great deserts and forests stretching far into the uncharted lands in the south of Middle-earth. It was divided into numerous warrior kingdoms; some were primarily foot soldiers, others cavalry, and still others were mounted on the backs of the tusked Mûmakil, the giant ancestors of the elephants. One of the greatest ports of Harad was Umbar, the home of those sea-going Haradrim, known as the Corsairs of Umbar.

Haradrim

In the histories that were written in the days of the War of the Ring, much is told of the brown-skinned Men of the South who were named the Haradrim, and how they came forth fiercely in war. Some Haradrim appeared on horseback and others on foot, and those who were named Corsairs came in dread fleets of their black ships called dromunds.

But most famous were those Haradrim who rode in war towers on the broad backs of the great Mûmakil. Such Haradrim armies caused terrible destruction, because Horses would not come near the Mûmakil. From their towers the Haradrim shot arrows and threw stones and spears. With tusk and trunk and great pounding feet the Mûmakil would break the shield-walls of its foes and overthrow mighty armies on Horse and foot.

In the Battle of Pelennor Fields, the Haradrim were most numerous among the servants of the Witch-king of Morgul. They were fierce and they rallied under a red banner marked with a black serpent. These warriors were clothed in scarlet cloaks and had gold rings in their ears and golden collars and great round shields, both yellow and black, studded with steel spikes. All had black eyes and long black hair in plaits braided with gold, and some as well had paint like crimson blood upon their faces. Their helmets and corselets of overlapping plates were of bronze. They were armed variously with bows, crimson-headed spears and pikes, curved daggers and scimitars. They were said to be as cruel as Orcs and in battle gave no quarter and expected none.

Although most of the Haradrim in the army that came to Mordor were of brown skin, the lands of the Haradrim were vast, and part of the army came from Far Harad, where the tribesmen of the Sunlands were black. These were mighty warriors, who were compared with Trolls in strength and size.

All these people, strong though they had grown, owed their source of power to the coming of the Dark Lord Sauron. Their King of Kings was always Sauron throughout the Second and Third Ages, and allegiance to Mordor and the Dark Lord's emissaries – the Ringwraiths – was their law.

HARADRIM The brown- and black-skinned races from the southern region of Middle-earth, allied to Sauron the Dark Lord and his servants. In the Third Age they made constant war on the Men of Gondor.

In the Second Age, Sauron came among the Haradrim and gave them many gifts of power. To him they made sacrifice and gave worship. In time the might of the Haradrim increased and they ventured north against the kings of Gondor. Among them came other emissaries of the Dark Lord Sauron including a few of the Númenóreans who had turned against the Powers of Arda. In the Second Age two of these Black Númenóreans became great lords among the Haradrim and these were Herumor and Fuinur.

The 'Book of the Kings' tells how the power of the Haradrim in the North was destroyed in the Second Age. As they rallied about the power of Sauron in Mordor, the Last Alliance of Elves and Men was formed and there was a mighty battle before the Black Gate. The Gate was broken, and the Haradrim, Easterlings and Orc-hordes were crushed, and Mordor fell. And finally, after a seven-year siege, Sauron and the Ringwraiths were defeated and driven into the shadows.

This was not the end of the Haradrim, for the One Ring was not destroyed. Sauron and the Ringwraiths eventually returned in the Third Age and they again called the Haradrim to arms, promising them great wealth and making evil threats. So the Haradrim came to Mordor once again.

In the 'Book of the Kings' it is told that when the Men of Gondor sailed to Umbar and broke the power of the Black Númenóreans, the Haradrim arose, in the year 1015 of the Third Age, and made war on Gondor. In battle they slew Ciryandil, third in line to the Ship-kings of Gondor, but the Haradrim could not break Gondor's hold on the port at that time. The next king of Gondor destroyed their armies in 1050 and the Haradrim had no power to come again against the Men of Gondor for nearly four hundred years, when there was a rebellion in Gondor itself. A great navy of rebels – sons of one named Castamir the Usurper – came to Umbar and made an alliance with the Haradrim against the Men of Gondor. So for all the centuries of the Third Age, with the rebels who were named the Corsairs of Umbar and with some of the Black Númenóreans, the Haradrim raided the borderlands and shores of Gondor's realms.

In the year 1944, the histories of Gondor again speak of the land armies of the Haradrim. At that time the Haradrim and the Variags of Khand made a pact with the Easterling barbarians called the Wainriders. The purpose of their alliance was to achieve a simultaneous two-pronged attack on Gondor, from the East and from the South. Thus, the forces of Gondor were split, and the Wainriders succeeded and broke the army of East Gondor and slew the king, but they had not counted on the valiant general Eärnil of the southern army of Gondor. Eärnil, having swept the Haradrim and Variags from the field at the Battle of Poros Crossing, then turned to the east marches and struck down the unprepared Wainriders at the Battle of the Camp.

In the year that the War of the Ring was declared many legions of the Men of Harad went to Mordor: brown Men in crimson from Near Harad on Horse, on foot and riding the great Mûmakil in war towers; and terrible black tribesmen from Far Harad. With them came the Corsairs out of Umbar, the fierce Variags from Khand and the Easterlings from near and far: bearded axe-men, footmen and cavalries. And finally there were the legions of Orcs, Uruk-hai, Olog-hai and Trolls. No greater army was amassed in that time in Middle-earth. But as is told in the 'Red Book of Westmarch' their doom was sealed by power beyond strength of arms, and, though valiant in battle, they were crushed and destroyed at the Battle of Pelennor Fields and at the Black Gate of Mordor. Sauron was cast down for ever and with him all his servants. But it is told a new king who was both strong and merciful came to Gondor and he made a peace with the Haradrim that long endured into the Fourth Age of the Sun.

Haradwaith

All the lands of Middle-earth that lay south of Gondor were, in the histories of the West, called Harad, meaning the 'south'. Its people were sometimes called Haradwaith, sometimes Southrons, and most commonly Haradrim.

Harfoot

Most numerous and typical of the Hobbit strains were those who were named the Harfoot. They were the smallest of the Halflings and their skin and hair were nut-brown. The Harfoot were the first of the Hobbit people to leave the Vales of Anduin and cross over the Misty Mountains into Eriador. This migration was in the year 1050 of the Third Age. They were friendliest with the Dwarves, for they loved hillsides and highlands, and hole-dwelling to them was a joy.

Helcar

The Inland Sea in the far northeast of the continent of Middle-earth was called Helcar. It was located where the mighty northern pillar of the Lamp of the Valar once stood as a light to the world through the most ancient days of Arda. After the destruction of the Lamps and at the time of the Rekindling of the Stars, it was in the Mere of Cuiviénen, a bay on the eastern shores of this same Sea of Helcar, where the race of the Elves was first awakened. These waters of the Inland Sea of Helcar were constantly fed and refreshed by a multitude of crystal springs, streams and rivers.

HEL'CARAXË 'The Grinding Ice'.

Helcaraxë

Until the end of the Second Age of the Sun and the Change of the World, there was a northern narrow gap of sea and ice between the Undying Lands and Middle-earth. This was called Helcaraxë, the Grinding Ice. It was over this bridge of ice that Melkor and Ungoliant the Great Spider fled after they destroyed the Trees of the Valar and stole the Silmarils.

Helm Hammerhand

Northman, king of Rohan. Helm Hammerhand was born in 2691 of the Third Age. He became the ninth king of Rohan in 2741. Helm ruled for seventeen years before Rohan suffered from a devastating Dunlending invasion. After the Rohirrim defeat at the Crossings of Isen in 2758, Helm and his army retreated to the fortress of Hornburg, where he held the enemy at bay through the Long Winter. He often terrorized his Dunlending besiegers by going out in the snow at night and silently slaying his enemies with his bare hands. On one of these raids, Helm froze to death. Helm's Deep, Helm's Dike and Helm's Gate were all named after Helm Hammerhand.

Helm's Deep

The huge fortified gorge in the White Mountains in the Westfold of Rohan was called Helm's Deep. Named after the Rohirrim king Helm Hammerhand, Helm's Deep and Dunharrow were Rohan's two major places of refuge during times of war. Helm's Deep referred to the entire fortified system which included the gorge, the Deeping Wall built across the gorge, the fortress of Hornburg, the cavern refuge known as Aglarond ('glittering caves') and the Deeping Stream that flowed from the gorge. The defences of Helm's Deep were largely built by the Men of Gondor, although the caverns of Aglarond were believed to have been delved during the Second Age by the Númenóreans. In 2758, the Rohirrim under Helm Hammerhand defended it against the Dunlendings, and during the War of the Ring, King Théoden fought the Battle of Hornburg here against the forces of Saruman.

Helmingas

In the twenty-eighth century of the Third Age of the Sun, a king of great stature came to the Rohirrim, the Horse-lords of Mark. He was ninth in the line of kings, and his people called him Helm Hammerhand. Though his rule ended in tragedy during the Long Winter and Dunlending Invasions, his legend grew strong among his foes. He was compared with a great Troll, for he hunted the Dunlendings by night and with his bare hands slew them in the snow. Even after his death the Dunlendings feared his wraith, who they claimed pursued them for many years.

The Rohirrim often called upon the spirit of that fearful king in war, and in his honour they called his mountain stronghold Helm's Deep, and named themselves the Helmingas.

High-Elves

Of all the Elves, the mightiest were the High-Elves, those of the Eldar who first reached the shores of Aman, the Undying Lands, in the days of the Trees of the Valar. These were called the High Elves, and they were those Elves who arrived in that place named 'Elvenhome' and were granted great wisdom and many skills by the Valar and Maiar. In large part they dwell there still, though the Trees have been destroyed and the Undying Lands have been taken from the Circles of the World and cannot now be reached by any device of Men.

Hildor

When Arien the Sun first shone on the World, there came forth the race of Men far to the East of Middle-earth. They were late-comers to the World, for many other races had arisen before them. Therefore, the Elves named them Hildor, for its meaning is the 'followers'.

Hillmen

In the Ettenmoors in Eriador there lived an evil race of Hillmen who served the Witch-king of Angmar in the Third Age of the Sun. These barbarian Hillmen were fierce and numerous and they were allied with the Orkish legions. In the fourteenth and fifteenth centuries, it is told, they subdued the provinces of Rhudaur and Cardolan of the Dúnedain of the North Kingdom. In 1974, after six centuries of intermittent war this alliance finally brought down Arthedain, the last of the proud Dúnedain provinces of the North Kingdom.

HELM Helm ruled for seventeen years before Rohan suffered from a devastating Dunlending invasion.

But this too was the time of the Hillmen's own ruin. Hardly had the Hillmen and their Witch-king taken Fornost, the last citadel of the Dúnedain, when they were attacked by a great army led by Eärnur of the South Kingdom of Gondor, Círdan of Lindon and Glorfindel of Rivendell. In this Battle of Fornost the power of the Hillmen was broken, the Orcs exterminated and the kingdom of Angmar was destroyed. The Hillmen became a hunted people, scattered and forgotten.

Hobbiton

The most famous village in the land of the Hobbits of the Shire was a humble Hobbit village built on and around Hobbiton Hill with a mill and granary on a stream called the Water. The village became famous because on that hill was the street of Bagshot Row and the Hobbit hole of Bag End. This was the home of the most celebrated of all Hobbits on Middle-earth, Bilbo and Frodo Baggins, who played such critical roles in the War of the Ring.

HOBBITS A diminutive, burrowing, hole-dwelling people with a lifespan of roughly a century. Between two and four feet high, they were plump and cheerful, with curly brown hair on top of their head and feet.

Hobbits

When the bright fire of Arien the Sun came into the World there arose the race of Men, it is claimed that in that same Age there also arose in the East the Halfling people who were called Hobbits. These were a burrowing, hole-dwelling people said to be related to Men, yet they were smaller than Dwarves, and the span of their lives was about a hundred years.

Nothing is known of the Hobbit race before 1050 of the Third Age, when it is said they lived with the Northmen in the northern Vales of the Anduin between the Misty Mountains and the Greenwood. In that century an evil force entered the Greenwood, and it was soon renamed Mirkwood. It was perhaps this event which forced the Hobbit people out of the Vales. For in the centuries that followed, the Hobbits migrated westwards over the Misty Mountains into Eriador, where they discovered both Elves and Men in an open fertile land.

All Hobbits, both male and female, shared certain characteristics. All measured between two and four feet in height; they were long-fingered, possessed of a well-fed and cheerful countenance, and had curly brown hair upon their heads and peculiar shoeless, oversized feet. An unassuming, conservative people, they judged their peers by their conformity to quiet Hobbit village life. Excessive behaviour or adventurous endeavour were discouraged and considered indiscreet. The excesses of Hobbits were limited to dressing in bright colours and consuming six substantial meals a day. Their one eccentricity was the art of smoking Pipe-weed, which they claimed as their contribution to the culture of the World.

It is said that Hobbits were of three strains. These three were named the Harfoots, the Fallohides and the Stoors. The Harfoots, the most numerous of Hobbit strains, were also the smallest. They had nut-brown skin and hair. They loved hill lands and often enjoyed the company of Dwarves. These Harfoots were the first of the Hobbit people to cross over the Misty Mountains and enter Eriador.

Nearly a century later, in the year 1150 of the Third Age of the Sun, the Fallohides followed their kindred Harfoots and crossed the mountains. They entered Eriador by way of the passes north of Rivendell. The Fallohides were the least numerous of Hobbit strains. They were taller, thinner and were thought to be more adventurous than their kin. Their skin and hair were fairer, and they preferred woodlands and the company of Elves. They preferred hunting to ploughing, and of all Hobbits demonstrated the greatest traits of leadership.

The Stoors were the last of the Hobbits to enter Eriador. The most Mannish of their race, they were bulkier than the other strains and could actually grow beards. They were the most southerly of the Hobbits in the Vales of Anduin and they chose to live on flat river lands; again in a very un-Hobbit-like fashion they knew the arts of boating, fishing and swimming. They were the only Hobbits to use footwear; in muddy weather, it was claimed, they wore boots. It is said that the Stoors did not begin their western migration until the year 1300, when many passed over the Redhorn Pass; yet small settlements remained in such areas as the Gladden Fields as many as twelve centuries later.

For the most part the Hobbits of Eriador moved into the Mannish lands near the town of Bree. In the year 1601 most of the Hobbits of Bree marched westwards again to the fertile lands beyond the Brandywine River. There they founded the Shire, the land that was recognized thereafter as the homeland of Hobbits. Hobbits reckon time from this date.

By nature the Hobbits had peace-living temperaments and by great luck they had discovered a land that was as peaceful as it was fertile. So, except for the Great Plague of 1636 which devastated all the peoples of Eriador, it was not until the year 2747 that an armed encounter took place in the Shire. This was a minor Orc raid which the Hobbits rather grandly named the Battle of Greenfields. More serious by far was the Long Winter of 2758 and the two famine years that followed. Yet, compared to the other peoples of Middle-earth, they lived in peace for a long time. Other races, when they saw them, believed them to be of little worth, and in return the Hobbits had no ambitions towards the great wealth or power of others. Their limitations proved their strength, for, while greater and more powerful races fell about them, the Hobbits lived on in the Shire quietly tending their crops. Throughout the Shire lands their little townships and settlements expanded: Hobbiton, Tuckborough, Michel Delving, Oatbarton, Frogmorton and a dozen more; and after their fashion Hobbits prospered.

Of famous Hobbits little can be said before the thirtieth century of the Third Age of the Sun, for before that time the entire race was almost totally unknown to the World at large. Yet, of course, the Hobbits themselves had their own sense of the famous. In the lore of the Shire the first Hobbits to be named were the Fallohide brothers, Marcho and Blanco, who led the Hobbits out of Bree over the Bridge of Stonebows into the Shire. This land had been ceded by the Dúnedain of Arnor, to whose king the Hobbits paid nominal allegiance in return. In the year 1979 the last king of Arnor vanished from the North and the office of the Thain of the Shire was set up. The first Thain was the Hobbit Bucca of the Marish from whom all the Thains descended.

A giant among Hobbits was Bandobras Took, who stood four feet and five inches tall, and, astride a horse, he had led his people valiantly against the Orcs in the Battle of Greenfields. With a club, it is claimed, he slew their chieftain Golfimbul. For his size and deeds he was called Bullroarer Took. Another Hobbit notable for his deeds within the small lands of the Shire was Isengrim Took, who was named Isengrim II, the twenty-second Thain of the Shire, architect of the Great Smials of Michel Delving and grandfather of Bandobras Took.

Yet, typically among Hobbits, perhaps the most honoured of heroes before the War of the Ring was a humble farmer named Tobold Hornblower of Longbottom, who in the twenty-seventh century first cultivated the plant Galenas, also called Pipe-weed. For this deed he was praised, and delighted Hobbit smokers named one superior strain 'Old Toby' in his memory.

In the thirtieth century of the Third Age, however, fame in a very real sense came to the Hobbit folk. For, by chance, a great and evil power fell into Hobbit hands with which the fate of all Hobbits became entwined.

The first Hobbit to become famous in the World was Bilbo Baggins of Hobbiton, who was tempted into a leading role in the Quest of Erebor by the Wizard Gandalf and the Dwarf-king Thorin Oakenshield. This is the adventure that is told in the first part of the 'Red Book of Westmarch'. It is the memoir that Bilbo himself called 'There and Back Again', wherein Trolls, Orcs, Wolves, Spiders and a Dragon are slain. In that adventure, Bilbo Baggins achieved many deeds that those of stronger and wiser races in Middle-earth could not, and unexpected strength and bravery were revealed in the Hobbit character.

Part of that adventure tells how Bilbo Baggins acquired a magic ring, and, though this seemed of little importance at the time, it was an act that imperilled all who inhabited Middle-earth. For Bilbo Baggins, gentleman Hobbit of the Shire, had unknowingly become possessor of the One Ring.

In time, the identity of the One Ring was discovered and it was passed on to Bilbo's heir, Frodo Baggins. Bilbo then went to the Elven refuge of Rivendell, where he indulged his literary pursuits. For besides his memoirs in 'There and Back Again' he composed a good number of original poems and a major work of scholarship, the three-volume 'Translations from the Elvish'.

Frodo Baggins had become the Ringbearer at the time that Sauron the Ring Lord was preparing to make war on all the World. In the year 3018 the Wizard Gandalf came to Frodo and set him on the road to Rivendell on the Quest of the Ring. If the mission was successful the One Ring would be destroyed and the World would be saved from the domination of Sauron.

So, in Rivendell the Fellowship of the Ring was formed, wherein eight others were chosen as companions of Frodo Baggins, the Ringbearer, in his Quest. Three of that fellowship were also Hobbits destined for fame nearly as great as the Ringbearer himself. Samwise Gamgee, Frodo's man-servant, was one of these. A simple and loyal soul, Samwise more than once saved both his master and the Quest itself, and for a time was a Ringbearer.

Peregrin Took, the heir to the Thain of the Shire, and Meriadoc Brandybuck, were the other two Hobbits of the Fellowship. In the course of the Quest both Pippin and Merry (as they were most often called) were made Knights of Gondor. Merry was also made the squire of King Théoden of Rohan, and, to the amazement of all, with the shield-maiden Éowyn he slew the Witch-king of Morgul at the Battle of Pelennor Fields. Pippin, as a Guard of Gondor, fought with the Captains of the West and in the last Battle before the Black Gate he slew a mighty Troll.

Merry and Pippin were the tallest of all Hobbits in the history of their race, for upon their journeys they drank Ent-draughts, the food of the giant Ents. So they towered above their people and by Mannish measure were four and a half feet tall. Further, Merry was a Hobbit scholar of note and compiled the 'Herblore of the Shire', the 'Reckoning of the Years', and the treatise 'Old Words and Names in the Shire'.

Frodo Baggins, champion of the Quest of the Ring, was also the chief historian of the War, for he wrote the greater part of the 'Red Book of Westmarch'. He named that history 'The Downfall of the Lord of the Rings and the Return of the King'. Yet though this humble and valiant Hobbit was heralded the noblest

HOLMAN GREENHAND Ancestral first gardener of Hobbiton-on-the-Hill.

of his race, in the end it was not Frodo but another Hobbit who destroyed the One Ring in a way both unexpected and unintentional.

This was Sméagol Gollum, the only Hobbit ever to have succumbed to truly evil ways. Of all his race, the tale of Sméagol Gollum is the strangest. For, as is told in the histories of the One Ring, he was once a Stoorish Hobbit who in the twenty-fifth century of the Third Age lived near the Gladden Fields. There Sméagol and his cousin Déagol first discovered the lost Ring, but Sméagol murdered Déagol and took the Ring for himself. By the power of the Ring his life was lengthened, yet by it as well he was twisted beyond recognition. His form became ghoulish; he lived by dark deeds of murder, on unclean meats and the dark influence of the Ring made him shun light. He lived by dark pools and in deep caverns. His skin became hairless, black and clammy, and his body thin and gaunt. His head was like a skull, yet his eyes grew great like those of fish that flourish far beneath the seas; they bulged yet were pale and his vision was poor. His teeth grew long, like Orc fangs, and his Hobbit feet grew flat and webbed. His arms became long and his hands larger and filled with evil grasping strength.

The 'Red Book of Westmarch' records that Gollum (for so he became named in this form because of the ugly guttural sound he made) resided for nearly five centuries hidden in caverns beneath the Misty Mountains, until the year 2941. Then, guided no doubt by a destiny beyond his understanding, the Hobbit Bilbo Baggins came to Gollum's cavern and took the One Ring. From Bilbo it passed to Frodo Baggins and in all the eighty years that the Ring was out of his groping hands, Gollum never ceased his searching for it. At last he came upon the Ringbearer himself. For a time Frodo Baggins almost seemed able to tame Gollum, but Gollum's soul was entirely given over to evil and he still lived by treachery. So it was that in the moment of decision, when the power of the Ring overcame the good Frodo Baggins upon Mount Doom, Gollum came upon him and fought him upon the edge of Doom. By his evil strength Gollum won the Ring, but he toppled backwards with his precious prize down into the fiery bowels of the Earth and the One Ring was destroyed. The World was thus saved from the horror of eternal darkness, and though Hobbits now are few, for many centuries of the Fourth Age they dwelt in honour and peace because of the deeds of their people in that mighty conflict.

Hobgoblins

The evil beings to whom Men now give the name Goblin were in the days of Middle-earth called Orcs, and there were many kinds. Most powerful of these were the Uruk-hai: Man-sized creatures of great strength and endurance; like the smaller breeds in wickedness, but stronger and unafraid of light. Often these were the cruel leaders of the lesser Goblin folk, and they formed élite fighting units within a larger army. They are sometimes called Great Goblins, or Hobgoblins, even though they could wreak far greater evil in ancient times than now.

Holbytlan

The 'Red Book of Westmarch' tells much of the history of the Halfling people called Hobbits. In one part is explained how that name was derived from the name Holbytlan, which means 'hole-dwellers' in the tongue of the Rohirrim.

Hornburg

The massive fortress of Hornburg was built by the Men of Gondor in the first millennium of the Third Age on the Hornrock in Helm's Deep, a gorge in the White Mountains. Hornburg was the centrepiece of a huge defence system in the Helm's Deep that included the Deeping Wall, and the great cavern refuge of Aglarond, the 'glittering caves'. In 2758, the Rohan King

Helm Hammerhand and his people defended the Hornburg against the might of the Dunlendings. However, the greatest conflict fought here was the Battle of Hornburg, one of the decisive battles in the War of the Ring. Here the army of the White Hand of Saruman the Wizard set against the Rohirrim defenders of the Hornburg. The army was made up of Dunlendings, Orcs, Half-orcs and Uruk-hai, and although the invaders succeeded in storming the earthwork defences of the Deeping Wall and smashing the gates of the fortress itself, the force of the Rohirrim cavalry drove them from the high walls out onto the battleground of Deeping-coomb where the enemy was trapped by a second army of Rohirrim supported by a legion of giant Huorn tree-spirits. Here the battle ended and Saruman's army was destroyed.

Horses

How Horses were first made is not told in the histories of Arda, but it is known that Nahar, the steed of Oromë, the Huntsman of the Valar, was the first such being to enter the World. And though all Horses take from Nahar their form, he is the mightiest and most beautiful of the race. Golden are his hooves and his coat is white by day and silver by night. Tireless, Nahar travels over the Earth as easily as the swiftest Eagle speeds through the air.

Men and Elves bred Horses to their needs, but it is said that the nobler breeds were descended from Nahar, and these were the Elven Horses of Eldamar and those named the Mearas that lived in Rhovanion. These noble breeds were for the most part white or silver-grey. They were long-lived and fleet, and they understood the language of Elves and Men.

Most famous of the High Elven Horses in the histories that have come to Men are those that the Noldor brought to Middle-earth, and best known of those Horses was one named Rochallor. This was the warhorse that Fingolfin, most valiant of the Noldor kings, rode in his great ill-fated duel with Morgoth the Enemy.

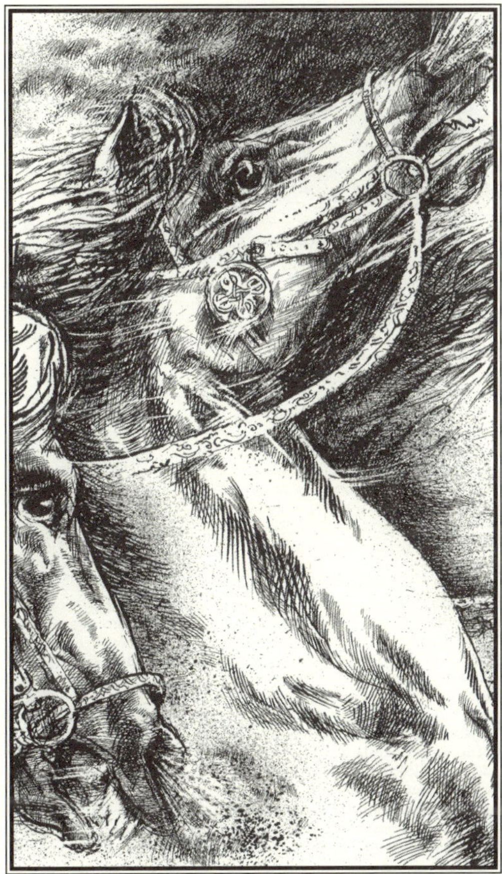

HORSES Descended from Nahar, the Valarian steed of Oromë, horses played a critical role in the histories of Middle-earth. Most famous were the Elven Horses of Eldamar and the magnificent Mearas of Rhovanion.

In the Third Age of the Sun, the noblest Horses of Middle-earth were those wild steeds of Rhovanion that were named the Mearas. In the twenty-sixth century of the Age, Eorl, the first king of the Riders of the Mark, tamed the Mearas, and for many centuries only the king of the Mark and his sons could ride these Horses.

There were other breeds of Horses in various parts of Middle-earth, where Men, Elves and some other races – both good and evil – took them into service. Many of the people that came out of Rhûn and Harad came to

THE BLACK RIDERS The Horses of the Ringwraiths were fearsome indeed.

war mounted on Horses or in Horse-drawn chariots. The Horses of the Ringwraiths were fearsome indeed, but more terrible still were the Horses that were taken into the domain of Sauron in Mordor. The Orcs of Mordor often came to the Horses of the Rohirrim in the night and took them to their master, Sauron, and he twisted their noble form to evil purpose. Such a steed was the mount of the lieutenant of Barad-dûr, the Black Númenórean who was called the Mouth of Sauron. This beast was huge and black, but its tortured head was like a great skull and from its nostrils and eyes came forth red flames.

Huan

Wolfhound of the Valar. Hound of Oromë the Huntsman, Huan was given to the Noldor prince, Celegorm. Huan went with his new master to Beleriand. Because of his love for the Elven princess Lúthien, he became fatefully caught up in the Quest of the Silmaril. One by one, he slew the Werewolves of Tol Sirion, including their sire, the mighty Draugluin, and even managed to defeat Sauron in Wolf form. Finally, he took on Carcharoth, the largest and mightiest Wolf of all time who was hand-reared by Morgoth. In the ensuing battle Huan prevailed, but he was also fatally wounded by Carcharoth's poisonous fangs.

Hummerhorns

According to a Hobbit rhyme, a race of winged insects called Hummerhorns was said to have battled a questing knight. Whether these ferocious insects were of giant size, or the knight was of some diminutive race, or whether the tale was the product of Hobbit humour cannot now be learned.

Huorns

Among the most ancient of the Olvar that lived within Arda were the trees of the Great Forests that came from the seeds that Yavanna devised in the Ages of the Lamps. For many Ages they grew peacefully, but in Middle-earth at the beginning of the Ages of Starlight there came among the trees great spirits, which were called Ents, the Shepherds of the Trees. These protectors appeared because many other races

OLD MAN WILLOW He held all the Old Forest in an enchantment by the power of his song and led all travellers to him.

in that time came into the World and Yavanna feared that the forests would be destroyed. So through the Ages of Starlight and the Sun the Ents walked the forests, and in time it is said some Ents became more tree-like than they were before, and some of the ancient trees became more Ent-like and limb-lithe. Like the Ents, they learned the art of speech. Whether tree or Ent in the beginning, by the Third Age of the Sun there was a race apart from either, that was named the Huorns. Mostly, the Huorns stood like dark trees in the deepest forests, gnarled and unmoving, yet watchful. When aroused in wrath they moved swiftly as if wrapped in shadows, falling on foes with deadly and merciless strength.

The tale of the War of the Ring tells how with the Ents of the Huorns, like a great forest, marched on Isengard, and how under the direction of the Ents of Fangorn they exterminated the entire Orc legion at the Battle of the Hornburg.

Yet these were wild wood spirits bent on the destruction of all who threatened the forests. They were dangerous to all who went on two legs unless the travellers were protected by the Ents and the wrath of these Huorns was rightly feared.

Huorns were ancient and long-brooding, and some were black-hearted and rotten. Once such sentient tree spirit inhabited the Old Forest by the banks of the Withywindle. He was the Willow Man who some called Old Man Willow. The Old Forest was but the remnant of the most ancient forest of Middle-earth, and Old Man Willow wished to prevent any further inroads into his realm. He held all the Old Forest in an enchantment by the power of his song and led all travellers to him, where with limb-lithe roots and branches he ended them.

Húrin

Edain lord of Dorthonion. Born in the middle of the fourth century of the First Age, Húrin was son of Galdor, lord of the Edain. He married Morwen, a lady of the First House, and fathered three children: Túrin, Lalaith and Nienor. He was a short, but powerfully built man. In 462, Húrin's father was slain breaking the siege of the Elven tower of Barad Eithel. During the Battle of Unnumbered Tears in 473, Húrin's brother Huor was killed, along with all the Edain of the rearguard, except Húrin, who slew seventy Trolls before being captured and taken to Angband. Withstanding terrible tortures and deceptions, he was imprisoned on a crag of Thangodrim for twenty-eight years. A year after the death of his son Túrin, Húrin unwittingly helped Morgoth find the location of Gondolin. Living a cursed existence, he found his wife only on the day of her death. He then went to Nargothrond where he killed the Petty-dwarf Mîm for betraying his son, then retrieved the necklace, the Nauglamír, and took it to Thingol in Menegroth. There, in 503, Melian the Maia cleared his mind of the tormenting deceptions of Morgoth, before Húrin wandered away to die.

I·J·K

Ilmarë

Maia handmaid of Varda. Ilmarë is the greatest of the Maiar maiden spirits, and most loved by the Elves. As the handmaid of Varda, the Queen of the Heavens, she is guardian spirit of the stars.

Ilmarin

Atop the Taniquetil, the highest mountain in the Undying Lands, stands Ilmarin, the 'mansion of the high air', the home of the King and Queen of the Valar: Manwë the Lord of the Air and Varda the Lady of the Stars. Here, those servants and messengers called the Great Eagles come and go upon command. Within the vast domed halls of Ilmarin, in Olympian splendour, Manwë and Varda sit upon burnished thrones from which they can look down upon all the lands of Arda.

Imrahil

Dúnedain prince of Dol Amroth. Of mixed Dúnedain and Elvish blood, during the War of the Ring, Prince Imrahil was a champion of the Battle of Pelennor Fields, and temporarily took over the rule of the White Tower of Gondor after Denethor II's death. As one of the Captains of the West, he fought before the Black Gates of Mordor. His daughter the Princess Lothíriel married Éomer, the King of Rohan.

Ingwë

Elven king of Eldamar. Ingwë was the High King of the Vanyar Elves, the first kindred to undertake the Great Journey to the Undying Lands. They were the first to settle in Eldamar, although they were later joined by the Noldor and Teleri. Of all the Elves, the Vanyar were most loved by Manwë, and so Ingwë finally led his people into Valinor where they settled at the foot of the sacred mountain of Taniquetil.

Iron Hills

After the Dragon invasions forced the Dwarves out of the gold-rich Grey Mountains, a part of those people led by Grór travelled eastward in Rhovanion and settled in the Iron Hills in 2590 of the Third Age. The Dwarves of the Iron Hills fought in the War of the Dwarves and Orcs, and indeed, at the gates of Moria in the final Battle of Azalnulbizar in 2799 their arrival at the last moment proved the decisive blow, crushing the Orc legions. Then too, in the year 2941, an army of Dwarves from the Iron Hills led by Dáin came to the aid of Thorin Oakenshield in a successful defence of the Kingdom under the Mountain at Erebor after the death of Smaug the Golden. In this Battle of Five Armies Thorin was slain. Dáin, his kinsman, became King of Erebor and many of his people came to repopulate the Kingdom under the Mountain.

Iron Mountains

During the Ages of the Lamps Melkor went into the north of Middle-earth and raised up a mighty range of high mountains covered in snow and ice. These mountains were the Iron Mountains, called the 'Ered Engrin' in Elvish. The Iron Mountains were the first defences of Melkor's fortress kingdom of Utumno which was built in the eastern parts. It also defended his armoury of Angband which was built during the Ages of Darkness, and was to be found in the west. Here were found many of

Melkor's greatest servants: Balrogs, Vampires, Great Spiders, Werewolves and Dragons. Not content with the towering heights of the Iron Mountains as they were first conceived, Melkor raised the great volcanic peak of Thangorodrim as Angband's chief defence. However, this was all in vain, for at the end of the First Age of the Sun, Thangorodrim, Angband and the Iron Mountains were all broken in the War of Wrath. The Iron Mountains and all the evil spirits within them were destroyed and finally sank into the sea.

Isengard

The strategic fortress of Isengard lay at the southern end of the Misty Mountains near the source of the River Isen and was in a commanding position above the Gap of Rohan and the Fords of Isen. It was through this gap that the main North-South Road made its way between the Misty Mountains and the White Mountains. The fortress was built by Gondor near the beginning of the Third Age. The fortress's main defence was a large natural ring-wall of stone enclosing a flat plain. This ring-wall accounted for the fortress name of Isengard, meaning 'iron-fence', on which were built huge gates and additional defences. However, in the centre of the fortress stood the tower of Isengard built of four pillars of unbreakable black stone. This tower was over five hundred feet tall and was called Orthanc, the 'forked-tower', because of its pronged spire. Isengard and Orthanc housed one of the seven palantíri stones. Through the Third Age, the power of Gondor faded and Isengard was abandoned. In about 2700 the Dunlendings took possession of it, but they were driven out by the Rohirrim in 2759. At that time, the Wizard Saruman was given the keys to Orthanc and permission to occupy Isengard by the Steward of Gondor. In 2963 he began to refortify it and fill it with Dunlendings, Orcs, Wolves, Half-orcs, and Uruk-hai. During the War of the Ring, the mighty army Saruman had built in Isengard was entirely destroyed at the Battle of Hornburg and those few that remained behind were also destroyed when the Ents of Fangorn Forest attacked and literally tore down the walls of Isengard with their bare hands. Unable to entirely destroy the tower of Isengard, the Ents then dammed the Isen River and its waters engulfed the tower and all of Isengard, until Saruman surrendered. After the War of the Ring, the Ents tore out all the defences of Isengard and planted the Watchwood, and thereafter called the place the Tree-garth of Orthanc.

Isildur

Dúnedain king of Gondor. In 3319 of the Second Age, the Númenórean prince Isildur, his brother Anárion, his father Elendil and their followers, escaped the Downfall of Númenor. In Middle-earth, Isildur and Anárion built Pelargir, Minas Ithil, Minas Anor and Osgiliath in the south, and ruled jointly as kings of Gondor. As Lord of Ithilien, Isildur lived in Minas Ithil until 3429 when Sauron seized the city. He fled to his father's northern kingdom of Arnor, leaving his brother to defend the rest of Gondor. He returned in 3434 with the Last Alliance of Elves and Men, which destroyed Sauron's army at the Battle of Dagorlad. However, both his father and brother had died in the conflict. In 3341, Isildur finally overcame Sauron by cutting the One Ring from his hand. After this victory, Isildur succumbed to the power of the One Ring by refusing to destroy it. Two years later, Isildur was ambushed by a horde of Orcs in the Gladden Fields. He attempted to escape by using the One Ring's power of invisibility to cross the river. However, the One Ring slipped from his finger in the water, and the Orcs killed him.

ISILDUR **Isíldur succumbed to the power of the One Ring by refusing to destroy it.**

Istari

After a thousand years had passed in the Third Age of the Sun, an Elven ship came out of the Western Sea and sailed to the Grey Havens. Upon that ship were five aged Men with long white beards and great cloaks. They were cloaks of various colours, and each Man wore a tall pointed hat, high black traveller's boots, and carried a long staff. These were the Istari, whom Men called Wizards; their hats and staffs were their signs of office. They were an order and a brotherhood sent to Middle-earth from the Undying Lands, for it was perceived that a great evil was growing in Mortal Lands.

Though the Istari came secretly and in humble form, in the beginning, before their arrival in Middle-earth, they were mighty spirits. They were Maiar, spirits older than the World itself, and of that first race that came from the mind of Ilúvatar in the Timeless Halls. Yet in the diminished World of Middle-earth in the Third Age they were forbidden to come forth in power as Maiar. They were limited to the form of Men and the power found within the mortal World.

Although five Istari are said to have come to Middle-earth, two play no part in the histories of the Westlands that have come to Men, for the others were said to have gone to the far east of Middle-earth. These two were the Ithryn Luin, 'The Blue Wizards', and though it is known that they were called Alatar and Pallando in the Undying Lands and were chosen by the Vala Oromë the Horseman, nothing else is known of their lives and deeds.

Most famous and praised of the Istari is Gandalf the Grey, who by the Elves was called Mithrandir, by the Dwarves, Tharkûn, and Incánus by the Haradrim. As a Maia, in the Undying Lands he was named Olórin and was accounted wisest of his people. At that time he resided in the gardens of Lórien, the Master of Visions and Dreams, and also went often to the house of Nienna, the Weeper. Tutored by the Vala Lórien in the Gardens, Olórin's wisdom for many Ages grew greater

still. Also, counselled by Nienna in her house, which looks out on the Walls of the Night, to his wisdom was added pity and endurance beyond hope.

Of all the Istari Gandalf is counted the greatest, for by his wisdom the free peoples of Middle-earth were guided to victory over the Dark Lord Sauron, who wished to enslave them. In this Gandalf was aided by Narya, the Elven-ring of Fire, that Círdan, lord of the Grey Havens, gave him, for Narya had power to make Men brave and resolute. By Gandalf's instigation, Smaug the Dragon was slain and the battles of Five Armies, the Hornburg and Pelennor Fields were won. By Gandalf's hand alone the Balrog of Moria was destroyed. Yet his greatest deed of all was his discovery of the One Ring and his guiding of the Ringbearer to the place of its destruction. By this action the Ring was unmade, and Sauron and all his servants and all his kingdoms were brought to utter ruin. Gandalf's task upon Middle-earth was completed by this one act and so the Third Age ended with Gandalf's departure to the Undying Lands.

Another of the Istari is Radagast the Brown, who lived in Rhosgobel in the Vales of Anduin. He played a part in the White Council, which was formed to stand against Sauron, but it seemed his greatest concern was with the Kelvar and Olvar of Middle-earth and little is told of him in the chronicles of that time. He was wiser than any Man in all things concerning herbs and beasts, for his Elvish name was Aiwendil and he was a spirit faithful to Yavanna, the Queen of the Earth. It is said he spoke the many tongues of birds. Even the Beornings and Woodmen of Mirkwood and the mighty Ent guardians of the Forest of Fangorn spoke with reverence of the wisdom of Radagast the Brown, for in forest-lore he had no equal.

ISTARI The five Wizards of Middle-earth. The two greatest were the good Wizard Gandalf and the evil Wizard Saruman.

Last named of the Istari is Saruman the White, whom Elves called Curunír, 'Man of skill'. When the Istari were formed, Saruman was counted the greatest of the Order. For many centuries Saruman wandered the lands of Middle-earth and eagerly sought to destroy Sauron the Dark Lord, but after a time he grew proud and desired power for himself. In the year 2759, Saruman came to Isengard, and Beren, the Ruling Steward of Gondor, granted him the key to the tower of Orthanc, for it was thought the Istari would aid the Men of Gondor and the Rohirrim in war against the Orcs, Easterlings and Dunlendings. However, Saruman made a mighty place of evil power there and summoned Orc legions and Uruk-hai, Half-orcs and Dunlendings to him. In Isengard he flew the standard of his tyranny, the black banner marked with a ghostly white hand. In his pride he grew foolish, until he was ensnared by Sauron, who commanded sorcery far greater than his own. So the greatest of the Istari who had come to destroy the Dark Lord became one of his agents. Yet Saruman's power was annihilated by the wrath of the Ents, the valour of the Rohirrim and Huorns, and the wisdom of Gandalf. Isengard was destroyed by the Ents, his army was exterminated by the Rohirrim and Huorns, and his staff was broken and his sorcerous power was taken by Gandalf. So low did Saruman fall that in his defeat he looked for petty vengeance in the tiny realm of the Shire, where the Hobbits, the least of his enemies, resided. Here in a pathetic bid for domination Saruman was bested by the Hobbits and slain by his own servant, Gríma Wormtongue. When Saruman died, his body shrivelled to a form without flesh. It swiftly became skin, skull and bones wrapped in a ragged cloak, and from it rose a grey mist in a column. For a moment, it is said, this grey form of Saruman's Maia spirit stood over his mortal remains, but a wind came and it vanished.

Kelvar

Before Elves and Men entered the World all things were called either Kelvar or Olvar. Kelvar were animals and living creatures that moved, and Olvar were living things that grew and were rooted to the Earth. Kelvar were granted swiftness of foot and subtlety of mind with which they might elude destruction, while the Olvar were granted powerful guardian spirits.

Khamûl

Nazgûl or Ringwraith. Khamûl was an Easterling king who came under Sauron's influence during the Second Age of the Sun and was given one of the Nine Rings of Mortal Men. Sometimes called the Black Easterling or the Shadow of the East, Khamûl was second only to the Witch-king in rank among the Nazgûl. He fought for Sauron until the Ring Lord was overthrown at the end of the Second Age. In the Third Age, Khamûl appears to have been Sauron's chief lieutenant in Mirkwood from about 1100. Certainly, after 2951, Khamûl was the master of Dol Guldur. During the Quest of the Ring, Khamûl was the Dark Rider who entered Hobbiton, and then pursued Frodo Baggins and nearly caught him at Bucklebury Ferry. Through the War of the Ring, the Ringwraiths brought despair to the enemies of Sauron. After the destruction of the Witch-king at the Battle of Pelennor Fields, Khamûl became the new captain of the Ringwraiths. Khamûl was among the surviving eight Ringwraiths who flew on their Winged Beasts into the battle before the Black Gate. However, all their evil power came to nothing, for once the One Ring was destroyed in the fires of Mount Doom, all of Sauron's empire was ended. Khamûl the Black Easterling and the Shadow of the East and the other Wraiths were sent shrieking into the shadows forever after.

Khand

To the southeast of Mordor lay a barbarous land called Khand which during the Third Age had allied itself with Sauron the Ring Lord. Although little is told of this land, its people were known to be fierce warriors called the Variags who with the Easterlings and the Haradrim had long been under the evil influence of Sauron and often came at his bidding to make war on the land of Gondor. In the year 1944, the Variags of Khand came to war, along with the Haradrim, but were defeated at the Battle of Poros Crossing by the forces of Gondor. Over a thousand years later during the War of the Ring, the Variags again came forth, first at the bidding of the Witch-king of Morgul to Pelennor Fields and then at Sauron's command to the Black Gate. Both of these battles ended in disaster for the men of Khand, and during the Fourth Age they were forced to sue for peace with King Elessar and live in peace with their neighbours.

Khazâd

In the mountain heart, Aulë the Smith made the race that called itself the Khazâd. These people, who Men and Elves called Dwarves, were strong and proud, but they were also a stunted and unlovely race. Yet Dwarves were the most gifted masons and carvers of stone the World had ever seen, and their great halls and delvings beneath the mountains were counted amongst the greatest wonders of Middle-earth. The most far-famed of their dwellings was the kingdom of Khazad-dûm, which in the Third Age of the Sun was called Moria.

Khazad-dûm

The most ancient and famous of all Dwarf kingdoms was Khazad-dûm, meaning 'dwarf mansion', the ancestral home of Durin the Deathless, the first of the Seven Fathers of the Dwarves. Durin began the delvings of Khazad-dûm after discovering natural caves on the eastern side of the Misty Mountains, above the beautiful valley of Azalnulbizar. Through five Ages of Stars and three Ages of the Sun the Dwarves of Khazad-dûm were prosperous and delved a network of caverns through to the western side of the Misty Mountains. After the destruction of Beleriand, many Dwarves fled from the ruin of Nogrod and Belegost to Khazad-dûm, and its population grew, as did its wealth when the rare and magical metal called mithril was discovered in its mines. In the Second Age of the Sun, these were the Dwarves who had a long friendship with the Elven-smiths of Eregion, who forged the Rings of Power. But in the Accursed Years of Sauron's dominion in the Second Age, the Dwarves closed their great doors to the world, and so avoided the devastations of the War of Sauron and the Elves and the Last Alliance of Elves and Men. At this time, the great mansion was renamed Moria, the 'dark chasm'. Yet still the Dwarves quarried and worked the forges beneath the Misty Mountains until 1980 of the Third Age. In that year the Dwarves delved too deep beneath Mount Barazinbar and an entombed Balrog was released within the halls of Khazad-dûm. So terrible was the Balrog's strength and wrath that the Dwarves were either slain or driven from their kingdom. When the Fellowship of the Ring entered Moria at the end of the Third Age it was a chasm of darkness that had long been abandoned by the Dwarves. Its treasures had been stripped by Orkish hordes and through its barren corridors there still walked the Balrog and many bands of Orcs and Trolls. However, the reign of the Balrog ended when, after a series of duels in the Hall of Mazarbul, on Durin's Bridge, and the Endless Stair, the Wizard Gandalf finally overcame the monster and threw it from the top of Durin's Tower on the high peak of Zirak-zigil.

Kíli

Dwarf of Thorin and Company. Kíli embarked on the Quest of the Lonely Mountain in 2941 of the Third Age, which resulted in the death of Smaug the Dragon and the re-establishment of the Dwarf-kingdom under the Mountain. As the son of Thorin's sister, Dís, Kíli was fiercely loyal to his uncle. Both Kíli and his brother Fíli were killed in the Battle of Five Armies while defending Thorin Oakenshield.

Kine of Araw

Of the animals of forest and field, there were many that Oromë, the Horseman of the Valar, brought to Middle-earth. One breed of these animals was called the Kine of Araw by the Men of Gondor (Araw being the Sindarin name for Oromë). These Kine were the legendary wild white oxen that lived near the Inland Sea of Rhûn. Their long horns were much prized. In Gondor one such ox horn was made into a silver-mounted hunting horn by the first of the Ruling Stewards, Vorondil the Hunter; this was the heirloom called the Horn of the Stewards, which was destroyed in the War of the Ring.

Kingsfoil

From the lost land of the Númenóreans, a herb was brought to Middle-earth that for a long while was used as a simple folk-cure for mild pains of the head and body. In the Grey-elven tongue it was named Athelas, but Men called it Kingsfoil, for their legends told of its magical healing properties in the hands of the Númenórean kings.

Kirinki

In the lands of Númenor lived a small bird about the size of a wren, but covered in brilliant scarlet plumage and gifted with a beautiful piping voice. This bird was called the Kirinki.

Kraken

According to the most ancient tales, Melkor, that most evil of powers, in his kingdom of Utumno in Middle-earth bred many terrible creatures for which there are no names in the Time of Darkness before Varda rekindled the Stars. In the following Ages these creatures were a bane on the land and in dark waters to those who lived peacefully in the World.

Some of these beings of Melkor's survived below the thunders of the deep far beneath the abysmal seas in ancient, dreamless, uninvaded sleep even into the Third Age of the Sun. The 'Red Book of Westmarch' tells that when a fiery Balrog was loosed in the Dwarf-kingdom of Moria, another being came out from the dark waters that lay below the great mountains. This was a great Kraken, many tentacled and huge with a slimy sheen. It was luminous and green and an inky stench came from its foul bulk. Like a legion of serpents it lay in the black water beneath the mountain. Eventually, it came to the clear water of the River Sirannon, which flowed from the West Gate of Moria. There is built a great wall in the river bed and made for itself a black pool, hideous and still. The Kraken was guardian of the West Gate and none could pass without challenge. For this reason, in the 'Book of Mazarbul' it was named Watcher-in-the-Water. During the Quest of the Ring, this evil being was awakened by the Fellowship of the Ring, who managed to escape to Moria.

Kûd-Dûkan

In each of the lands of Middle-earth the Halfling people, who were called Hobbits by Men, bore different names according to the language of the various peoples. In the land of Rohan the Hobbits were named Kûd-dûkan, which means 'hole-dwellers'. From this root word it is thought that the Hobbitish term Kuduk became commonly used both by Hobbits of the Shire and by the Men of Bree in the latter part of the Third Age of the Sun.

KRAKEN A huge, many-tentacled monster, known as the 'Watcher-in-the-Water'. This evil being inhabited a foul dark pool near the West Gate of Moria and challenged all who tried to enter the ancient Dwarf Kingdom.

L

Laiquendi

Of the Three Kindred of Elves who chose to come out of the eastern lands of Middle-earth and search out the Land of Eternal Light in the West, there were many who, out of love for Middle-earth or in fear of the perils of the journey, forsook the quest and never came to the Undying Lands. The Nandor, one factor of the Teleri, were such an Elven people.

Denethor, son of the Nandor king Lenwë, gathered many of the Nandor to him in the Age before the Rising of the Sun and took them from the wilderness of Eriador to Beleriand, where they were welcomed by the Grey-elves of that land and given protection and many gifts of steel and gold. There they were granted a land that was called Ossiriand, 'land of seven rivers', which was in the south of Beleriand. While there the Nandor were renamed the Laiquendi – 'Green-elves' – because of their garments, which were green to hide them from their foes, and for their love and knowledge of all that was green and grew. They were second only to the Shepherds of Trees, the Ents, as protectors of the Olvar of the forest, and of the Kelvar as well, for the Laiquendi did not hunt the creatures of the woodlands.

For a time they were a happy people again, as no evil creatures dared to enter Beleriand in those days. The Laiquendi sang in the woodlands like the nightingales and tended the forest as if it were a great garden. Their singing was so beautiful and so constant that the Noldor, when they came to that land, renamed it Lindon, which in Quenya is 'land of song'. It always remained Lindon, even after all but this small part of Beleriand fell beneath the sea in the time of the Great Battle and the War of Wrath.

After the release of Melkor a great evil came to Middle-earth once again, as the 'Quenta Silmarillion' relates. Melkor's armies of Orcs, Trolls and Wolves appeared and the First Battle in the Wars of Beleriand took place. Though the Grey-elves and the Laiquendi were victorious over the evil army on Amon Ereb in Ossiriand, the Laiquendi lord Denethor was slain. His people were full of great sorrow and would take no new king. They swore that they would never again come into open battle with the Enemy but would remain under cover of the forest, where they could ambush their foes with darts and arrows.

Ever after, the Laiquendi kept this pledge and became a tribal people, and their enemies were harassed but could not defeat them, for they made no cities that the Enemy could find and destroy. These people were as the wind in the trees, which sometimes can be heard but never seen. And in time, after the disasters of the Fourth and Fifth Battles of Beleriand, many of the Noldor and Edain hid from the Enemy in the realm of the Laiquendi and learned much woodlore from them.

Lairelossë

In the lost land of Númenor, in the forested westlands of Andustar, was a part that was so filled with a multitude of scented evergreen trees that it was called Nísilmaldar, or land of 'the Fragrant Trees'. Among the many trees that grew there was the fragrant flowering evergreen called Lairelossë, meaning 'summer-snow-white', which was first brought to Númenor by the Sea Elves of the island realm Tol Eressëa.

Lake Men

Between Mirkwood and the Iron Hills lay the Long Lake and the city of Esgaroth, and it was here that the Lake Men lived in the Third Age of the Sun. These were Northmen who had been traders upon the lake and the Running

River. They had become wealthy trading with the Elves of the Woodland Realm in Mirkwood and with the Dwarves of Erebor, the Lonely Mountain.

Esgaroth was built upon pylons driven into the lake bottom, and a wooden bridge stood between the city and shore. It was not, however, proof against the winged Fire-drake Smaug, who in 2770 came to Erebor. In 2941 Smaug attacked Esgaroth, and, though the warrior of Dale called Bard the Bowman slew the beast, the city was ruined. Yet the Lake Men were saved from starvation, for with a part of the Dragon's hoard of jewels, the town was rebuilt.

The ruler of the Lake Men, called the Master of Esgaroth, was an elected merchant. In the time of the slaying of Smaug, the Master was cowardly and corrupt, but a new Master followed him who proved honest and wise, and the Lake Men prospered again.

Landroval

Eagle of the Misty Mountains. Landroval was the brother of Gwaihir the Windlord, the lord of the Eagles of Misty Mountains. Landroval and his brother were the largest Eagles of the Third Age, and often came to the aid of the Free Peoples against the evil servants of Sauron. Landroval flew with Gwaihir on many of his adventures; notably, the Battle of Five Armies and the battle before the Black Gates of Mordor. After the destruction of the One Ring, Landroval and Gwaihir rescued Frodo Baggins and Samwise Gamgee from the fiery lava flows on the slopes of Mount Doom.

Laurinquë

In Hyarrostar, the southwest lands of Númenor, there once blossomed the golden-flowered tree called Laurinquë. Its flowers hung in long clusters and were much loved for their beauty, and its wood was much valued by the mighty Númenórean sea lords as it provided excellent timber for their ships.

Leaflock

Ent of Fangorn Forest. Leaflock was the Westron name for one of the three oldest Ents still surviving on Middle-earth at the time of the War of the Rings. Leaflock's Elvish name was Finglas. By the end of the Third Age, he moved about very little for he had become sleepy and 'treeish'.

LAIQUENDI The 'Green Elves' of Ossiriand, in later times, Lindon, 'land of song'. Always dressed in green, the Laiquendi were protectors of all creatures of the forest and were the wisest of all Elves in woodlore.

Legolas

Elven prince of the Woodland Realm. Legolas (whose name meant 'green leaf') was the son of Thranduil, the Sindar Elf king of the Woodland Realm of Northern Mirkwood. In 3019 of the Third Age of the Sun, Legolas became a member of the Fellowship of the Ring. His keen Elf eyes, his woodland skills and his deadly bow all proved of great value to the Fellowship in their many adventures. After the death of Boromir and the breaking of the Fellowship, Legolas went on with Gimli the Dwarf and Aragorn to fight at the Battle of Hornburg. The three rode on through the Passes of the Dead to take the Corsair ships at Pelargir, then sail on into the Battle of Pelennor Fields. In the aftermath of the war, Legolas started a colony of Woodland Elves in Ithilien. After the death of Aragorn in the year 120 of the Fourth Age of the Sun, Legolas, along with his friend, Gimli the Dwarf, sailed to the Undying Lands.

Light Elves

The tale of the Great Journey tells how most of the Vanyar, Noldor and Teleri reached the shores of the Undying Lands in the time of the Trees of the Valar. There they dwelt in Eldamar and were tutored by the Powers of Arda, the Valar and their people, the Maiar. The Elves grew wise and noble and learned many skills: the making of jewels, and precious metals, the building of majestic cities and the finest arts of music and language. These people were called the Light Elves for they were shining both in body and spirit, and, of all peoples to live within the Circles of the World, they were the fairest by all accounts.

Lindar

As is told in the 'Ainulindalë', all things that came into the World came out of the grand themes of the Music of the Ainur. Elves were the fairest of all beings and their singing was almost a match for the beauty of the Great Music. Among the Elves, the loveliest singers were the Teleri, who listened tirelessly to the sounds of water against river banks and on the sea shore, and their voices became fluid, subtle and strong. Because of their skill in singing they were sometimes known by the name Lindar, which means the 'singers'.

Lindon

After the War of Wrath and the destruction of Angband, all but a small part of Beleriand sank into the Western Sea. This was a part of Ossiriand just west of the Blue Mountains called Lindon. Its name means the 'land of song' because the Laiquendi Elves, famous for their singing, had from the earliest time made these woodlands their home. By the Second Age Lindon was a narrow coastal realm west of that small part of the Blue Mountains which stood in western Eriador. Both Lindon and the Blue Mountains were divided in two by the great cleft of the Gulf of Lune. The northern part was Forlindon and served by the port of Forlond and the southern part was Harlindon and had the port of Harlond. The most important city and port, however, was Mithlond, or the 'Grey Havens', which was at the head of the Gulf of Lune. As the only remnant of Beleriand to survive, it was especially important to the Elves. From the beginning of the Second Age Gil-galad, the last High King of the Noldor on Middle-earth, came to rule in Lindon, and Círdan, the Ship-lord of the Falathrim, became master of the Grey Havens. After the destruction of the Elven Smiths in 1697 of the Second Age, and the outbreak of the War of Sauron and the Elves, the Númenóreans sent a fleet to Lindon and helped Gil-galad drive Sauron from Eriador. At the end of the Second Age, however, Gil-galad had to ride forth again from Lindon, with the army of the Last Alliance of Elves and Men, against Sauron in Mordor. Although the forces of Mordor were overthrown, Gil-galad was slain. Lindon no longer had a High King and the realm was thereafter governed by Lord Círdan from the Grey Havens. During the Third Age, the Elves of Lindon were a much diminished people and more and more were taking their magical white ships and sailing west to Eldamar, in the Undying Lands. However, from time to time Círdan sent what aid he could to the Dúnedain, and in the Battle of Fornost it was the Elves of Lindon which turned the tide of battle and finally broke the power of the Witch-kingdom of Angmar.

Surviving the War of the Ring, Lindon, along with all the kingdoms of the Eldar on Middle-earth, diminished during the Fourth Age, as one by one the High Elves departed from the Grey Havens. Finally, Círdan himself gathered together the last of his people upon his last ship and sailed westward over the sea to the Undying Lands.

Lissuin

Many of the most beautiful of the flowers of Middle-earth were brought as gifts to mortals from the shores of the Undying Lands by the High Elves of Eldamar.

Such was the case of the sweet-smelling flower Lissuin, for the histories of Númenor tell how the Elves of Tol Eressëa brought the flower Lissuin and the golden star-flower Elanor into mortal lands. The two flowers – one because of its fragrance, the other because of its colour – were woven into garlands and were worn as crowns at wedding feasts.

Little Folk

The Hobbits were known to be the smallest of the people of Middle-earth in the Third Age of the Sun. In height they measured between two and four feet, and, though quick and nimble, they were of far less strength than Dwarves. Both Men and Elves often called them the Little Folk.

Lómelindi

To the ears of Elves, the loveliest of the song birds of Arda are the Lómelindi, the 'dusk-singers', whom the Elves have also named Tinúviel and Men have called Nightingales. The name of these fair creatures is woven into many tales and the voices of the most beauteous women of Elf-fame, Melian, Lúthien and Arwen, are compared to the Lómelindi's song.

Lórellin

In Valinor, the land of the gods, is the garden of Lórien, the Vala who is Master of Dreams, and in that vast garden is the lake called Lórellin. Surrounded by these wonderful gardens, and with the misty, wooded isle of Estë, the Healer, in the middle of its glimmering waters, Lórellin is considered the fairest lake on Arda.

Lórien

During the Second and Third Age of the Sun, the Elf-realm in the Golden Wood to the east of the Misty Mountains was often called Lórien, but its true name was Lothlórien, and its history is told under that name. The true Lórien was a far more ancient place in the Undying Lands. Lórien, which means 'Dreamland', was a vast garden of extraordinary beauty in southern Valinor where the Valar, Maiar and Eldar came for physical and spiritual restoration of their powers. It was the garden of the Vala, Irmo, who was himself most often called Lórien, the Master of Dreams. It was a gentle, restful place filled with silver trees and multitudes of flowers. The waters of its crystal fountains magically refreshed all visiting Valar and Eldar. In the midst of this most beautiful of gardens were the glimmering waters of the lake Lórellin and in the midst of that lake was the isle of tall trees and gentle mists that is

LOTHLÓRIEN The Mallorn trees of Lothlórien shimmered gold.

the home of his wife Estë, the Healer, the Vala who grants rest to those who suffer. Lórien's brother is Mandos, the Master of Doom and his sister is Nienna, the Weeper.

Lossoth

On the icy Cape of Forochel to the north of the Westlands there lived a people called the Lossoth, in the Third Age of the Sun. They were a reclusive, peaceful folk, wary of all the warlike Men of Middle-earth. In the common tongue of Men they were called the Snowmen of Forochel, and they were said to be descended from the Forodwaith of the Northern Waste.

The Lossoth were poor people of little worldly knowledge, but they were wise in the ways of their cold lands. They built their homes from snow and, in sliding carts and skates of bone, they crossed the ice lands and hunted the thick-furred animals from which they fashioned their clothes. It is claimed that the Lossoth could foretell the weather by the smell of the wind.

Lothlórien

The fairest Elf-kingdom remaining on Middle-earth in the Third Age of the Sun was to be found in the Golden Wood just to the east of the Misty Mountains beyond the Gates of Moria. It was called Lothlórien, the 'land of blossoms dreaming', which was also called Lórien, 'dreamland', and Laurelindórinan, 'land of the valley of singing gold'. In this wooded realm the golden-leaved, silver-barked Mallorn trees grew. They were the tallest and fairest trees of Middle-earth and upon their high branches the Elves of Lothlórien, who were called the Galadhrim, or 'tree-people', made their homes on platforms called telain or flets. For the most part the Galadhrim were all but invisible, for they moved about among the high limbs and wore Grey-Elf cloaks possessed of magical chameleon-like qualities. Here the Noldor Queen, Galadriel, and the Sindar King, Celeborn, ruled; and some part of the brilliance of the Eldar-kingdoms of ancient times could be glimpsed in this realm. Lothlórien had one great city-palace called Caras Galadhon, the 'city of trees'. It was a royal hall built on the crest of a high hill where stood the tallest trees in the wood. This hill was walled and gated and then encircled with other great trees. Modelled on the Grey-Elf kingdom of Doriath in lost Beleriand, Lothlórien was similarly protected by powerful enchantment. Galadriel was the highest ranking Eldar remaining upon Middle-earth and by the power of Nenya, her Ring of Adamant and of Water, she cast a spell of protection around Lothlórien, so enemies might not be able to enter and making it invisible to the Eye of Sauron. For nearly all the years of the Third Age, Lothórien remained apart from the struggles of the other peoples of Middle-earth, but during the last years of the age, the Fellowship of the Ring entered the realm. Fleeing the servants of Sauron, they found rest and shelter, and by Queen Galadriel they were granted magical gifts that renewed their strength and will.

In the War of the Ring, Lothlórien was attacked three times by Sauron's servants from Dol Guldur, in Mirkwood. These forces were driven away, and, after the fall of Mordor, the Elves of Lothlórien destroyed Dol Guldur and renamed Mirkwood the Forest of Green Leaves. When, early in the Fourth Age, Galadriel left Middle-earth for the Undying Lands and Celeborn took a greater part of the Galadhrim to the Forest of Greenleaves and founded East Lórien, the Golden Wood of Lothlórien was slowly abandoned, and the magical light in that place faded.

Lúthien

Elven princess of Doriath. Lúthien was the daughter of the Sindar Grey-elf king, Thingol and Melian the Maia. She was born during the Ages of Starlight and was considered the most beautiful maiden of any race ever born. In the year 465 of the First Age of the Sun, she met the mortal Edain hero Beren, and the couple fell in love. King Thingol did not approve and set Beren an impossible task: the Quest of the Silmaril. Despite many perils, Lúthien also embarked on this quest. With Huan, the Hound of the Valar, she overcame Sauron on the Isle of Werewolves, and freed Beren from its dungeons. She then went on with Beren to Angband, where she cast spells of enchantment which allowed Beren to cut a Silmaril from Morgoth's Iron Crown. Although the quest was achieved in the end, it cost Beren his life. Lúthien was filled with such remorse, she faded and died. However, when she stood before Mandos, Lord of the Dead, she sang a song of such sadness that in pity he granted the couple a second mortal life. United at last with Beren, Lúthien soon gave birth to Dior, their only child. The two lovers lived quietly for another forty years in Ossiriand, before they were granted their second and final death.

LÚTHIEN Luthien dances before Morgoth, casting spells of enchantment, which allowed Beren to cut a Silmaril from Morgoth's Iron Crown.

Maiar

When the World was first made, the Ainur, the 'holy ones', came out of the Timeless Halls and entered this new land. The Ainur had been without shape or form in the Timeless Halls, but within the Spheres of the World they took many and various forms. These people were the Powers of Arda and the mightiest among them were the Valar, who numbered fifteen. The lesser Ainur were a multitude called the Maiar and they were the servants of the Valar. Though the Maiar were many within the Undying Lands, few are named in the histories of Men, for their concerns are seldom with mortal lands and mortal matters, but with Valar in the Undying Lands.

Mightiest of the Maiar is Eönwe, the Herald of Manwë, the Wind Lord. Eönwe's strength in battle rivals that of even the Valar, and the blast of his trumpets is a terror to all his foes, for in the wake of its sound comes the Host of the Valar. It was he who taught the Edain great wisdom and knowledge. Ilmarë, who throws down her spears of light from the night sky, is chief of the Maiar maids. She is also handmaid to Varda, the Star Queen, who rules the Heavens.

Arien, the fire spirit who once was a Maia of Vána's golden gardens in Valinor, is most worshipped by Men. It is she who guides the flight of the Sun, for, as the 'Narsilion' tells, the Sun was the last fruit of Laurelin, the Golden Tree of Valar; it was placed in a great vessel shaped by Aulë, which was then hallowed by Manwë before being carried by Arien into the sky.

As Arien goes by day, so by night flies Tilion, the Huntsman of the silver bow. Tilion was once a Maiar of Oromë, but he now carries the vessel of the Moon, which was the last flower of Telperion, the Silver Tree of Valinor.

The Maiar Ossë and Uinen, servants of Ulmo, the Ocean Lord of the Valar, are known to all who sail on the seas. Ossë is master of the waves of Belegaer, the Western Sea, and though it is said that Ossë truly loves the Sea-elves and it was he who first brought the art of shipbuilding to the World, he is feared by all mariners. For both in joy and in wrath, he is a fearsome power. However, all mariners have a great love of Uinen, Lady of the Calms. She is the spouse of Ossë, and only she may restrain his raging tempers and his wild spirit. Beleaguered mariners pray to her that she may lay her long hair upon the waters and calm the tumult. As Ossë loved the Sea-elves, so did Uinen love the Númenóreans; until the Downfall of Númenor and the Change of the World she always travelled before the ships of these sea folk.

Of all the tales of the Maiar, perhaps the strangest is that of Melian, who served both Vána and Estë in Valinor, but who in the Ages of Starlight came to Middle-earth. There in the forests of Beleriand she met the Eldar lord Elwë Singollo and married him. This is the only union of Elf and Maia that ever was, and, through four long ages of stars and one of Sun, Melian was queen of the Grey-elves and wife of Elwë, who was called Thingol and King Greymantle. In that time their realm was the fairest kingdom of Middle-earth because of the light and beauty of Melian. Yet, tragically, Thingol was slain near the end of the First Age of the Sun. Melian wrapped herself in grief and the light of the kingdom faded. The queen rose up and returned to Valinor once again, leaving Mortal Lands for ever.

Many other good and strong spirits came to inhabit Middle-earth. These were perhaps Maiar, like Melian, yet from the histories this cannot now be learned. Chief of these, in the tales of Middle-earth, is he whom the Grey-elves named Iarwain Ben-adar, which means both 'old' and 'without father'. By Dwarves he was named Forn, by Men Orald, and by Hobbits he was called Tom Bombadil. He was a short, stout Man, with blue eyes, red face and brown beard. He wore a blue coat, a tall battered hat with a blue feather, and great yellow boots. Always singing or speaking in rhymes, he seemed a nonsensical and eccentric being, yet he was absolute master of the Old Forest of Eriador where he lived, and no evil within the World was strong enough to touch him within his realm.

Other spirits, who may have been servants of the Vala Ulmo, also lived within the Old Forest. One of these was the River-woman of the Withywindle, and another was her daughter, Goldberry, who was Bombadil's spouse. Goldberry was golden-haired and as beautiful as an Elf-queen. Her garments were silver and green, and her shoes were like fish-mail. In her hair and in her belt were many flowers, and her singing was like bird song.

At the end of the first millennium of the Third Age of the Sun, it is told that five Maiar came to Middle-earth. They came not in grand forms but in the shape of ancient Men. Each was white-bearded and wore a traveller's cape, a peaked hat, and carried a long staff. These were the Istari, whom Men called the Wizards and much of their tale is told in the 'Red Book of Westmarch'. Yet only three of the five are named in the histories. Radagast the Brown was a master of birds and animals of the forest and lived near Mirkwood in Rhosgobel. Saruman the White was in the arising of the Istari Order counted the greatest, and for a time he was indeed skilful and wise, but he fell into evil ways, brought ruin down upon many and was himself completely destroyed in his efforts to make himself a great power. Gandalf the Grey was most famous of the Istari. In the beginning he was called Olórin and he served both Lórien, the Master of Dreams and Nienna, the Weeper; he was acknowledged the wisest of the Maiar race. The last two of the Istari were Alatar and Pallando, called the Blue Wizards and servants of Oromë, the Horseman. Of their fate and deeds upon Middle-earth little is told.

Yet not all the Maiar are good and fair spirits. Many were corrupted by the rebellious Vala, Melkor the Enemy. Foremost among these were the Balrogs, who were once bright spirits of fire, as fair as Arien who guides the Sun, but were twisted into demon forms by hatred and wrath. Cloaked in a foul darkness, the Balrogs were maned in fire and they wielded whips and blades of flame. Gothmog was their lord and the tale of the deeds of the Balrog host is long and bloody.

The spirit that took the form of a huge and fearsome Spider was named Ungoliant. She devoured light, vomited forth darkness and spun a black web of unlight that no eye could pierce. None could tame this spirit who perhaps was once a Maia of Melkor. Ungoliant had long since turned to serving only herself and, though she destroyed the Trees of the Valar with Melkor, she turned on Melkor at the last. In the end, driven into the great deserts of the South, it is said that having no other to turn on she consumed herself.

The Vampires and Werewolves of Angband may also have been Maiar in their beginning, like the Balrogs. It is said they were malevolent spirits that took on terrible forms, yet no tale tells of their making. Out of all the Vampires the one called Thuringwethil, 'lady of the shadow', alone is named, and of the vast Werewolf host Draugluin is named both lord and sire.

One Maia is known above all others because of his great evil, as the histories of Middle-earth tell. This is Sauron, whose name means the 'abhorred'. Sauron, the Dark Lord, who was once a Maia of Aulë the Smith, was chief servant and eventual successor to Melkor.

In the Ages of Darkness, while Melkor ruled in Utumno, and in the Ages of Stars, while Melkor was chained by the Valar, Sauron ruled the evil realm of Angband. On the return of his master, and through all the Wars of Beleriand until Melkor was cast into the Void, Sauron was his greatest general. He was also called

Gorthaur the Cruel, and he survived longest of all the Maiar who served Melkor. Many were the wars and holocausts through the Ages of Lamps, Trees, Stars and Sun that Sauron survived. After the terror of the First Age of the Sun, it is said that Sauron reappeared in the Second Age in fair form and assumed the name Annatar, 'giver of gifts'. Eventually, when he made himself Lord of the Rings, his evil spirit was revealed and war, like a black shadow, again covered Middle-earth.

In the Downfall of Númenor Sauron's body was destroyed. Yet his spirit fled to Mordor and by the power of the One Ring he made himself again a form, though he could no longer appear fair. Thereafter, he took the shape of the Dark Lord and became a fearsome warrior with black armour on burning black skin and had terrible, raging eyes. But even this form was destroyed at the end of the Second Age when Mordor fell and the One Ring was taken from his hand. Yet, so great was the power of Sauron's spirit, that in the Third Age he again made himself a form. His spirit became manifest in the sorcerous power of one great lidless Eye. Like the eyes of all the great hunting cats of forest, mountain and plain made into one, and made entirely evil, was the Eye which was wreathed with deadly flame and ringed in darkness. But even this form depended on the power that was in the One Ring, and, in the war that ended the Third Age, the Ring was destroyed. Once more, and finally, Sauron's spirit was swept into the shadows and never again did this Maia arise.

Mallorn

On the banks of the Silverlode, which flowed east of the Misty Mountains, was a forest land where the tallest and loveliest trees of Middle-earth grew. These were the Mallorn trees, which had barks of silver and blossoms of gold, and from autumn to spring the leaves were also golden-hued. In the Third Age of the Sun, this land was called the Golden Wood and Lothórien, 'land of blossoms dreaming'. This woodland of Mallorn trees was made a safe refuge from evil creatures by Elven powers, and the trees thrived and grew as they grew in no other place on Arda, except in the Undying Lands. There lived Galadhrim, the Elves of the kingdom of King Celeborn and Queen Galadriel. And within the shelter of the Mallorn tree limbs, where the trunks forked near the crest, the Galadhrim built their dwellings, which were called telain or flets. Their king and queen lived in a great hall in the tallest Mallorn. The Galadhrim were like spirits of the woods and in that realm there was no cutting or burning of wood. It truly was a kingdom of trees, and a golden glow of Elven power shone there like none other in that Age.

Mallos

In the fields of Lebennin, near the delta of the River Anduin, there grew the flowers that Grey-elves named Mallos, the 'gold-snow'. Their blooms were fair and never fading, and in Elven songs they were likened to golden bells calling the Elves to the Western Sea.

Mandos

On the deserted western shore of the Undying Lands and facing the Encircling Sea and the Walls of Night there are the Halls of Mandos where, in the lore of Eldar, the spirits of slain Elves are called to inhabit the Hall of Awaiting, until the summons of Ilúvatar at the time of the World's End. This is the House of the Dead, the vast mansions of the Vala Namo who is also called Mandos, the Master of Doom, who knows the fate of all. He is the stern Judge of the Dead, who only once felt pity, when Lúthien sang to him. His wife is Vairë, the Weaver. His brother is Lórien, the Dream-master and his sister is Nienna, the Weeper.

Manwë

Vala, King of Arda. Manwë Sulímo is the Lord of the Air, and with his wife, Varda, Queen of the Heavens, rules all of Arda from their mansions of Ilmarin on top of Taniquetil, the tallest mountain in the world. Manwë, meaning 'the Good', is also referred to as the Wind Lord, for his element is the clear air, wind, clouds and storms. Eagles and all birds are sacred to him. His eyes and his clothing are blue and his sceptre is made of sapphire. Manwë sees all the world beneath the skies and he is the breath of all the peoples of the world. The Vanyar Elves are the dearest to his heart for their greatest skill is in poetry which is his chief delight.

Mearas

All the Horses of Arda were created in the image of Nahar, the white steed of Oromë, the Valarian Horseman. The true descendents of Nahar, it was believed, were the Mearas, the 'Horse-princes' of Rohan, for they were magical and wonderful. White and silver-grey, they were fleet as the wind, long-lived and tireless and filled with great wisdom.

The tales of Rohirrim record how the first Mearas came to the Men of Rhovanion. In the twenty-sixth century of the Third Age of the Sun, the lord of the Éothéod, who was named Léod, tried to tame the most beauteous Horse his people had ever seen, but the Horse was wild and proud and threw Léod, who was killed. So the Horse was named Mansbane. However, when Léod's son, Eorl, came to the Horse, it surrendered to the young lord as if in atonement. Eorl renamed him Felaróf, Father of Horses, for from him came forth the Mearas, who allowed none but the kings and princes of Eorl's Line to ride them. Though they could not speak, they understood the speech of Men, and did not need a saddle or bridle as they obeyed the spoken word of their masters, the Rohirrim of the royal house.

The Mearas were loved and honoured by their masters and the banner of the Rohirrim was always the fleet white form of Felaróf galloping upon a green field.

In the War of the Ring, the Mearas did great service. One named Snowmane carried Théoden, the king of the Rohirrim, into the Battles of the Hornburg and Pelennor Fields, where they won great glory for the Rohirrim, though in the end both Horse and rider were slain by the Witch-king of Morgul. Another Meara in the War performed greater deeds still. He was Shadowfax and, breaking the law that none but kings and princes might ride the Mearas, he carried the White Rider, the Istari Mithrandir, who was also named Gandalf. Shadowfax was stout-hearted and strong-limbed, for he stood firm with the White Rider against the terror of the Nazgûl and outran even the loathsome Winged Beasts. He carried Gandalf into the lands of Gondor during the siege of the White Tower. After the Battle of Pelennor Fields, he carried the Wizard with the army of the Captains of the West to the Black Gate of Mordor, and to the final confrontation with the evil armies of Sauron.

Meduseld

Among the strongest allies of the Dúnedain in the Third Age were the Kings of Mark who ruled the land of Rohan from the palace called Meduseld, the Golden Hall. Meduseld was a huge gold-roofed feasthall built by Brego, the second king of the Rohirrim horsemen, in the year 2569. It stood at the highest point in Edoras, the hill-fort and capital city of Rohan. Within was the golden throne of the king, tall pillars gilded in gold, and carved walls hung with rich tapestries. It was to the Golden Hall of Meduseld and King Théoden that four of the Fellowship of the Ring came as emissaries of the Dúnedain to call the Rohirrim to arms in the War of the Ring.

Melian the Maia

Maia queen of Doriath. In Valinor, Melian was a Maia spirit who tended the flowering trees in the Dreamland of Lórien, and served the Valarian queens, Vána the Youthful and Estë the Healer. However, during the Ages of Starlight she went to Beleriand in Middle-earth and fell in love with Elwë Singollo, the High King of the Teleri. Together, Melian and Thingol (as Elwë was then called) founded the realm of Doriath and built Menegroth. This was the realm of the Sindar, or Grey-elves, which was protected by an invisible barrier of a powerful spell, called the Girdle of Melian. Melian and Thingol had one daughter, the incomparable Lúthien. For many Ages of Starlight and most of the First Age of the Sun, Melian's enchantment of Doriath protected the realm from harm. Finally, however, the strife of the War of the Jewels found its way into the Sindar kingdom. When King Thingol was slain by treachery in Menegroth in the year 505 of the First Age, she could no longer bear to live in Middle-earth. Queen Melian fled from Beleriand. Her spell of protection of Doriath melted away, and she returned to the Undying Lands.

Melkor

Vala, Lord of Darkness. Even as an Ainur spirit, Melkor – which means 'he who arises in might' – was filled with pride, and brought discord to the Great Music and the Vision. Upon Arda, Melkor took Darkness and Cold as his domain. During the Shaping of Arda, he thwarted its making so it became marred and imperfect. And while the Valar set about building their kingdom of Almaren, Melkor corrupted many of the Maiar spirits. He took them into the north of Middle-earth and built his rival kingdoms of Utumno and Angband. In Arda, Melkor waged five great wars against the Valar, laid waste to Almaren and destroyed both the Great Lamps and the Trees of the Valar. In the beginning Melkor appeared in forms both fair and foul, but after the destruction of the Trees of Light, he always assumed his evil form, which the Elves called Morgoth, 'the Dark Enemy of the World'.

Tall as a tower, Morgoth wore an iron crown and black armour. He carried the mace called Grond, the Hammer of the Underworld, and a huge black shield. The fire of malice was in his eyes, his face was twisted and scarred, and his hands burned perpetually from the fire of the Silmarils. Yet, in the War of Wrath, all of Melkor's power was destroyed, and he alone of the Valar was driven from the Spheres of the World, and dwells for ever in the Void.

Men

As the Elves had come forth with the Rekindling of the Stars, so Men came with the Rising of the Sun. In the land the Elves called Hildórien, 'land of the followers', which was in the far East of Middle-earth, Men first opened their eyes to the new light. Unlike the Elves, Men were mortal and, even by Dwarf measure, short-lived. In strength of body and nobility of spirit Men compared poorly with Elven-folk. They were a weak race that succumbed readily to pestilence and the rough elements of the World. For these reasons Elves called them the Engwar, the 'sickly'. But Men were stubborn as a race, and they bred more quickly than any other people except the Orcs, and though great numbers perished they multiplied again and finally thrived in the eastern lands, and so by some were called the Usurpers.

Morgoth made his way to those lands and in Men, for the most part, he found a people he could easily bend to his will.

Some fled from this evil and scattered to the West and to the North. Eventually, they reached Beleriand, and the Kingdoms of the Noldorin Elves. The Noldor accepted the allegiance of these Men and called them the Atani, the 'Secondborn', but later, as the greater part of the people of Beleriand spoke the Grey-elven tongue, they were more commonly named the Edain, the 'second ones'.

The Edain were divided into three hosts: the First House of Bëor, the Second House of the Galadin and the Third House of Hador. The deeds of the Three Houses of Elf-friends were renowned. Of the tales of Men in the First Age is the 'Narn i Hîn Húrin', which tells of Húrin the Troll-slayer; of Túrin who slew Glaurung, the Father of Dragons; of Beren, who cut a Silmaril from Morgoth's Iron Crown; and of Eärendil the Mariner who sailed 'Vingilot' and carried the Morning Star into the heavens.

MELKOR, THE LORD OF DARKNESS Among the greatest of the Valar, Melkor revolted against all the others. The Elves named him Morgoth the Dark Enemy, for all evil in Arda found its beginning in him.

In the First Age still more of the race of Men came out of the East. They were a different people whom Elves called Swarthy Men and Easterlings. In times of war, most of these men proved unfaithful and, though feigning friendship with the Elves, they betrayed them to Morgoth, the Dark Enemy.

When the First Age of the Sun was ended and Morgoth was cast into the Void, the land of Beleriand went down beneath the Western Sea. All the enemies who inhabited Beleriand were slain, as well as most of the Elves and the Edain. Even the Edain who survived that Age became divided. Some fled the sinking of Beleriand and went to the East. They lived in the Vales of Anduin with others of their kin who had never entered Beleriand; they were known as the Northmen of Rhovanion. Others of the Edain went to the South with the Elves. These Men were granted a land that lay in the Western Sea. They were named the Dúnedain, the Men of Westernesse, for their island was called Westernesse, which in the elvish tongue was Númenor. In the Second Age the Dúnedain were more often called the Númenóreans and they became a mighty sea power. Then, too, the span of the Númenóreans' lives was increased and their wisdom and strength also grew. Their history in the Second Age was glorious but, corrupted by Sauron, they went to war against the Valar and were destroyed. Númenor was cast into a great abyss, the Western Sea came over it and it was no more.

Most of the Númenóreans perished, yet there were those who were saved from that disaster, including some known as the Black Númenóreans. These people lived in the land of Umbar in the South of Middle-earth.

However, the noblest of the Númenóreans returned to Middle-earth in nine ships; their lord was Elendil the Tall and with him were two sons, Isildur and Anárion. These Elendili, the 'faithful', who were of the true line of the Dúnedain, made two mighty kingdoms in Middle-earth: the North Kingdom was Arnor, and the South Kingdom, Gondor.

However, the power of Sauron grew again, and so they made the Last Alliance of Elves and Men, which combined all the armies of the Dúnedain and the Elves. The Men were led by Elendil and the Elves by Gil-galad, the last High King. Many Men called Haradrim, from the south lands, fought against them, as did others from Rhûn, who were Easterlings, and some who came from the Kingdom of Umbar – the Black Númenóreans.

The Alliance defended Sauron's legions. However, Gil-galad, Elendil and Anárion were killed in that war and among the rulers of the Dúnedain only Isildur remained. It was he who cut the Ring from Sauron's hand and sent his spirit to wander without form in the waste places of Middle-earth. So began the Third Age. After taking the One Ring from Sauron's hand Isildur did not destroy it and in the first years of the Age tragedy befell him. The Orcs cut him down with black arrows at the Gladden Fields and for a long time the Ring was lost.

Of the Dúnedain who survived there were the sons of Isildur, who ruled the North Kingdom of Arnor, and the sons of Anárion, who ruled the South Kingdom of Gondor. There were also other races of Men who had arisen in the East and South, and many now appeared. The Balchoth, Wainriders and other Easterlings came out of Rhûn against the Dúnedain of Gondor, whilst from the South, the Haradrim and the Variags advanced with the Black Númenóreans. However, the Men of Gondor were strong and defeated all enemies.

But in the North another power grew in the land of Angmar. A Witch-king ruled in that land, and he summoned an army of Orcs and evil creatures, as well as Hillmen of the Ettenmoors and Easterlings, to make war on the North Kingdom of Arnor, which they had laid waste. Although Angmar was finally destroyed by the Dúnedain of Gondor, the North Kingdom of Arnor was ended, and only a small number of that people wandered the empty lands and they were named the Rangers of the North.

In the South and from the East there came a constant flow of barbarian Men, corrupted long before by Sauron's evil power. The Dunlendings advanced, prepared for war, as did the Haradrim and Easterlings. Yet in this time Gondor gained an ally, for the horsemen known as the Rohirrim came to their aid. These were the Northmen of Rhovanion and were like the Woodmen and the Beornings of Mirkwood, or the Lake Men of Esgaroth and the Bardings of Dale, for they perpetually fought the evils made by Sauron, the Dark Lord.

At the end of the Third Age, the War of the Ring was waged and all the peoples of Middle-earth allied themselves with either Sauron or the

Dúnedain. Sauron's army was overthrown. The One Ring was found and destroyed, and the One King came to the Dúnedain. This was Ranger Chieftain Aragorn, son of Arathorn, who was named King Elessar, the true heir of Isildur.

Elessar proved a strong and wise ruler. For though he crushed many enemies in war, and feared nobody in battle, he made peace with the Easterlings and Haradrim, and in the Fourth Age of the Sun, which was ordained the Age of the Dominion of Men, there was peace in the Westlands and also for many years after that time, because of the wisdom of Elessar and his sons.

Menegroth

During the Ages of Starlight, the most magnificent mansions on Middle-earth were to be found in Menegroth, the 'Thousand Caves', the city fortress of the Grey-elves of Doriath in Beleriand. Menegroth was cut into the rock cliffs on the south bank of the Esgalduin, a tributary of the Sirion River. It could only be entered by a single stone bridge over the river. It was the secret fortress-palace of the Sindar King Elu Thingol and his Queen Melian the Maia. Built for Thingol by the Dwarves of Belegost, its chambers were a wonder to behold. Because the Sindar loved the forests, the halls and caverns were carved with trees, birds and animals of stone and filled with fountains and lamps of crystal. Through Ages of Starlight, Menegroth prospered, and even through the greater part of the First Age of the Sun when all Beleriand was in conflict, all of Doriath was protected by the magical powers of Melian the Maia. However, the curse of the Silmarils resulted finally in the murder of Thingol within Menegroth itself and the departure of Melian. Thereafter, Menegroth was twice sacked: first by the Dwarves of Nogrod, and secondly by the Noldor Elves. Menegroth was abandoned, and with the rest of Beleriand sank beneath the waves.

Meneltarma

The highest mountain on the island kingdom of Númenor was the holy mountain called Meneltarma, the 'Pillar of Heaven'. It was to be found in the centre of Númenor and from its peak, the Hallow of Eru, it was claimed it was possible to see the Tower of Avallónë, on the Elf island of Tol Eressëa. The Noirinan, the Valley of the Tombs of Kings, was at the foot of Meneltarma, and the royal city of Armenelos was built on a hill nearby. The snows of Meneltarma were the source of the Siril, Númenor's longest river.

Mere of Dead Faces

Between the Falls of Rauros on the River Anduin and the mountains of Mordor was a vast fenland called the Dead Marshes. On this foul, tractless wasteland few ever dared to travel, for not only were the waters stagnant and poisoned but they were also haunted. Through the Third Age, the Dead Marshes had gradually spread out over the Dagorlad, the 'battle plain' that lay north of Mordor and vast graveyard for fallen warriors. By some evil power, the creeping marshlands invasion animated the spirits of these long dead Men, Elves and Orcs whose phantom faces appeared just beneath the surface as if lit by candlelight, although their images had no substance. It was through this Mere of Dead Faces that Hobbit adventurer Frodo Baggins was guided during the Quest of the Ring by that tormented creature Sméagol Gollum.

Meriadoc Brandybuck

Hobbit of the Shire. Meriadoc Brandybuck was born in 2982 of the Third Age, the son of Saradoc Brandybuck, Master of Buckland. In 3018, Merry became one of the four Hobbit members of the Fellowship of the Ring. Merry survived many adventures until the breaking of the Fellowship, when both he and Pippin (Peregrin Took) were captured by Orcs of

Isengard. When the Orcs were attacked by the Rohirrim, the Hobbits escaped into the Fangorn Forest and helped convince the Ents to attack Isengard. Merry later became the squire of King Théoden of Rohan. He became an heroic figure when, with the shield-maiden Éowyn, he slew the Witch-king of Morgul at the Battle of Pelennor Fields. This encounter nearly killed Merry, but he was healed by Aragorn. Upon returning to the Shire later that year, Merry fought in the Battle of Bywater. Merry later married Estella Bolger and succeeded his father as Master of Buckland. Merry and Pippin were the tallest Hobbits in history, measuring a towering four and one-half feet. In the year 64 of the Fourth Age, Merry and Pippin left the Shire to spend their last few years in Rohan and Gondor, where they were buried with high honour in the House of Kings.

Mewlips

According to the lore of Hobbits, an evil race of cannibal spirits called the Mewlips settled in certain marshlands of Middle-earth. Hoarding phantoms very like the dreaded Barrow-wights they seemed, but they made their homes in foul and dank swamps. Travellers in their lands always walked in peril, for many were said to be waylaid and slain by these beings.

Middle-earth

The great continent of Middle-earth was first shaped in the most ancient days of the World of Arda. It lay to the east of that other great continent of Aman, which was most often called the Undying Lands, and which was separated from the Middle-earth by Belegaer, the Great Sea. At the end of the Second Age of the Sun, however, when Númenor was destroyed, the Undying Lands were torn out of the Circles of the World. Middle-earth, the mortal lands, remained, though much changed and continued to change through the ages. It eventually evolved into Europe, Asia and Africa.

Mîm

Petty-dwarf king of Amon Rûdh. Mîm was the last king of the Noegyth Nibin, or Petty-dwarves, who lived in the caverns beneath Amon Rûdh in Beleriand. By the end of the fifth century of the First Age of the Sun, the entire population of this vanishing race consisted of Mîm and his two sons, Ibun and Khîm. In 486 of the First Age, Mîm was captured by the outlaws of Túrin Turambar and he led them to

MERE OF DEAD FACES The stagnant, haunted waters of the Dead Marshes. The Mere covers an ancient battleground and graveyard. Evil spirits animate it, so that the flowing faces of long-dead warriors are visible.

the safety of his secret caverns. The following year, Mîm was captured by Orcs and saved his own life by betraying Túrin and his band, who were ambushed and slaughtered. However, Mîm won his freedom to no great purpose. Both Mîm's sons perished, and Túrin's father Húrin hunted down the betrayer of his son, and slew him with a single blow.

Minas Anor

The fortress-city of Minas Anor, the 'Tower of the Sun', was one of the three great cities of Gondor built in that strategic gap between the eastern end of the White Mountains and the western wall of the Mountains of Mordor. Standing at the foot of the easternmost mountain of the White Mountain range, it was the first city of the fief of Anórien and controlled the plain on the western side of the Anduin River. When it was built in 3320 of the Second Age, Minas Anor was the city of the Dúnedain Prince Anárion. Its twin, Minas Ithil, the 'Tower of the Moon' – built in the same year on the westernmost spur of the Mountains of Mordor and controlling the plain on the eastern side of the Anduin River – was the city of his brother, Prince Isildur. Together they jointly governed Gondor from the royal capital of Osgiliath, the 'citadel of the stars', which bridged the River Anduin at a point mid-way between the two towers. After centuries of war and the devastation of a great plague, both Minas Ithil and Osgiliath were in serious decline by the middle of the Third Age. By 1640 the royal court moved to Minas Anor, which became the new capital of Gondor. In the year 1900, King Calimehtar built its famous White Tower. When at last the Witch-king took Minas Ithil in the year 2002 and renamed it Minas Morgul, it was apparent that the fate of all of Gondor depended on the defence of Minas Anor, and it was renamed Minas Tirith, the 'Tower of the Guard'. It is under that name that the rest of the fortress-city's tale is told.

Minas Ithil

Within the realm of Gondor, the fortress-city of Minas Ithil, the 'Tower of the Moon', was built on a western spur of the Mountains of Mordor and controlled the fief of Ithilien on the eastern bank of the River Anduin. When it was built in 3320 of the Second Age, Minas Ithil was the city of the Dúnedain Prince Isildur. Its twin fortress-city of Minas Anor was built in the same year for his brother, Prince Anárion. While their father Elendil ruled as High King of the Dúnedain from the North Kingdom of Arnor, the brothers jointly governed Gondor. Just a century after it was built, in the year 3429, the forces of Sauron seized Minas Ithil, but at the beginning of the Third Age Isildur restored it. However, as the heirs of Isildur from this time ruled from the North Kingdom of Arnor, its royal status, if not its military significance, diminished thereafter. In the year 2000, Minas Ithil was attacked by the Witch-king of the Nazgûl whose forces poured through the pass of Cirith Ungol out of Mordor. After a siege of two years Minas Ithil fell to the Witch-king and was renamed Minas Morgul. For more than a thousand years thereafter, it was the main base for Sauron's forces within Gondor and was a constant threat to the survival of the Dúnedain realm. The evil powers were not driven from the fortress-city again until the end of the War of the Ring and although it was once again renamed Minas Ithil, it was never again inhabited by the Men of Gondor.

Minas Morgul

In the year 2002 of the Third Age, the fortress-city of Minas Ithil, the 'Tower of the Moon', was captured after a two-year siege by the forces of the Nazgûl Witch-king, and renamed Minas Morgul, the 'Tower of the Wraiths'. It was also called the Tower of Sorcery and the Dead City. Similar in structure to its great rival, Minas Tirith, it became a haunted and evil place that shone in the night with a ghostly light. By some magical power or fiendish

machinery, the upper rooms of its great tower revolved slowly in constant vigilance. For over a thousand years, Minas Morgul was ruled by the terror of the Ringwraiths and this resulted in the almost total ruin and depopulation of the fief of Ithilien. In the year 2050 the Witch-king of Morgul slew Eärnur, the last king of Gondor, and in 2475 Osgiliath was sacked and its stone bridge broken by the Witch-king's army of giant Orcs, called Uruk-hai. During the War of the Ring, Minas Morgul played a key position in Sauron's strategies. The forces out of Morgul were the first to move directly against Gondor and overrun Osgiliath. Then in the siege of Minas Tirith, the Witch-king's leadership during the Battle of Pelennor Fields proved critical. When he was slain it was an indication of the disaster that was to come. After the destruction of Sauron and the fall of Mordor, all evil influences were swept out of Minas Morgul, and once again it came to be called Minas Ithil. However, it was never again repopulated by the people of Gondor.

Minas Tirith

In the histories of Middle-earth there are two fortresses called Minas Tirith. The first was built by the High Elves of Beleriand in the First Age of the Sun. It was built on an island in the Sirion River and its story may be found under that isle's name: Tol Sirion. The second and more famous Minas Tirith stood in the land of Gondor during the Third Age. In the year 2002, when the fortress city of Minas Ithil, the 'Tower of the Moon', fell to the Nazgûl Witch-king and was renamed Minas Morgul, the 'Tower of Wraiths', the Men of Gondor changed the name of their remaining tower from Minas Anor, the 'Tower of the Sun', to Minas Tirith, the 'Tower of the Guard'. This proved to be an appropriate name; for over a thousand years Minas Tirith stood on guard against the evil forces that threatened to entirely destroy Gondor.

Since the decline of Osgiliath in the seventeenth century, this fortress had become the first city of Gondor, and all through the Third Age Sauron had concentrated his mind on destroying this last bastion of power. In 1900, the city was strengthened by the raising of the White Tower, and again in 2698, the Ruling Steward Ecthelion I rebuilt the White Tower and improved the defences of Minas Tirith.

By the time of the War of the Ring, Minas Tirith was a formidable hill-fortress, built on seven levels. Each level was terraced above the next and surrounded by massive ring-walls. Each of these walls had only one gate, but for reasons of defence each gate faced a different direction from the one below it, with the Great Gate on the first wall facing east. This seemingly invulnerable fortress-city rose level by level like a great cliff for over seven hundred feet to the seventh wall, which was called the Citadel, and within that final ring-wall was raised the mighty spire of the White Tower itself. So mighty were the defences of Minas Tirith that it took all the power of the Witch-king of Morgul himself to breach them, and even so, he got no further than breaking the Great Gate on the first wall when the charge of the Rohirrim cavalry drove him back and onto the Pelennor Fields, where his forces were destroyed. The saving of Minas Tirith was essential to the winning of the War of Ring and the revival of the Reunited Kingdom of Arnor and Gondor.

Mirkwood

In the year 1050 of the Third Age of the Sun, an evil power came to that huge forest of Greenwood the Great in Rhovanion, just east of the Misty Mountains and the River Anduin. The power, known as the Necromancer, was

THE WHITE TREE OF MINAS ITHIL Isildur took Nimloth's seedling to Middle-earth where he planted it at Minas Ithil, as a symbol of the rebirth of Númenor and its true, original values in Middle-earth.

in fact Sauron the Ring Lord who built the fortress of Dol Guldur in its southern reaches. So great was Sauron's evil sorcery that he turned the once beautiful forest into such a place of dread and darkness that for over two thousand years it was called the Mirkwood. Great Spiders, Orcs, Wolves and evil spirits haunted Mirkwood and, though the Silvan Elf Woodland Realm of Thranduil survived in the north of the forest, the power of those Elves was not enough to halt the spreading darkness. By the middle of the Third Age there were few who dared to travel along its dark paths, although the Silvan Elves and the Northmen, called the Woodmen and the Beornings, did what they could to keep its passes and roads open. It was Gandalf the Wizard who in 2850 entered south Mirkwood and discovered at last that it was Sauron and the Ringwraiths who ruled Dol Guldur.

The Mirkwood was among the major obstacles that were standing before the Dwarf company of Thorin Oakenshield on the long road to the Lonely Mountain. Yet, with stealth and valour, the Hobbit Bilbo Baggins guided the company through its many perils. During the War of the Ring, Sauron's forces from Dol Guldur came forth in great numbers against the Elven kingdoms of the Woodland Realm in the north and the Golden Wood of Lothlórien in the south. However, both these campaigns failed and the retaliating Elves destroyed the evil armies of Mirkwood, knocking down the walls of Dol Guldur and ripping up its pits and dungeons. By the beginning of the Fourth Age, the great forest was no longer called Mirkwood, but Eryn Lasgalen, the 'Wood of Greenleaves'. The north was the undisputed territory of Thranduil's Woodland Realm, the southern part was settled by the Elves of Lothlórien who called it East Lórien, while the forest lands between these two kingdoms were given to the Woodmen and Beornings.

Misty Mountains

Nearly one thousand miles long, the mountain range called the Misty Mountains ran from the far north of Middle-earth south to the Gap of Rohan and separated the lands of Eriador from Rhovanion. The Misty Mountains were the home of Orcs, Great Eagles and the Dwarves of Khazad-dûm. For a time its northernmost part made up the defences of the Witch-kingdom of Angmar and the Orc-hold of Gundabad, while in its southernmost part, the evil Wizard Saruman defended his stronghold of Isengard. Called the Hithaeglir, the 'misty peaks', by the Elves, the major peaks of the Misty Mountains were Methedras, Bundushathûr, Zirak-zigal, Barazinbar and Gundabad; while the High Pass, the Redhorn and the tunnels of Khazad-dûm were the three main passages through them.

Mordor

At the end of the first millennium of the Second Age, Sauron founded an evil kingdom on Middle-earth, just to the east of the River Anduin. This was called Mordor, the 'black land', and for two ages was Sauron's base of power in his quest for dominion over all of Middle-earth. Mordor was defended on three sides by two unassailable mountain ranges: the Ash Mountains in the north, and the Shadowy Mountains in the west and south. Through these mountains, there appear to have been only two passes: Cirith Ungol in the west and Cirith Gorgor in the northwest. Besides the small circular plain called Udûn inside Cirith Gorgor, Mordor's two major regions were the Plateau of Gorgoroth and the wide plain and slave fields of Nurn.

Gorgoroth was a vast dreary plateau of slag heaps and Orc pits always under the pall of smoke from the volcanic mountain of Orodruin (or Mount Doom) near its centre. Here too, on the northeast side of the plateau on a spur of the Ash Mountains, was Sauron's stronghold, the Dark Tower of Barad-dûr. Nurn, however, was a vast farmland populated

MORDOR Mordor was, for two ages, Sauron's base of power in his quest for dominion over all of Middle-earth.

by slaves and slave-drivers who supplied the massive foods and basic materials for Sauron's armies. Nurn was drained by four rivers, and each flowed into the inland sea of Nûrnen.

After forging the One Ring in the fires of Mount Doom in 1600, Sauron completed Barad-dûr and began the War of Sauron and the Elves. Although surrendering to the astonishing power of the Númenóreans in 3262, Sauron managed to destroy them by guile and return to Mordor after Númenor's destruction. In 3429, Sauron's forces made war on Gondor, but retribution came in 3434 when the Last Alliance of Elves and Men destroyed his army on Dagorlad and broke down the Black Gate in order to enter Mordor. After a seven-year siege Barad-dûr was taken, the One Ring was cut from Sauron's hand, and all of his evil servants driven out of Mordor. During the early part of the Third Age, Mordor was empty and Gondor built the Tower of the Teeth and the fortress of Durthang in the north pass, and the Tower of Cirith Ungol in the west pass, to watch over Mordor and prevent any of Sauron's scattered allies from entering the kingdom. Unfortunately, after the devastation of the Great Plague of 1636, Gondor abandoned these fortresses and they were taken over by Orcs and prepared for the entry of the Nazgûl and Sauron himself. In 2942 Sauron returned and in 2951 began rebuilding Barad-dûr. However, the unmaking of the One Ring proved a final blow. Sauron was destroyed for the last time and Mordor was never again a threat to the peace of Middle-earth.

Morgoth

Vala Lord of Darkness. Morgoth, meaning 'the Dark Enemy', was the name the Noldor Elves gave the evil Valarian Lord who destroyed the Trees of Light, stole the Silmarils and slew their king. However, his history is accounted here under his original name, Melkor.

Moria

In the year 1697 of the Second Age of the Sun, in the midst of the War of Sauron and the Elves when all of Eregion was being laid waste by dark forces, the Dwarves of the mighty mansions of Khazad-dûm in the Misty Mountains sealed their great doors and went out no more into the world beyond. Thereafter, it was considered a secret and dark place, its histories and people were unknown to those of the outside world, and so it was called Moria, the 'dark chasm'. In this way, the Dwarves of the Misty Mountains survived the devastation of the Second Age, and happily delved beneath the mountains until the year 1980 of the Third Age. That year, while pursuing a rich vein of mithril in one of their mines, they accidently released an evil Balrog spirit that had hidden and slept beneath the roots of Barazinbar since the end of the First Age. Though they battled for a year against the demon, after the deaths of two of their kings, the Dwarves deserted Moria. Thereafter, Moria became the domain of the Balrog, the Orcs and other servants of Sauron. The once dazzling beauty of its halls and grottoes was ruined and mutilated and it became an evil, dank and haunted place. For five years, from 2989 to 2994, a group of Dwarves attempted to re-establish a kingdom in Moria, only to be trapped and slaughtered when they were caught between an army of Orcs at the East Gate and a new threat, the terrible Kraken, called the Watcher in the Water, at the West Gate. It was not until 3019 of the Third Age that the Balrog was at last slain by Gandalf the Wizard. Yet, although the evil tyrant of Moria was slain, it appears that its vast halls remained abandoned and empty forever after.

Moriquendi

In the High Elven tongue of Quenya, all Elves who did not come to the Undying Lands in the time of the Trees of the Valar were named Moriquendi, the Dark Elves. They were Elves of lesser power than those who witnessed the Undying Lands in the time of their greatest glory. Among the Moriquendi were: the Avari, the Silvan Elves of Lothlórien and Mirkwood, the Nandor, the Laiquendi, the Falathrim and the Sindar.

Mount Doom

The massive volcanic mountain that stood in the centre of the blackened plateau of Gorgoroth, within Mordor, was the mighty, natural forge upon which Sauron made the One Ring in the year 1600 of the Second Age of the Sun. Called Mount Doom in the language

MÛMAKIL: Massive, bad-tempered beasts, half-way between a pre-historic Mammoth and an Elephant. The Mûmakil were often used with devastating effect by the Men of Harad as machines of War.

of Men, its elvish name was Orodruin, the 'mountain of red flame', and under that name its history may be found.

Mûmakil

In the Third Age of the Sun in the south lands of Harad, there lived beasts of vast bulk that are thought to be ancestors of the creatures Men now name Elephants. Yet it is said the Elephants that now inhabit the World are much smaller in size and might than their ancestors.

In the years of the War of the Ring the fierce warriors of Harad came north to the lands of Gondor at the call of Sauron, and with their armies they brought the great Mûmakil, which were used as beasts of war. The Mûmakil were harnessed with the gear of war: red banners, bands and trappings of gold and brass; on their backs they had great towers from which archers and spearmen fought. They had a natural thirst for battle, and many foes were crushed beneath their feet. With their trunks they struck down many enemies and in battle their tusks were crimsoned with the blood of their foes. They could not be fought by mounted Men, for Horses would not come near the Mûmakil; nor by foot soldiers, who would be crushed. In war they would frequently stand as towers that could not be captured: shield-walls broke before them and armies were routed.

These thick-skinned beasts were almost invulnerable to arrow-shot. In only one place, their eyes, could the Mûmakil be blinded or even killed by arrows released with great force. When blinded they became enraged with pain, and often destroyed masters and foes alike.

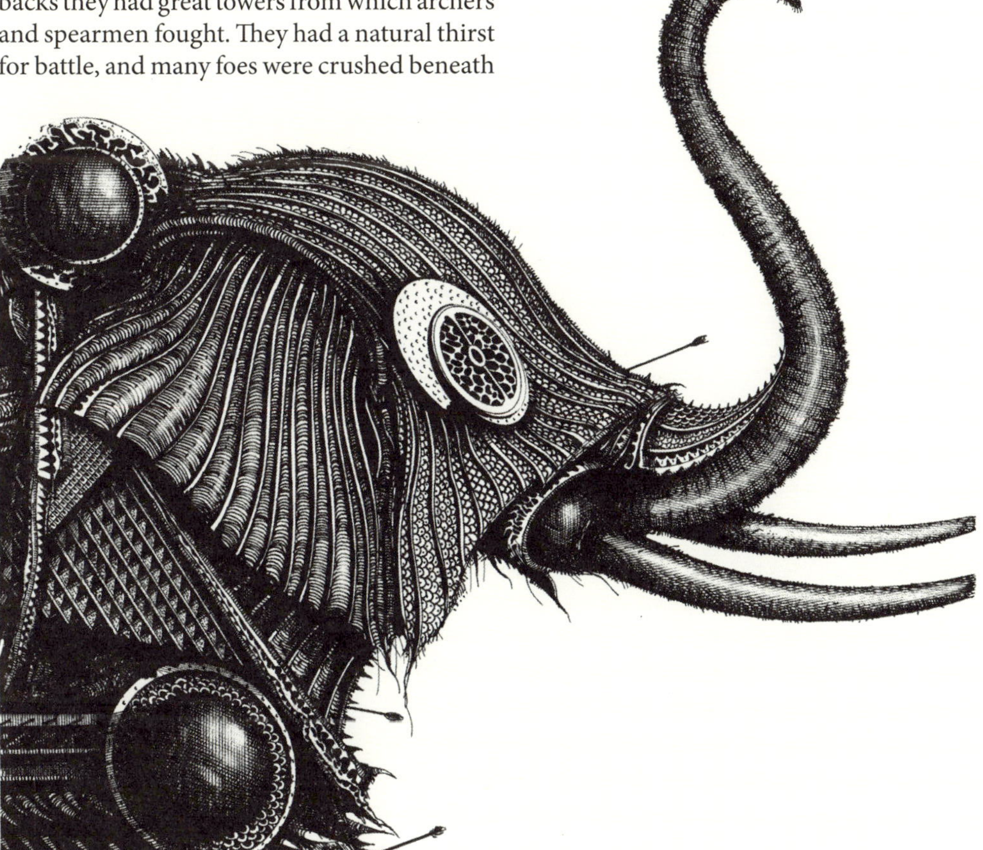

N

Nahar

Horse of Valar. The gigantic white Horse of Oromë, the Huntsman of the Valar. Nahar is the first Horse in creation and the progenitor of all horses. Oromë rode Nahar often into the forest lands of Middle-earth through the Ages of Darkness and Starlight. On one such journey, Oromë and Nahar discovered the Elves by the Waters of Awakening.

Nandor

Among the Elves to undertake the Great Journey in search of the Undying Lands there were Three Kindred. The third and largest kindred were the Teleri, and because these people were so numerous their passage was slowest, and those unable or unwilling to complete the Journey were in greater numbers than the other two kindred. The first division recorded in that Journey came when the Teleri halted before the Great River Anduin and, looking beyond, saw the Misty Mountains. This mighty barrier terrified the Elves and so, rather than risk crossing the mountains, Lenwë, a lord of the Teleri, led his people away. They went southwards down the Great River Anduin and lived in places unknown to others of their kin; they were named the Nandor, 'those who turn back'. They were a wandering woodland folk and they had no equal in ways of woodlore and woodcraft, or in knowledge of the Kevlar and Olvar of Middle-earth. They hunted with bows and had weapons made from certain base metals, but they did not know how to forge arms of steel with which to fight the evil creatures that, in later Ages, came out of the North.

For more than two Ages of Starlight the Nandor lived in harmony in the lands of their wanderings, in the Vales of Anduin. Some crossed over the White Mountains and came into Eriador. They grew wiser in the ways of the forests and waters, but when

evil beings attacked them in the forests they were unprepared and their numbers began to dwindle. Many were slaughtered by legions of steel-shod Orcs, gangs of Stone-trolls and packs of ravening Wolves.

Many Nandor, practising their woodcraft, hid as best they could from the lurking terror. However, Denethor, son of King Lenwë, gathered many of the Nandor to him and set off once again on the long-abandoned westward march. He sought what kindred he could to aid him, for tales had reached the Nandor of the might of the Sindar, led by one who had once been king of all the Teleri, Elwë Singollo, now named Thingol. Denethor crossed the Blue Mountains and entered Beleriand, bringing a great number of Nandor under the sovereignty of their rightful king once again.

There, they were welcomed by the Sindar, who protected them, and taught them some of the arts of war and granted them Ossiriand, the 'land of seven rivers', as their realm. They were called Nandor no more but Laiquendi and Green-elves because of their love of green woodlands and their habit of dressing in green cloth so they might be one with the forest in the sight of an enemy. So in that Age before the coming of the Sun, they lived happily by rivers and in the forests of Ossiriand, and the sweet singing of the Laiquendi rivalled the melodies of the nightingale.

Nargothrond

The largest kingdom of Noldor Elves in Beleriand during the First Age was that controlled by Finrod from his fortress city of Nargothrond. This was a powerful underground fortress carved in the caverns of the Narog River and from it Finrod ruled most of West Beleriand. Modelled on the Thousand Caves of Menegroth, the vast complexes of this fortress-palace were expanded by the Noldor and the Dwarves of the Blue Mountains from the original delvings of the Petty-Dwarves who had once lived there. Although its people were involved in many skirmishes and battles with Morgoth's forces, Nargothrond remained undiscovered and secure until late in the fifth century when they went often and openly to war. This proved their undoing, for in 496 they fought the Battle of Tumhalad against Glaurung the Dragon and a massive army and were destroyed. Glaurung then entered Nargothrond before its stone bridge could be destroyed. All within were slaughtered or enslaved and for five years Glaurung ruled its caverns before he himself was slain. Briefly thereafter, Mîm, the last of the Petty-dwarves, returned to the caverns that were once the home of his ancestors, but when he too was slain the ancient halls were empty forever after.

Naugrim

During the Ages of Starlight before the kingdom of the Grey-elves had grown to its full power, a race of Dwarves who were long-bearded and armed with steel weapons came over the Blue Mountains into Beleriand. The Grey-elves thought these people deformed and unlovely, and named them the Naugrim, the 'stunted people'. But the Naugrim came not to fight but to trade and barter, and by this traffic both races thrived. And though the Naugrim lived in prosperous peace with the Elves, there was only an uneasy alliance and no great friendship between them.

NANDOR Woodland Elves of the Vales of the Anduin. The Nandor ('those who turn back') were a nomadic people and masters of woodcraft and woodlore who finally settled in Ossiriand as the Laiquendi.

Nazgûl

In the twenty-third century of the Second Age of the Sun, in Middle-earth there arose nine mighty wraiths who in the Black Speech of Orcs were named the Nazgûl, which is 'Ringwraiths'. And of all the evil servants and generals of Sauron the Ring Lord, these Nazgûl proved to be the greatest.

It is said that the Nazgûl were once powerful kings and sorcerers among Men and they were each given a Ring of Power by Sauron. These Rings were nine of the magical nineteen Rings that Celebrimbor and the Elven-smiths of Eregion forged for Sauron. For many centuries these Men used their Rings to fulfil their own desires, yet all were ruled by the One Ring that Sauron made. Though these chosen Men lived by the power of the Rings far beyond the span of ordinary mortals, their forms faded. By the twenty-third century they were wraiths entirely, and thralls that thought only of how they might serve Sauron the Ring Lord. So they roamed the World committing terrible deeds. They wore great cloaks, black and hooded, and hauberks of mail and silver helms, yet beneath were the grey robes of the dead and their bodies were invisible. Any who looked into their faces fell back in horror, for nothing seemed to support helm and hood. Yet sometimes there appeared, where faces should be, the glow of two luminous and hypnotic eyes or, in rage and power, a red and hellish flame.

The weapons of the Nazgûl were numerous: they carried swords of steel and of flame, black maces and daggers with magical poisoned blades. They used spells of beckoning and spells of blasting sorcerous fire, and the curse of their Black Breath was like a plague of despair and the curse of its terror froze the hearts of their foes. The Nazgûl were untouchable to mortal Men, for arms could not harm them unless blessed by Elvish spell, and any blade that struck them withered and perished.

So for a thousand years of the Second Age of the Sun the Nazgûl, on nine black Horses, swept over the lands of Middle-earth like a nightmare of terror. And in all that time, they fared in the wars as did Sauron the Ring Lord himself. They did not perish until the realm of Sauron's Mordor fell and the seven-year Siege of Barad-dûr was broken by the Last Alliance of Elves and Men at the end of that Age. Isildur, the Dúnedain lord of Gondor, cut the One Ring from Sauron's hand, and the Nazgûl, with the Ring Lord, were swept away to the shadows and the waste places in the eastern lands of the World where they had no form or power.

The Nazgûl were both formless and powerless for thirteen centuries in the Third Age of the Sun. Yet the One Ring had not been destroyed and Sauron was able to make himself a shape again. So in the fourteenth century he summoned again his great servants, the Nazgûl, out of the shadows. The nine Black Riders arose in the East and the greatest of these came to the north of Eriador, where he made the kingdom of Angmar and built a great citadel in Carn Dûm. He called forth Orc legions and the evil Hillmen of the Ettenmoors. For more than six centuries there was continuous war in Eriador. This Nazgûl lord, who was at that time called the Witch-king of Angmar, made constant war against the Dúnedain of Arnor and out of Carn Dûm came much evil. One by one the great provinces and cities went down until 1974, when the last – the province of Arthedain and the city of Fornost – fell to the barbarous hordes. Yet the Witch-king's possession of the Dúnedain Kingdom of the North was short-lived, for in 1975 his army was routed and destroyed by the Elf-lords Círdan and Glorfindel and by Eärnur, the king of Gondor, at the Battle of Fornost. But still the Witch-king and his master Sauron counted this as a great deed, for they were

NAZGÛL: Six of the Nazgûl, the Black Riders who were the evil servants and generals of Sauron. They were also called 'Ringwraiths', for these damned spirits were once humans who were given a cursed Ring of Power by the Dark Lord.

little concerned with the slaughter of Orcs and Hillmen, and the destruction of the power and the kingdom of the Dúnedain of the North in Arnor was indeed a great victory by the Dark Powers.

The Witch-king of Angmar, called the High Nazgûl, deserted the ruined lands of Eriador and returned to Mordor. And though Sauron was not yet come, but hid still in Dol Guldur in the darkness of Mirkwood (where the Nazgûl called Khamûl, the Black Easterling, was his chief lieutenant) there were in Mordor other Nazgûl who had come secretly three centuries before. In that time they had laboured to rebuild the evil power of that land and had gathered Orkish hordes about them.

In the year 2000 the Nazgûl came out of Mordor to fight the Dúnedain of the South in Gondor, and two years later the eastern citadel, Minas Ithil, the 'tower of the Moon', fell. The Nazgûl made this place their own and renamed it Minas Morgul, the 'tower of black wraiths', and sometimes the Tower of Sorcery and the Dead City. The High Nazgûl, the Witch-king of Angmar, was now called the Morgul Lord and wore a crown of steel. It was he who slew Eärnur, the last king of Gondor, and for a thousand years he made war on the Men of Gondor with both sorcery and the might of his army, and he eroded their power, laid waste their cities and ruined their lands.

It was not, however, until the year 2951 that Sauron the Dark Lord declared himself and came to Mordor. It is said that Sauron feared to declare himself openly before that time lest someone possessed the One Ring, which could destroy him. And it was not until later still that even the wisest among Men knew that he commanded the wraiths of Morgul, and that these wraiths were the Nazgûl of the Second Age.

In the year 3018 of the Third Age the War of the Ring had its beginning. For in that year Sauron learned where the One Ring was hidden and such was his desire that he sent all nine Nazgûl to take it. Yet they were thwarted in their errand. When they came to the borders of Rivendell the nine Black Riders were unhorsed at the Ford of Bruinen and were driven away by the Elvish powers that commanded the river.

The search for the One Ring brought the Nazgûl to the Shire, where their suspicion fell on the Hobbit Frodo Baggins. Rightly, they suspected Frodo of being the Ring-bearer and pursued him and his companions. On several occasions they nearly succeeded in capturing the Ring-bearer. Indeed, on Weathertop, the Witch-king wounded Frodo Baggins with a poisoned dagger. Still, the Ring-bearer and his companions managed to take refuge by entering the kingdom of Elrond Half-Elven.

Yet they reappeared in still mightier forms, on steeds as dreadful as themselves. These steeds were the Winged Beasts for which Elves and Men had no name. They were ancient beings that had come into the World before the Count of Time began. Though they had beak and claw and wing, they were not birds, nor even Bats: they were serpentine beings like Dragons, yet older. They were made by Melkor, Sauron's master, in Utumno's foul pits, where serpent, Kraken and other vile creatures of hidden places had arisen. Fed on the cannibal meats of the Orcs and grown larger than all creatures of the air, the Winged Beasts carried the Nazgûl high over the lands with the speed of the winds. Despite their might and fierceness, in the War of the Ring the Nazgûl were in deadly peril, because the One Ring was in the hands of their foes. In the Battle of Pelennor Fields, the Morgul Lord, who could not be slain by the hand of Man, was brought to an end by the shield-maiden Éowyn of Rohan and the Hobbit warrior Meriadoc Brandybuck. Though eight of the Nazgûl remained they, too, were soon destroyed. As they rose to fight the enemy at the Black Gate of Mordor, there was a great alarm within Mordor itself. Sauron commanded the Nazgûl to hasten to Orodruin, the Mountain of Fire, that is called Mount Doom, for there stood the Hobbit Frodo Baggins. On their Winged Beasts the

Nazgûl flew like the wind to Sauron's aid, but to no avail, for Frodo Baggins dropped the One Ring into the Fire of Mount Doom. In that moment Sauron and all his dreadful world were destroyed. As the Black Gate collapsed, the Dark Tower toppled, and in the midst of their flight the mighty Nazgûl fell shrieking in flames that ended them for ever.

Neekerbreekers

In the foul Midgewater Marshes in northern Eriador there lived vast numbers of blood-sucking insects. Among them were some noisy creatures akin to crickets that were named Neekerbreekers by Hobbits. Travellers in the Midgewater Marshes were driven all but mad by the awful repetitious din of the creatures' 'neek-breek, neek-breek'.

Neldoreth

Among the most loved of the trees growing in the Middle-earth were those that Elves called Neldoreth but Men knew as Beech. According to the tales of lost Beleriand, the great halls of Menegroth, the Thousand Caves, had carved pillars like the Beech trees that grew within the vast Taur-na-Neldor, the Forest of Neldoreth, which was thought to be the fairest forest in Beleriand. And in the minds of Elves the Neldoreth was loved the more because in part it was like the Golden Tree of the Valar, called Laurelin, which once lit the Blessed Realm with Golden Light.

The triple-trunked Beech of Doriath that was named Hírilorn was mightiest of the Neldoreth that ever grew in Middle-earth, and in it was built the guarded house of Lúthien – as the tale of the Quest of the Silmaril relates.

Nessa

Vala called 'the Dancer'. Nessa is the sister of Oromë the Huntsman, and the spouse of Tulkas the Wrestler. A spirit of the woodlands, the deer are sacred to the beautiful Nessa, who is light-footed, agile and a wonderful dancer.

Nessamelda

One of the many fragrant evergreen trees that was brought from Tol Eressëa to the land of Númenor by the Sea Elves in the Second Age of the Sun was the Nessamelda. This was the 'three of Nessa', the dancing Vala goddess of the woodlands, the sister of Oromë the Huntsman and was most numerous in that part of Númenor called Nísimaldar, land of 'Fragrant Trees'.

Nienna

Vala called 'the Weeper'. Nienna's chief concern is mourning, which is the meaning of her name. She is the sister of Lórien and Mandos. She lives alone in the west of Valinor where her mansions look out on the sea and the Walls of Night. Her tears have the power to heal and fill others with hope and the spirit to endure.

Nimbrethil

In lost Beleriand there grew many fair white birch trees, which were called Nimbrethil in the tongue of the Grey-elves. 'Vingilot', the mighty ship that Eärendil the Mariner sailed over Belegaer, the Western Sea, to the Undying Lands, was built with timber from these huge trees.

Nimrodel

Elven maid of Lothlórien. During the second millennium of the Third Age of the Sun, Nimrodel and her lover Amroth became betrothed in Lothlórien. However, the pair were separated at the time of the rising of the monstrous demon, the fiery Balrog of Moria in 1980. Nimrodel, meaning 'white lady', lost her way through the White Mountains and was never seen again.

NOLDOR The High Elves of Eldamar who created the Silmarils and ruled in Beleriand. Illustrated here is their High King Fëanor who led them into the disastrous War of the Jewels against Morgoth the Enemy.

Niphredil

At the end of the Second Age of Starlight, the fairest child that ever entered the World was born to Melian the Maia and Thingol, king of the Sindar. She was born in the woodlands of Neldoreth in Beleriand and was named Lúthien. To the woodland at that time came the white flower Niphredil to greet fair Lúthien. This flower was said to be a Star of the Earth, as was this only daughter born of Eldar and Maia union. Though many Ages of Stars and Sun passed, and Lúthien with her lover Beren had long ago gone from the Spheres of the World, the Star flower Niphredil remained as a memory to the fairest daughter of the Earth. In the Third Age of the Sun, the white flower grew still in the Golden Wood of Lothlórien, where, mixed with the gold flower Elanor, it thrived. In the Fourth Age of the Sun the fairest Elf-maid of that age came to the forest. This was Arwen Undómiel, and she, like Lúthien, shared the same fate of tragic love for a mortal, and in that forest Arwen plighted her troth to Aragorn, the Dúnedain. Years later in that same forest she chose to die on a bed of these white and gold flowers.

Noegyth Nibin

The ancient tales of the lost realm of Beleriand tell of a race whom the Grey-elves called Noegyth Nibin. They were small people – smaller even than Dwarves, from whom they descended. Men called them Petty-Dwarves and in the First Age of the Sun Mîm, the last of this dwindled race, was bloodily slain by Húrin.

Nogrod

One of the two great kingdoms of Dwarves in the Blue Mountains was Nogrod, the 'Dwarf-dwelling'. The Dwarves of Nogrod, just like those of nearby Belegost, were skilled smiths and craftsmen who prospered in their trade with the Elves of Beleriand, and fought valiantly against Orcs and Dragons during the First Age. Most famous of the smiths of Nogrod in the making of weapons was Telchar, who forged Narsil, the sword of Elendil which cut the One Ring from Sauron's hand, and Angrist, the knife of Beren which was used to cut a Silmaril from Morgoth's crown.

The downfall of Nogrod came about when some of its Dwarf craftsmen, staying in Menegroth, were asked by King Thingol of the Grey-elves to set the priceless Silmaril gem in the golden necklace called the Nauglamír. The craftsmen were overcome by greed, slew Thingol and stole the necklace. Before they could escape, they were slain in retaliation and the necklace was returned to Menegroth.

Enraged, the Dwarves of Nogrod sent out a large army, sacked Menegroth and once again took the necklace. However, before they could safely return to Nogrod, the Dwarf army was ambushed by Beren and Dior and, with the aid of the Laiquendi, and the Ents, the entire army was slaughtered. At the end of the First Age, the Dwarf Kingdom of Nogrod, along with Belegost, and most of Beleriand, sank into the sea.

Noldor

Mightiest of the Elves who inhabited Middle-earth were the Noldor, and most far-famed in the songs and tales that have come to the ears of Men. For these were the Elves who wrought the Great Jewels called the Silmarils, as well as the Rings of Power. The mightiest wars that were ever known to Elves and Men were fought over these great works.

Of the Eldar who came to the Undying Lands, the Noldor were the Second Kindred. The name Noldor means 'knowledge', which, above all the Elves, they strove hardest to possess. In the years of the Trees of the Valar their king was Finwë, and at that time great was their joy in learning from their tutors, the Valar and the Maiar. In that golden and silver light everlasting the Noldor grew strong and noble. Their city of Tirion on the green hill of Túna, which looked over the starlit sea, was mighty and beautiful. For the city was built in the Pass of Light named Calacirya, the only passage through the vast Pelorí Mountains, which enclosed the lands of Eldamar and Valinor. Through this gap flowed the Light of the Trees and it fell on the west of the city. To the east, in the shadow of Túna, the Elves looked on the Stars that shone over the Shadowy Seas.

So it was that the Noldor became wise people, but they especially excelled in the crafts of Aulë, Maker of Mountains. They cut the great towers of Eldamar from rock and carved many things of beauty out of radiant white stone. They were the first to bring forth the gems that lay in the mountain heart. They gave the stone freely, and the mansions of the Elves and the Valar glinted with the gems of the Noldor, and the very beaches and pools of Eldamar, it is said, shone with the scattered light of gems.

To the king of the Noldor and his queen, Míriel, was born a son named Curufinwë, who was called Fëanor, which is 'spirit of fire'. Of all craftsmen who learned the skills of Aulë, Fëanor was mightiest. Even among the Maiar there were none to surpass him. For he was first to make those magical Elven-gems that were brighter and more magical than the Earth stone. They were pale in the making, but when set under Stars they were compared to the eyes of the Elves, for they took on the light of the Stars and shone blue and bright. Fëanor also made other crystals called Palantíri, the 'seeing stones', which were the magical stones that, many Ages later, the Elves of Avallónë gave to the Dúnedain. But greatest of the deeds of Fëanor was the making of those three fabulous gems that captured the mingled Light of the Trees of the Valar within their crystals. These were the Silmarils, the most beautiful jewels that the World has ever seen, for they shone with a living light. Yet, as is told in the 'Quenta Silmarillion' and the 'Noldolante', the high ambitions of Fëanor, coupled with the evil deeds of Melkor, led to the greatest bane that was ever known to the Elven peoples. However, tragedy befell the Noldor when Melkor came forth and with the Spider, Ungoliant, destroyed the Trees of the Valar, slew Finwë and stole the Silmarils. Fëanor swore an oath of vengeance that was a curse on his people for ever more. In anger he followed Melkor, whom he named Morgoth, the 'dark enemy of the World', to Middle-earth. So began the War of the Jewels and the Wars of Beleriand, which were fought through all the days of the First Age of the Sun.

During this age of war the Noldor also brought great gifts to Middle-earth. And for a time there arose the Noldor Elven kingdoms in Hithlum, Dor-lomin, Nevrast, Mithrim, Dorthonion, Himlad, Thargelion and East

Beleriand. Fairest of the Noldor realms were the two hidden kingdoms: Gondolin, which was ruled by Turgon; and Nargothrond, which was held by Finrod Felagund.

In the War of the Jewels Fëanor was slain, as were all his seven sons: Amras, Amrod, Caranthir, Celegorm, Curufin, Maedhros and Maglor. His brother Fingolfin and Fingolfin's children, Fingon, Turgon and Aredhel, were also killed by Morgoth. And though Finarfin, the other brother (and third son of Finwë), had remained in the Undying Lands where he ruled the remnant of the Noldor in Tirion, all his children went to Middle-earth and his four sons, Aegnor, Angrod, Finrod Felagund and Orodreth, were killed. So of all the Noldor lords and their children only Finarfin's daughter, Galadriel, the eventual Queen of Lothlórien, survived on Middle-earth.

Through the years of the First Age Morgoth and his servants destroyed all the Noldorin kingdoms. At that time there were in Beleriand many other people whose doom in part was tied to that of the Noldor. Because of these wars, the realms of the Grey-elves, who were also called the Sindar, were destroyed, as were the Dwarf-realms of Nogrod and Belegost and most of the kingdoms of the Three Houses of the Edain.

But finally the Valar and the Maiar came forth out of the Undying Lands against Morgoth. Thus occurred the Great Battle and the War of Wrath. Before this mighty force Angband fell and Morgoth was cast into the Eternal Void for ever. Yet the struggle was so great that Beleriand was broken and most of the land was swallowed up beneath the sea.

Of all the royal lines of the Noldor few who survived the War of the Jewels could claim direct descent. So it was that Gil-galad, son of Fingon, son of Fingolfin, set up the last Noldor high kingdom in Mortal Lands. This was in Lindon, the last part of Beleriand to remain after the Great Battle. With Gil-galad lived Celebrimbor, son of Curufin, only prince of the House of Fëanor to live into the Second Age. Galadriel (daughter of Finarfin), Elrond and Elros the Half-elven and many Sindar lords also came, as well as Círdan of the Falathrim, the Laiquendi and the Edain – the Men who were loyal to the Elves during the War of the Jewels.

At that time many of the Elves took ships from the Grey Havens and sailed to Tol Eressëa in the Bay of Eldamar in the Undying Lands and built there the city of Avallónë. The Edain were also given a fair island in the Western Sea, called Númenorë, and they too left the lands of Middle-earth.

Yet all those of royal Noldorin line remained. Gil-galad ruled Lindon, and Círdan held the Grey Havens. But in the year 750 of the Second Age, it is said Celebrimbor came out of Lindon and made a kingdom at the foot of the Misty Mountains in the land of Eregion, near the Dwarf-realm of Khazad-dûm. These Elves were named the Gwaith-i-Mírdain, the 'people of the jewel-smiths', and the Elven-smiths, in the legends of later times. It was here, through the subtle persuasions of Sauron, that the Rings of Power were forged by Celebrimbor, grandson of Fëanor, who created the Silmarils, and so was wrought the second great work of the Noldor, over which another cycle of bitter wars was fought. For Sauron at that time made the One Ring that would rule all the other works of the Noldor. In anger and fear the Elves arose, and the War of Sauron and the Elves was fought. Celebrimbor and most of the Gwaith-i-Mírdain were slain, Eregion was laid waste and, though Elrond Half-elven came with an army, all he could do was rescue those few who remained and take refuge in Imladris, which Men called Rivendell. There the only Noldor stronghold between the Blue and the Misty Mountains was made.

In this time, Lindon itself was in peril, but descendants of the Edain, the Númenóreans, brought their immense fleets and drove Sauron into the East. Later still they returned and captured the Dark Lord, but did not destroy him. They held him prisoner, and in this way came their Downfall, for he turned them against the Valar and they were swallowed by the sea for their folly.

So Sauron returned to Middle-earth, where only the Noldorin realms of Lindon and Rivendell stood, though the kingdoms of Greenwood the Great and Lothlórien had been built with Noldorin and Sindarin nobles and Silvan subjects. But with Sauron's return there was war again. The Last Alliance of Elves and Men was made and in that war, which ended the Second Age, Gil-galad and the king of the Dúnedain were slain by Sauron, but Sauron himself was destroyed with all the realm of Mordor.

Thereafter, there was no High King of the Noldorin Elves in Middle-earth, yet the kingdoms remained. The lordship of Lindon and the Grey Havens fell to Círdan, while Elrond still ruled in Rivendell. During the Third Age the most beautiful kingdom was Lothlórien, where Queen Galadriel reigned, the noblest Noldor still to live in Middle-earth. Though few Noldor lived among those named the Galadhrim in the Golden Wood, it was the brightest and most like the Noldorin realms of old.

As is told in the 'Red Book of Westmarch', when at the end of the Third Age the One Ring was unmade and Sauron was destroyed, Elrond was summoned out of Rivendell and Galadriel came out of Lothlórien to the white ships that would take them into the Undying Lands. With the queen gone, Lothlórien faded, and the Noldorin kingdoms of Middle-earth dwindled in the years of the Fourth Age. It is said that Círdan the Shipwright took the last of the Noldor to the Undying Lands. There dwell now the remnant of the Noldorin people who suffered most grievously, inflicted the greatest sorrow, did the greatest deeds, and won the most fame of all the Elves in the tales that have come down through the Ages. What their deeds have been since the sailing of the last ship, only the Great Music at the End shall make known to those who live in Mortal Lands.

Nómin

When Men entered the lands of Beleriand in the First Age of the Sun, they saw for the first time the Elves of Finrod Felagund, lord of the Noldor. These Men were amazed at the beauty and knowledge of these Elves, whom they named the Nómin, which means the 'wise'.

Nori

Dwarf of Thorin and Company. Nori embarked on the Quest of Erebor in the year 2941 of the Third Age, which resulted in the death of Smaug the Dragon and the re-establishment of the Dwarf-kingdom under the Mountain. Nori settled in Erebor for the rest of his life.

Northmen

In the Third Age of the Sun many Men who were descended from the Edain of the First Age inhabited the northern Vales of Anduin. These Men were of many tribes and kingdoms and they were called the Northmen of Rhovanion. Though no single lord governed these Northmen, they were constant enemies of Sauron and all his servants. For through all Rhovanion these proud Men often fought the Orcs, Easterlings and Wolves of the Dark Lord, and at times they even dared to join battle with the great and ancient Dragons that came out of the Northern Waste.

These Northmen remained in Rhovanion for many centuries and did not succumb to the evil power of Sauron. In the histories that concern the last centuries of the Third Age of the Sun, the names of some of these strong and noble people are recorded: the Beornings and the Woodmen of Mirkwood; the Lake Men of Esgaroth; the Bardings of Dale; and, perhaps the most powerful and far-famed, the Éothéod, from whom the Rohirrim, the Riders of the Marks, were descended. These were all strong and noble Men, and, in the War of the Ring, the Northmen proved to be true allies of the Dúnedain, attacking minions of Sauron on the battle-field, in woodland and in mountain pass.

From the eleventh century of the Third Age the Northmen were allies of the Gondor Men against the Easterling invaders. Many entered the army of Gondor and their fortunes from that time followed the doom of the Gondor kings.

Númenor

After the First Age of the Sun, there was a remnant of that race of Men called the Edain who allied themselves with the Elves in the War of the Jewels against Morgoth. As a reward for their bravery, the Valar raised a great island in the midst of the Western Sea, so these people, called the Dúnedain, might have a land of their own. This was Númenor – 'Westernesse' in the language of the Men of Middle-earth – founded in the year 32 of the Second Age and the mightiest kingdom of Men in all of Arda. The Men of Númenor were given a life span many times that of other mortals, along with greater powers of mind and body that had previously been only granted to Elves. The island of Númenor, which was also called Andor, 'land of gift' or Elenna, 'land of star', was roughly shaped like a five-pointed star. It was approximately 250 miles across at its narrowest and five hundred miles at its widest, and was divided up into six regions. At the centre was Mittalmar, the 'inlands', which contained: Arandor, the 'kingsland'; Armenelos, the royal city; Meneltarma, the sacred mountain; and the port of Rómenna. Each of the five peninsulas that radiated from Mittalmar was a separate region: Forostar, the 'northlands'; Orrostar, the 'eastlands'; Hyarrostar, the 'southeastlands'; Hyarnustar, the 'southwestlands'; and Andustar, the 'westlands' with its major city and port of Anúnie, which means 'sunset'.

Númenor was blessed with many beautiful forests of fragrant blossoming trees. It had many fair meadows and two major rivers: the Siril, which flowed south from the slopes of Meneltarma to the sea near the fishing town of Nindamos, and the Nunduinë which

flowed west to Eldalondë the Green, the fairest port of Númenor. Through the Second Age Númenor was so great that the kings grew vain beyond reason. Corrupted by the evil promptings of Sauron the Ring Lord, in 3319 King Ar-Pharazôn dared to send a great navy against the Valar in the Undying Lands. The result was the utter destruction of Númenor as the sea literally swallowed up the island kingdom. This was the time that was known as the Change of the World, for not only was Númenor obliterated, but the Undying Lands were taken out of the Spheres of the World into a dimension that is beyond the reach and the understanding of mortals. Although a part of its people escaped the cataclysm and went to Middle-earth and built kingdoms and empires there, Númenor never arose again. For many ages legends spoke of it as a magical downfallen land beneath the sea under the names of Akallabêth, Mar-nu-Falmar and Atalantë or Atlantis.

Númenóreans

When the First Age of the Sun was ended and the power of Morgoth was broken, there remained but a remnant of the race of Men called the Edain, who were the allies of the Elves in the terrible Wars of Beleriand.

After the Great Battle, the Valar took pity on the Edain who had suffered so grievously and whose lands had been lost, and the Valar created a great island for them in the Western Sea, between Middle-earth and the Undying Lands. With this land they were given a gift of long life and greater powers of mind and body and many skills and much knowledge that had previously only been granted to Elves. These people were much changed and were now called the Númenóreans, for their land was Númenor or Westernesse. But it was also named Andor 'land of gift', Elenna, 'land of star', Mar-nu-Falmar 'land under waves' and Atalantë 'the downfallen'.

The deeds of the Númenóreans in the Second Age of the Sun were outstanding, for the Númenóreans were greatly strengthened by the gifts of the Valar and the Eldar. First of the kings of Númenor was Elros Half-elven, the brother of Elrond who later ruled in Rivendell. Elros chose to become mortal, yet his rule lasted 400 years. In that land he was named Tar-Minyatur. All over the World the Númenóreans sailed, even as far as the Gates of Morning in the East. However, they were never able to sail westwards, for a ban had been made that could not be broken: no mortal might tread the blessed shore of the Undying Lands of Eldamar and Valinor.

In Númenor the fortunes of Men increased, while darkness rose in Middle-earth once again. For though Morgoth the Enemy was gone from the World, his great servant, the Dark Lord Sauron, had returned and the Men in the southern and eastern lands of Middle-earth worshipped his evil shadow.

The tale of the Rings of Power tells how, at this time, Sauron made a sorcerous Ring with which he hoped to rule all Mortal Lands, and he made war on the Elves and slew them terribly and drove them back into the Blue Mountains. But the power of the Númenóreans had also grown, and they came to the aid of the Elves and made war on Sauron, and he was driven out of the western land. For a time there was peace and the Númenóreans again increased, building the ports of Umbar in the South and Pelargir in the North of Middle-earth. But they grew proud and wished to declare themselves lords of Middle-earth as well as lords of the seas. So in the year 3262 of the Second Age of the Sun they came to the Dark Land of Mordor with such a mighty host of arms and Men that Sauron could not withstand them. To the amazement of all the world, Sauron came down from his Dark Tower and surrendered to the Númenóreans rather than daring to fight such a host. So the Dark Lord was made

NÚMENOR 'Land of gift'.

prisoner and was taken in chains to the great tower of the king of Númenor.

Yet Sauron's surrender was only a ploy by the master deceiver to achieve by guile what he could not achieve by force of arms. For in the Númenóreans he perceived the fatal flaws of pride and ambition, and he believed that he could tempt them with the gifts of his powers. And so, once within the kingdom of Númenor, he managed to achieve the greatest evil that was ever committed against the race of Man: Sauron corrupted the king of Númenor, Ar-Pharazôn. In Númenor great temples were built to Morgoth the Lord of Darkness and human sacrifice was made on his altar. Then Sauron advised the Númenóreans to make war on the Valar and Eldar who lived in the Undying Lands. The greatest fleet that ever sailed the World was then assembled and it sailed into the West toward the land that was forbidden to Men. Passing through the Enchanted Isles and the Shadowy Seas, the fleet came to the Undying Lands. As the vast navy reached the Undying Lands the 'Akallabeth' tells how a great doom fell on the world. Though the king came to conquer, his first step brought the Pelóri Mountains down on him and all his vast armada. To a man the Númenóreans were lost, but this was not all, for a greater disaster followed. The waters rose up in wrath and Meneltarma – the mountain that was the centre of Númenor – erupted and great flames leapt up and all of Númenor sank in an immense whirlpool into Belegaer, the Great Sea.

Thus came what was called the Change of the World. For in that year, 3319 of the Second Age of the Sun, the Undying Lands were taken from the Circles of the World and moved beyond the reach of all but the Chosen, who travelled in Elven-ships along the Straight Road through the Spheres of both Worlds.

Yet a part of the Númenórean race lived on. Some had fled the sinking of Númenor and had sailed in nine ships to Middle-earth. These were the Elendili, the 'faithful', who were not corrupted by Sauron and refused to abandon the ancient ways of the Valar and Eldar. These people sailed away to Middle-earth in nine ships and made two mighty kingdoms in Arnor and Gondor. Others, too, survived the Downfall of Númenor and were in later times named the Black Númenóreans and they settled in the land of Umbar.

Nurn

The southern part of Sauron's evil realm of Mordor was known as Nurn. While Sauron ruled, this was a land filled with the slaves of the Ring Lord who joylessly worked its vast croplands to provide food for Mordor's armies. Through the fields of Nurn ran four main rivers which drained into the inland sea of Nûrnen. Little is told of this place or its people, but after the War of the Ring, King Elessar freed the slaves and turned the croplands of Nurn over to them for their own.

Oghor-hai

The name Oghor-hai was the Orkish name for the primitive Wildmen of the forests who often ambushed and raided Orc legions that wandered into their lands. They were known to Men as the Woses.

Oiolairë

Among the Númenórean sea kings, there was a custom of blessing a ship with safe passage and safe return. This was done by cutting a bough of the sacred, fragrant tree called Oiolairë and setting it on the ship's prow. This 'Green Bough of Return' was an offering to Ossë, the Master of the Waves, and Uinen, the Lady of the Calms. A gift to the Númenóreans from the Elves of Eressëa, Oiolairë means 'ever-summer'.

Óin

Dwarf of Thorin and Company. Óin, the son of Gróin, was born in 2774 of the Third Age, and joined the Quest of Erebor in 2941. After the slaying of Smaug the Dragon and the re-establishment of the Dwarf-kingdom under the Mountain, Óin settled for a time in Erebor. However, in 2989, he set out with Balin and Ori in an attempt to re-establish a Dwarf kingdom in Moria. He was killed there in 2994, by the monster called the Watcher in the Water.

Old Forest

By the Third Age of the Sun, the ancient forest that used to cover all of Eriador was reduced to a small area east of the Shire between the Brandywine River and the Barrow-downs. This was the Old Forest and within it were many malevolent tree spirits who made travel perilous. The most formidable of these was Old Man Willow who had the power of enchanting travellers with his whispering songs, entangling them with his mobile roots, and finally enclosing them within his trunk. Fortunately, another friendlier spirit called Tom Bombadil lived by the eastern side of the forest and had the power to command the malevolent tree spirits to release their prey.

Oliphaunts

Into the Hobbit lands of the Shire crept many legends about the mysterious hot lands that lay far in the south of Middle-earth. Most fascinating to the Hobbits were the tales of the giant Oliphaunts: tusked war beasts with huge pounding feet. It was rumoured that the savage Men of Harad placed battle towers on the backs of these creatures when they rode into battle. Sensible Hobbits believed these tales were the workings of fanciful minds, even though some of their own people claimed to have sighted these creatures, which the Men of Gondor commonly called Mûmakil.

Olog-hai

In the Third Age of the Sun, it is said that the Ring Lord Sauron, who ruled in Mordor, took some of the ancient Trolls that Melkor bred in Angband and from them made another race that was known as the Olog-hai in Black Speech. The creatures of this race were true Trolls in size and strength but Sauron made them cunning and unafraid of the light that was deadly to most of the Troll race. The Olog-hai were terrible in battle for they had been bred to be like ravening beasts that hungered for the flesh of their foes. They were armoured with stone-hard scale and were easily twice the height and bulk of Men. They carried round shields, blank and black, and were armed with huge hammers, clutching claws and great fangs. Before their onslaught few warriors of any race could hold firm a shield wall of defence, and blades unblessed by Elvish spell could not pierce their strong hides to release their foul black blood.

Yet strong as they were, the Olog-hai were wholly destroyed at the end of the Third Age. For these creatures were animated and directed solely by the will of the Dark Lord, Sauron. So when the One Ring was destroyed and Sauron perished, they were suddenly without senses and purpose; they reeled and wandered aimlessly. Masterless, they lifted no hand to fight and so were slain or lost. Therefore, the histories of the Fourth Age do not speak of the Olog-hai for they had already passed from the World for ever.

Olvar

In the Music of the Ainur were many prophecies. One was that before Elves and Men entered the World there would come spirits who would be guardians of all Olvar (living things that grow and are rooted in the Earth). For the Olvar, from the great forest trees to the smallest lichen, could not flee their enemies, and so Yavanna brought forth their guardians, called the Ents.

Olwë

Elven king of Alqualondë. Olwë was the brother of Elwë, the first High King of the Teleri Elves. The brothers led their people on the Great Journey at the beginning of the Ages of Starlight. However, in Beleriand, Elwë was enchanted by Melian the Maia and remained to found the kingdom of the Grey-elves. Olwë became the High King of the Teleri and led his people, first to Tol Eressëa, and finally to Alqualondë in Eldamar.

Onodrim

In the forests of Middle-earth in the time of the Rekindling of the Stars there came forth a giant people. These were the great Tree-herds, who were more often known as Ents but the Sindarin Elves called them the Onodrim. These fourteen-foot giants were secret protectors of the forest, and in form they were likened to both tree and Man. For the most part the Ents were gentle and slow to act. They were indifferent to the wars of other peoples, unless those disputes greatly diminished their forest realms. Yet once their anger was aroused, their wrath and power were beyond measure, and they annihilated their foes. During the War of the Ring the rebel Wizard Saruman learned the cost of incurring such anger, for the Onodrim destroyed both his army and his fortress of Isengard.

Orcs

Within the deepest Pits of Utumno in the First Age of Stars, it is said Melkor committed his greatest blasphemy. For in that time he captured many of the newly risen race of Elves and took them to his dungeons, and with hideous acts of torture he made ruined and terrible forms of life. From these he bred a Goblin race of slaves who were as loathsome as Elves were fair.

These were the Orcs, a multitude brought forth in shapes twisted by pain and hate. The only joy of these creatures was in the pain of others, for the blood that flowed within Orcs was both black and cold. Their stunted form was hideous: bent, bow-legged and squat. Their arms were long and strong as the apes of the South, and their skin was black as wood that has been charred by flame. The jagged fangs in their wide mouths were yellow, their tongues red and thick, and their nostrils and faces were broad and flat. Their eyes were

ORCS Their stunted form was hideous: bent, bow-legged and squat.

crimson gashes, like narrow slits in black iron grates behind which hot coals burn.

The Orcs were fierce warriors, for they feared more greatly their master than any enemy and perhaps death was preferable to the torment of Orkish life. They were cannibals, ruthless and terrible and often their rending claws and slavering fangs were gored with bitter flesh and the foul black blood of their own kind. Orcs were spawned as thralls of the Master of Darkness; therefore, they were fearful of light, for it weakened and burned them. Their eyes were night seeing, and they were dwellers of foul pits and tunnels. In Melkor's Utumno and in every foul dwelling in Middle-earth they multiplied. More quickly than any other beings of Arda their progeny came forth from the spawning pits. At the end of the First Age of Stars was the War of the Powers in which the Valar came to Utumno and broke it open. They bound Melkor with a great chain, and destroyed his servants in Utumno and with them most of the Orcs. Those who survived were masterless and went wandering.

In the Ages that followed were the great migrations of the Elves, and, though Orcs lived in the dark places of Middle-earth, they did not appear openly, and the Elven histories speak not of Orcs until the Fourth Age of Stars. By this time the Orcs had grown troublesome. Out of Angband they came in armour of steel-plate and linked chains, and helmets of iron hoops and black leather, beaked like a hawk or vulture with steel. They carried scimitars, poisoned daggers, arrows and broad-headed swords. This brigand race, with Wolves and Werewolves, dared, in the Fourth Age of Stars, to enter the realm of Beleriand where the Sindarin kingdom of Melian and Thingol stood. The Grey-elves knew not what manner of being the Orcs were, though they did not doubt they were evil. As these Elves did not use steel weapons at that time, they came to the Dwarf-smiths of Nogrod and Belegost and bartered for weapons of tempered steel. Then they slaughtered the Orcs or drove them away.

Yet, when Melkor returned to Beleriand in the last Age of Stars, out of the Pits of Angband, the Orcs came, rank upon rank, legion upon legion, in open war, and this was the beginning of the Wars of Beleriand. Because in the valley of the River Gelion they were met by King Thingol's Grey-elves and Denethor's Green-elves. In this First Battle the Orcs were decimated and driven shrieking in flight to the Blue Mountains, where they found no refuge but only the axes of the Dwarves. None of that army escaped. Yet Melkor had sent forth three grand armies. The second army of Orcs arose and overran the Western lands of Beleriand and besieged the Falas, but the cities of the Falathrim did not fall. So the second army of Orcs joined the third army and marched north to Mithrim, to slay the newly arrived Noldorin Elves. But the Orcs were little prepared for these Elves. In strength of body the Noldor were far beyond the darkest dreams of the Orcs. The eyes of these Elves alone seared the flesh of the Orcs, and the fierce light of Elven swords drove them mad with pain and fear. So the second Battle of Beleriand was fought against the Noldor whom Fëanor led, and this battle was called the Battle under Stars, the Dagor-nuin-Giliath. Though the Noldor king Fëanor was slain, the second and third armies of Melkor were entirely destroyed.

A second Noldor army led by the lord Fingolfin came out of the West and the great light of the Sun mounted the ramparts of the sky as if with a great shout that brought fear to every servant of Melkor. So the First Age of the Sun began and for a time the ambitions of the Orcs were checked by the new light of the Sun. Soon, however, under cover of darkness Orcs came in yet another grand army, more numerous than the other three and more heavily armed, hoping to catch the Noldor unaware. In the Glorious Battle, the Orc legions were slaughtered again. At this time the Siege of Angband was begun and, though Orcs at times sallied forth in bands, for the most part they were held within Angband's walls. Yet Melkor's might grew, for by dark sorcery he bred more of the Orc race and also Dragons, and about him were Balrogs, Trolls, Werewolves and monsters many and great. When he deemed himself ready the mighty host came into the Battle of the Sudden Flame, and this broke the siege of Angband and the Elven-lords were defeated. From this mighty battle is counted the reign of terror that the Orcs remember as the Great Years.

At that time Tol Sirion fell and the kingdoms of Hithlum, Mithrim, Dor-lómin and Dorthonion were overrun. The Battle of Unnumbered Tears was also fought: this was the Fifth Battle in the Wars of Beleriand and the Elves and Edain were completely defeated. The evil Orc legions of Angband then marched into Beleriand. The Falas fell to the Orcs, as did both the cities of Brithombar and Eglarest. The Battle of Tumhalad was fought and Nargothrond was sacked; because of his disputes with Dwarves and the Noldor, Menegroth was twice overrun and the Grey-elf lands were ruined. Finally Gondolin, the Hidden Kingdom, fell. So Melkor's victory was all but complete; his Orc legions went wherever they wished in Beleriand. All the Elven kingdoms were ruined; no great city stood and the lords and the greatest part of the Elves and Edain were slain. Such is the tale of days that are joyful to the black hearts of the Orcs and their allies.

Yet the terror of that Age finally came to an end. For the Valar, the Maiar, the Vanyar and the Noldor of Tirion, all came out of the Undying Lands and the Great Battle was joined. In it Angband was destroyed and all the mountains of the North were broken. Beleriand with Angband fell into the boiling seas; Melkor was cast out into the Void for ever more and his servants the Orcs were exterminated in the northwest of Middle-earth.

Still the Orcs survived, for part of the race lay hidden in foul dens beneath the dark mountains and hills. There they bred and multiplied. Eventually, they came to Melkor's general, Sauron, offering their services, and he became their new master. They served Sauron well in the War of Sauron and the Elves and in all his battles until the War of the Last Alliance, when the Second Age ended with the fall of Mordor and with most of the Orkish race again being exterminated. Yet in the Third Age of the Sun as in the Second, those Orcs hidden in dark and evil places lived on. Masterless, the Orcs raided and ambushed for many centuries but made no grand schemes of conquest until more than a thousand years of the Age had passed, when as a great and evil Eye, Sauron, re-appeared in the dark realm of Dol Guldur in southern Mirkwood. As in the Second Age of the Sun, the dark destinies of Sauron and the Orcs were again made one, and for two thousand years of the Third Age Orkish power increased with that of their Dark Lord.

Their power first grew in Mirkwood, then in the Misty Mountains. In 1300 the Nazgûl re-appeared in Mordor and the realm of Angmar in northern Eriador, and the Orcs flocked to them. After six hundred years of terror Angmar fell, but the evil realm of Minas Morgul arose in Gondor, and there again the Orcs increased, with those of Mirkwood, the Misty Mountains and Mordor, for the next thousand years.

Yet it was said that Sauron was not fully pleased with his Orkish soldiery and he wished to increase their strength. And though no tale tells of it, it was believed that Sauron through terrible sorcery made a new breed of greater Orcs. In the year 2475, those creatures, the Uruk-hai, came out of Mordor and sacked Osgiliath, the greatest city of Gondor. These were Orcs grown to the height of Men, yet straight-limbed and strong. Though they were truly Orcs – black-skinned, black-blooded, lynx-eyed, fanged and claw-handed – Uruk-hai did not languish in sunlight and did not fear it at all. So the Uruk-hai could go where their evil brethren could not, and, being larger and stronger, they were also bolder and fiercer in battle. Clad in black armour, often carrying straight swords and long yew bows as well as many of the evil and poisoned Orc weapons, the Uruk-hai were made élite men-at-arms and most often were the high commanders and captains of the lesser Orcs.

In the centuries that followed, the Uruk-hai and the lesser Orcs made alliances that they might ruin all the kingdoms of Men and Elves that were in the Westlands. Therefore, the Orcs made treaties with the Dunlendings, the Balchoth, the Wainriders, the Haradrim, the Easterlings of Rhûn and the Corsairs of Umbar to achieve their aim. The Orcs came even to the realms of the Dwarves. In the year 1980 Moria was taken by a mighty Balrog demon. With him were the Orcs of the Misty Mountains, who had come out of their capital of Gundabad in great number to inhabit the ancient Dwarvish city, heaping contempt on the Dwarf people and slaying whoever came near this most ancient realm.

Yet in the North this was to be the undoing of the Orcs, for the Dwarves were so enraged that they cared not at what cost they would have revenge. So it was that from 2793 to 2799 there was waged a seven years' war of extermination called the War of the Dwarves and Orcs. In this war, though it cost the Dwarves dearly, almost all the Orcs of the Misty Mountains were hunted out and slain, and at the East Gate of Moria the terrible Battle of Azanulbizar was fought. The Orcs were destroyed and the head of their Orc general, Azog, was impaled on a stake. So it was that for a century the Misty Mountains were cleansed of this vile race, yet in time they returned to Gundabad and Moria.

In the year 2941 a second great disaster befell the Orcs in the North. After the death of the Dragon Smaug, all the Orc warriors of Gundabad came to the Dwarf-realm of Erebor and the Battle of the Five Armies was fought beneath the Lonely Mountain. The Orcs were led by Bolg of the North, son of Azog, and he wished to have vengeance on the Dwarves, but all he achieved was his own death and that of all his warriors.

In the War of the Ring, the last great conflict of the Third Age of the Sun, the Orkish legions were everywhere, as the 'Red Book of Westmarch' relates. From the Misty Mountains and the shadows of Mirkwood the Orcs came to war under banners both black and red. Fearless Uruk-hai with shields and helmets carrying the emblem of the White Hand came out of Isengard, where the rebel Wizard Saruman ruled. In Morgul both greater and lesser Orcs were marked with a white moon like a great skull; and under Sauron's command were the countless Orcs of Mordor of whatever breed, who were marked with the symbol of the Red Eye. All of these prepared for war and many others as well. They fought numerous skirmishes and ambushes, as well as the Battles of the Fords of Isen, the Battle of the Hornburg, the Battle of Pelennor Fields, the Battle under the Trees and the Battles of Dale. In these assaults thousands on both sides fell, and, though in many of these battles the Orcs were utterly vanquished, it is told that Sauron held back the greatest part of his force within Mordor until the enemy came to the northern gateway of his realm.

Yet in the War of the Ring, all was to be resolved in one last battle before Morannon, the Black Gate. All the dreadful forces of Mordor were gathered there and at Sauron's command they fell on the army of the Captains of the West. However, at that very moment, in the volcanic fires of Mount Doom, the One Ring of Power which held all Sauron's dark world in sway, was destroyed. The Black Gate and Black Tower burst asunder. The mightiest servants of Sauron were consumed in fire, the Dark Lord became black smoke dispelled by a west wind, and the Orcs perished like straw before flames. Though some survived they never again rose in great numbers, but dwindled and became a minor Goblin folk possessed of but a rumour of their ancient evil power.

Ori

Dwarf of Thorin and Company. In 2941 of the Third Age, Ori embarked on the Quest of Erebor which resulted in the slaying of Smaug the Dragon and the re-establishment of the Dwarf-kingdom under the Mountain. Ori remained in Erebor until 2989, when he set out with Balin and Óin in an attempt to re-colonize Khazad-dûm. He died there in 2994, in the Chamber of Mazarbul.

Orocarni

Far to the east of Middle-earth were the Orocarni, the 'Red Mountains', or the Mountains of the East. In the Ages of Starlight they stood on the eastern shore of the Inland Sea of Helcar where, in the bay of Cuiviénen, the Elves were first awakened. The Orocarni were of a reddish hue and filled with the music of a multitude of rivers and springs that flowed down into the crystal waters of the Sea of Helcar.

Orodruin

Often called Mount Doom, that immense volcanic mountain of Mordor was more properly called Orodruin, the 'mountain of blazing fire'. Although Orodruin was less than five thousand feet high, it stood alone and dominated the vast, barren plateau of Gorgoroth in the northern part of Mordor. Orodruin was the fire and forge of Sauron who, within the Chambers of Fire and the fissures called the Cracks of Doom within its volcanic cone, made the One Ring in 1600 of the Second Age. A still active volcano through the Second and Third Ages, Orodruin's eruptions coincided with Sauron's various risings, and its black belching clouds darkened and fouled the skies far beyond the realm of Mordor. The fires of Orodruin proved to be critical in the War of the Ring, for only there could the One Ring be unmade and Sauron's power destroyed – and indeed, in the year 3019, the Quest of the Ring was achieved. When the One Ring was thrown into the Cracks of Doom, Orodruin underwent its final and most cataclysmic eruption, so great that the mountains of Mordor shook, and the Black Gate of Morannon and the tower of Barad-dûr toppled down in a smouldering heap of blackened stones.

Oromë

Vala called 'the Huntsman'. An Ainu spirit who descended from the Timeless Halls to Arda during the Ages of Darkness and Stars, Oromë loved to ride on his white horse, Nahar, through the forests of Middle-earth. Oromë's name means 'Horn blower', and the sound of his horn, Valaróma, was a terror to the servants of darkness. His sister is Nessa the Dancer, and his spouse, Vána the Ever-young. Oromë was the first of the Valar to discover the Elves, and it was he who summoned them to Eldamar. By the Sindar he is called Araw and by Men, Béma. He lives in the Woods of Oromë, in southern Valinor.

Orthanc

The tower in Isengard that was controlled by the evil Wizard Saruman during the War of the Ring was called Orthanc, meaning 'cunning mind' in Rohan. It was built in the midst of the fortified Isengard plain at the southern limit of the Misty Mountains and near the source of the River Isen. Orthanc was a five hundred foot tall tower built from four pillars of black rock by the Men of Gondor. It had a distinctive twin-pronged pinnacle with a flat roof between, marked with figures from astronomy. Abandoned by the Men of Gondor during the last part of the Third Age, the Wizard Saruman gained the keys to it in 2759 and took control of it and the Palantir, or 'Seeing Stone', that was kept in one of its chambers. Later he gathered a vast army within Isengard and made war on the Rohirrim. From Orthanc, Saruman controlled many destructive machines of war, but these were incapacitated by the Ents when

they flooded the plain about the tower. But the black stone of the tower proved invulnerable to assault, for the stone of Orthanc could not be broken. Eventually, Saruman was forced to surrender the tower, and Orthanc once again passed into the hands of the Men of Gondor.

Osgiliath

The first capital of Gondor was Osgiliath, the 'citadel of stars', which was built at the end of the Second Age and bridged the River Anduin midway between Minas Anor and Minas Ithil. Osgiliath remained intact until Gondor's civil war in 1437 when its legendary Dome of Stars was burned, along with most of the city. This was followed by the disaster of the Great Plague of 1636. The royal court was moved in 1640 to Minas Anor, which later was renamed Minas Tirith. In 2475, Osgiliath was completely sacked by the Uruk-hai legions out of Mordor, and although these were driven back the city was now totally deserted. In the War of the Ring, Osgiliath was briefly defended by Gondor Men on two occasions but soon fell to Sauron's servants and had its stone bridge broken. After the destruction of Mordor at the end of the war, Osgiliath was regained by Gondor, but it does not appear to have been rebuilt during the Fourth Age.

Ossë

Maia sea spirit. Ossë, Lord of the Waves, with his wife, Uinen, the Lady of the Calms, ruled the seas of Middle-earth. Ossë served Ulmo, Lord of All Waters. Ossë was feared by all who sailed the seas. Sailors prayed to Uinen that she might quell his rage and calm his wild, tempestuous joy. Ossë, who befriended the Teleri Sea Elves and taught them the art of ship-building, also raised the island of Númenor from the sea floor.

OROMË The sound of his horn, Valaróma, was a terror to the servants of darkness.

Ossiriand

In the east of Beleriand until the end of the First Age of the Sun was Ossiriand, the woodland home of the Laiquendi Green Elves. It was called Ossiriand, the 'land of seven rivers', because the River Gelion and six of its tributaries flowed through it. Because the Laiquendi were most famous for their singing Ossiriand was also called Lindon, the 'land of song'. Indeed, after the destruction and sinking of Beleriand at the end of the First Age, it was by this name that the small part of Ossiriand that survived was known. As the last surviving fragment of Beleriand, Lindon became the domain of the Eldar of Gil-galad, the last High Elven King on Middle-earth.

Ost-in-Edhil

In the year 750 of the Second Age, many Noldor Elves left Lindon and went into Eriador. There, near the west door of Khazad-dûm in the White Mountains, they founded the realm of Eregion and built the city of Ost-in-Edhil, the 'City of Elves'. These were the Gwaith-i-Mírdain, the Elven-smiths who in the year 1500 forged the Rings of Power. Ost-in-Edhil was a fair and prosperous city with its white Elven towers rising up in the midst of the holly forest of Eregion. However, when the Elven-smiths discovered Sauron had forged the One Ring to command the other Rings of Power, they rose up against him. In the ensuing War of Sauron and the Elves, in 1697 of the Second Age, Ost-in-Edhil was utterly destroyed and the realm of the Elven-smiths was no more.

P

Pelargir

Built near the mouth of the Great River Anduin in 2350 of the Second Age by the Númenóreans, the city and port of Pelargir became the most important haven for the ships of the Dúnedain on Middle-earth. It was here that Elendil landed after the destruction of Númenor and went out to found Gondor and Arnor. It was rebuilt during the tenth century of the Third Age by Eärnil I, and became the main base of power for the mighty Ship Kings of Gondor in their struggles with their rivals, the Black Númenóreans of the city-port of Umbar, far to the south in the land of Harad. During Gondor's civil war in 1447, Pelargir was seized by the rebels, but was regained after a year-long siege. Although suffering most of the same ills that afflicted all of Gondor, and often attacked by Haradrim, Easterlings and the Corsairs of Umbar, Pelargir survived as the chief port of Gondor until the War of the Ring. Only then were the black ships of the Corsairs able to overcome the defences of Pelargir, but even so their dominion did not last long. The Dúnedain chieftain Aragorn brought the phantom army of the Dead Men of Dunharrow and routed the Corsairs, who fled in terror and Aragorn seized the whole of their fleet. With these captured ships, Aragorn was able to bring the Men of Pelargir up the River Anduin in that last defence of Gondor on Pelennor Fields and turn the tide of battle. Through the Fourth Age, Pelargir once more grew wealthy and powerful as the chief port of the Reunited Kingdom.

Pelennor Fields

During the War of the Ring, there was a fair and green plain called the Pelennor Fields surrounding Gondor's fortress-city of Minas Tirith. Here the crucial Battle of the Pelennor Fields was fought, and the tide of the war turned. Pelennor means the 'fenced land' because the plain was encircled by a defensive wall called the Rammas Echor, that was built by the Ruling Steward Ecthelion II in the year 2594 of the Third Age. This wall was rapidly breached by the army of the Witch-king of Morgul when he advanced upon Minas Tirith during the War of the Ring. Fortunately, the Rohirrim cavalry drove the Witch-king's forces onto the fields where eventually his evil hordes were overcome and destroyed.

Pelóri Mountains

The greatest mountains in all of Arda were the Pélori Mountains, which were raised by the Valar to defend the Undying Lands from Melkor's forces in Utumno on Middle-earth. They were raised in a vast crescent that made up the boundary of Valinor on the north, east and south sides. Already the tallest mountains in the world, the Pelóri (meaning 'fenced peaks') Mountains were made taller and steeper still after the destruction of the Trees of the Valar. Of its many peaks, Taniquetil, the Mountain sacred to Manwë, was the tallest and stood in the central and eastern part of the range, not far from the only pass through these mountains. This gap was called Calacirya, which means the Pass of Light.

Peregrin Took

Hobbit of the Shire. Peregrin Took was born in 2990 of the Third Age, the son of the Thain of the Shire. As a loyal friend of Frodo Baggins, he undertook the Quest of the Ring in 3019. He survived many adventures with the Fellowship of the Ring until its collapse, when both Pippin and his Hobbit friend, Meriadoc Brandybuck, were captured by Orcs. Luckily, both Hobbits escaped into the Fangorn Forest, where they met Treebeard the Ent, and were instrumental in provoking the Ent attack on Isengard. Gandalf later took Pippin to Gondor where he was made a Guard of the Citadel, and helped save the life of the Steward's son, Faramir. At the Battle before the Black Gate of Mordor, Pippin distinguished himself by slaying a Troll. Later that year he fought in the Battle of Bywater. Pippin and Merry were the two tallest Hobbits in history – measuring nearly four and one-half feet – due to the drinking of Ent-draughts. In the fourteenth year of the Fourth Age, Pippin became the thirty-second Thain of the Shire and ruled until the year 64. He and Merry decided to spend their last years in Rohan and Gondor, where they were buried with honour in the House of Kings.

Periannath

In the histories of the War of the Ring it is told how the smallest and most timid of races, the Hobbits, were the means by which the War was won. And so the Periannath, as the Hobbits were known in the Grey-elven tongue, became famed in the songs of Elves and Men and were praised for their valour.

Petty-dwarves

The tales of Elves in the First Age of the Sun tell of a remnant of an exiled people of the Dwarves who lived in the land of Beleriand long before the Elves came. These were the Petty-dwarves and they inhabited the forest land of the River Narog and delved the halls of Amon Rúdh and Nulukkizdîn (which later became the Elven kingdom of Nargothrond). But when the Sindarin Elves came into the nearby land of Doriath, not knowing what manner of being these people were, they hunted them for sport. In time they learned they were but a diminished Dwarvish people who had become estranged from other Dwarves by some evil deed done long before in the land east of the Blue Mountains. So the Sindar ceased their persecution of this unhappy race, whom they called the Noegyth Nibin.

Yet in Beleriand these people dwindled. Having no allies in a land of strife, they enter the histories of Elves in the tales of Túrin. By that time the Petty-dwarves numbered only three: their lord, who was named Mîm, and his two sons, Ibun and Khîm. The 'Tale of Grief' relates how Mîm led Túrin Turambar and his followers into the ancient Dwarf-delvings of Amon Rûdh, where they found shelter. But later, Mîm was captured by Orcs and saved his own life by betraying Túrin and his band. So the Orcs made a surprise attack and slaughtered these Outlaws. Mîm won his freedom to no purpose, for both his sons perished, and, though he lived to gather a great Dragon hoard that Glaurung left behind in ruined Nargothrond, it happened that Túrin's father, the warrior called Húrin, came to Mîm's door. With a single blow Húrin slew Mîm in vengeance and so ended the life of the Petty-dwarf, the last to live within the Circles of the World.

Phantoms of the Dead Marshes

Between the vast falls of the Great River Anduin and the dark mountains of Mordor there was an immense dreary fenland called the Dead Marshes. These Marshes were terrible and perilous, and in the Third Age of the Sun they were an evil and haunted place. For it is told that at the end of the Second Age there was a mighty war before the Black Gate on the plain of Dagorlad. Innumerable warriors among the Last Alliance of Elves and Men died on that plain, and countless Orcs fell also. And so Elves, Men and Orcs and many other servants of Sauron were all buried on Dagorlad.

But in the Third Age the Marshlands spread eastwards and the graveyards of the warriors were swallowed by the fens. Great black pools appeared and they were crawling with evil beings. There were serpents and creeping life in these marshes, but no bird would visit the foul waters. From the evil stench and slime of these pools, where so many warriors rotted, haunting lights were seen. And these lights were said to be like candles lit, and in this light could be seen the faces of the dead: faces fair and evil; faces grim and decayed with death; evil Orkish faces and those of strong Men and bright Elves. Whether they were spirits or mirages of the dead is not known. These Phantoms of the Dead Marshes appeared in the pools but could not be reached. Their light beckoned travellers like a distant dream, and if any fell under their spell they would come to the dark water and disappear into the hideous pools. Such was the fate of those who journeyed that way to the east. Such was the fate of those Easterlings called Wainriders, who in the twentieth century of that Age were driven far into the Dead Marshes after the Battle of the Camp.

Pipe-weed

Before the days of the War of the Ring the Hobbits were a quiet folk who could claim little influence of the World beyond the Shire. But of one thing, however, they did boast to be the makers and masters, and that was the smoking of the herb nicotiana, which was named Galenas in Elvish. When originally brought from the land of Númenor by Men, it was prized only for the scent of its flower.

It was the Hobbits of Bree who grew it specially for the purpose of smoking it in long-stemmed pipes. Knowing not the Elvish name for the plant, or caring little if they did, they renamed it Pipe-weed after its most common use. They derived great enjoyment from this pastime, and in the way of Hobbits towards things of pleasure, smoking Pipe-weed was rated as a high art.

The Hobbits were also connoisseurs of fine Pipe-weeds, rating those of Bree and Southfarthing highest; then Longbottom Leaf, Old Toby, Southern Star and Southlinch. So from the centre of Bree this most famous Hobbit habit spread over Middle-earth and was widely practised by Men and Dwarves.

Ponies

On Middle-earth Ponies proved excellent servants of Hobbits and Dwarves, who, owing to their stature, could not ride on the backs of Horses. As beasts of burden, the Ponies also hauled the ore and trade ware of Dwarves and the field crops of Hobbits and Men.

In the annals of the Hobbits mention is given to those Ponies that aided the nine who went on the Quest of the Ring. By Tom Bombadil these were named: Sharp-ears, Swish-tail, Wise-nose, White-socks and Bumpkin. Bombadil's own Pony was called Fatty Lumpkin. The faithful beast that Samwise Gamgee befriended was just plain Bill.

Púkel-Men

On the great citadel of Dunharrow was set an ancient maze of walls and entrances that would break the advance of any army before it reached the Hold of Dunharrow. At each gate in the road huge stone guardians stood. These guardians were called Púkel-men by the Rohirrim who came to Dunharrow centuries after the race that built this maze had vanished.

The Púkel-men statues were of crouched, pot-bellied Man-like beings with almost comic, grimacing faces. They have been compared to the Wild Men called the Woses of Druadan. Indeed, it is likely that the Púkel-men were ancestors of that pygmy race, the Woses, but of their relationship with the builders of Dunharrow no tale tells. The builders of the vast fortifications were themselves only known as the Men of the White Mountains. They were thought to be the ancestors of the Dunlendings and in the early years of the Second Age of the Sun they thrived for a time in the White Mountains.

Quendi

As the 'Ainulindalë' tells, all things that came forth in the World were formed in the grand themes of the Music of the Ainur. And it was Ilúvatar alone who conceived of the themes that brought forth the race of Elves. So when the Elves came to the World, awakening to the sight of Stars and the sound of water, it was as if the Music of the Spheres had been born within them. Of all beings in the World they were the first to speak. The voices of the Elves were beautiful and subtle as water, and they were curious of all things and went about the World naming all that they saw. They were teachers to all the races and creatures on Earth who would learn the arts of speech and song.

So it was that the Elves came to name themselves the Quendi, which means the 'speakers', after their greatest art, and they then named their language Quenya, which means simply the 'speech'. All the tongues of the World came from this one source, which is the root of them and which is most fair to the ears of all who love beauty in its various forms. The giant Ents were the first race to learn speech from the Quendi, but soon the skill spread until even Men and evil Orcs and Trolls learned of its use. And though Quenya was the first tongue of the Quendi, it was not their only tongue. For the Avari and the Silvan Elves spoke dialects that changed through the Ages of Stars and the Sun as the lands of Middle-earth changed. Because of the Teleri's long exile upon Tol Eressëa the tongue of this Third Kindred who inhabited Alqualondë was also a dialect of the ancient speech. Only among the Vanyar and the Noldor in the Undying Lands did Quenya remain close to the language spoken at the time of the Awakening.

Because the Sindar Elves for many Ages ruled the western lands and because they were more numerous than the Noldor exiles, all the Eldar in Middle-earth commonly used the Sindarin tongue. Indeed, by the Third Age of the Sun, only the Eldar, the Ents and the Dúnedain lords still knew Quenya, and even to these it was the language not of daily use but that of high ceremony, ancient songs and romantic tales and High Elvish histories.

Quickbeam

Ent of the Fangorn Forest. Quickbeam was a protector of Rowan trees, and in the manner of Ents resembled those trees. During the War of the Ring, Quickbeam entertained the Hobbits Meriadoc Brandybuck and Peregrin Took. His Elvish name was Bregalad or 'swift-tree'. By the standards of his race, he was a very 'hasty' Ent. He was also one of the youngest. He had grey-green hair, red lips and a high, resonant voice. He took a prominent part in the destruction of Isengard.

R

Radagast

Istari, Wizard of Middle-earth. Radagast the Brown was originally a Maia spirit of Yavanna the Fruitful called Aiwendil, meaning 'lover of birds'. Chosen as one of the Istari, the order of Wizards, he came to Middle-earth in the year 1000 of the Third Age of the Sun. He seemed little concerned with the affairs of Elves and Men, but was extremely knowledgeable about herbs, plants, birds and beasts.

Radgbug

Orc of Cirith Ungol. During the War of the Ring, Radgbug gained brief note when he refused to carry out an order given by his Uruk-hai captain, Shagrat, after a fight between the Orcs of the Tower of the Spider's Pass and the Orcs of Minas Morgul. His mutiny was short-lived because Shagrat threw him to the ground and squeezed out his eyes.

Rangers of Ithilien

At the end of the twenty-ninth century of the Third Age of the Sun, Túrin II, the Ruling Steward of Gondor, decreed that a brotherhood of knights be formed in North Ithilien, for Gondor's power in that land was threatened by enemies from Mordor and Morgul. So the band called the Rangers of Ithilien was formed. These knights were dressed in foresters' green, and they fought with bows, spears and swords. In the years before the War of the Ring, their captain was Faramir, second son of Denethor, Gondor's Ruling Steward. Greatest of their dwellings was that refuge of caves and tunnels behind a great waterfall that looked far over the Vales of Anduin. This place was called Henneth Annûn, the 'window of the sunset'.

Rangers of the North

Through many centuries of the Third Age of the Sun, in the lands of Eriador, there roamed grim-faced men clothed in cloaks of forest-green or grey, with clasps like silver Stars on their left shoulders. They were grey-eyed, armed with sword and spear, and they wore long leather boots. By the common folk of Eriador they were called Rangers, and they were thought to be a strange, unfriendly people. For though they wandered over all the lands of Eriador on foot or on strange shaggy Horses, they did so silently. Indeed, few knew who these tough weather-worn Rangers were, or from where they had come. But as the 'Red Book of Westmarch' reveals, the Rangers were in fact the last nobles and knights of that once great Dúnedain realm of Arnor and their chieftain was the High Dúnedain king. In the years before and after the War of the Ring this was Aragorn, son of Arathorn, who as a Ranger was called Strider. At that time one named Halbarad, who was slain on Pelennor Fields, was Aragorn's chief lieutenant among the Rangers, while the famous sons of Elrond Half-elven, Elladan and Elrohir, also rode in that company.

At the War's end Aragorn was crowned King Elessar, lord of the twin Dúnedain realms of Arnor and Gondor, and the Rangers were honoured among the greatest Men of that Reunited Kingdom.

RADAGAST He seemed little concerned with the affairs of Elves and Men, but was extremely knowledgeable about herbs, plants, birds and beasts.

Rauros Falls

The most spectacular waterfalls on Middle-earth in the Third Age were the Rauros Falls on the Anduin River on the northern border of Gondor. The name Rauros means 'roaring foam', and accurately describes it as it fell in a shimmering golden haze from the long lake of Nen Hithoel on the heights of Emyn Muil to the marshlands below. The falls were unnavigable, but a portage route called the North Stair had been cut in the cliffs as a means of bypassing them. During the Quest of the Ring, the funeral boat of Boromir of Gondor was sent over the Rauros Falls to its final rest.

Ravenhill

Within Erebor, the Lonely Mountain, that stands just east of the forest of Mirkwood, was the Dwarf Kingdom under the Mountain. The Dwarves of Erebor built a fortified hill on the mountain's southern spur. This was called Ravenhill because the hill and its guardhouse rooftop was home to many Ravens who were always friends and allies of the Dwarves. It was here that the Raven called Roäc brought news to Thorin Oakenshield that Smaug the Golden Dragon had been slain. During the Battle of Five Armies, it was on Ravenhill that the Elves (with Gandalf the Wizard and Bilbo Baggins) made their stand.

Ravens

Many races of birds lived on Middle-earth. Among those named in the tales were the Eagles, which were noblest of all birds, and the Ravens, which were strong and long-living.
Part of the tale of the slaying of Smaug, the Dragon of Erebor, tells of the Ravens of Erebor, which in the Third Age of the Sun served the Dwarves of Durin's Line. These Ravens were wise counsellors and swift messengers of the Dwarves, and they were skilled in many tongues. At that time Roäc, son of Carc, was lord of the Ravens. He was ancient, his life

RAVENS The black birds of Erebor and allies of the Dwarves during the Quest of the Lonely Mountain. The Raven Lord at that time was the ancient balding Roäc, who understood and spoke the Western tongue.

having spanned more than one hundred and fifty years. By his will and wisdom he ruled the Ravens. And in the common tongue of Westron, Roäc spoke to his Dwarvish friends and brought them news and aid.

Region

Among the trees of Middle-earth was one that Elves called Region, and Men called Holly. Part of the realm of Sindar was named after that tree. This was the dense forest area of East Beleriand, which lay within the guarded realm of Doriath.

Region was widespread in Middle-earth, but in few places did it grow luxuriantly. One of the areas where it was most widely known was Eregion, which means 'land of the Holly'. The Elven-smiths lived there in the Second Age of the Sun, and it was there that the mighty Rings of Power were forged.

Rhovanion

The wide lands between the Misty Mountains and the Sea of Rhûn were called Rhovanion or 'wilder-land' and encompassed all lands south of the Grey Mountains and north of Gondor and Mordor. This included Mirkwood, Erebor, Lothlórien, Fangorn, the Brown Lands and all the northern vales of the Great River Anduin.

Rhûn

To the north-east of Mordor and west of Rhovanion lay the vast lands of Rhûn. Here was the inland Sea of Rhûn which was fed by the Redwater and Running Rivers. Out of the wide lands of Rhûn came many a barbarian people to make war on the Dúnedain through the Second and Third Ages of the Sun. Rhûn was the land of the Easterlings who were ever under the influence of Sauron, the Ring Lord. Many of his greatest servants were recruited among the kings of Rhûn. By the Fourth Age, King Elessar of the Reunited Kingdom had broken the power of most of the kingdoms of Rhûn and forced them to make a lasting peace with the westlands.

Ringwraiths

Nine was the number of the mighty wraiths that Sauron released in Middle-earth after the forging of the Rings of Power. In Black Speech they were named the Nazgûl, which in the common tongue is 'Ringwraiths', and they were the chief servants and generals of Sauron.

The tale of the evil deeds of the Ringwraiths is long, and the phantom shadows of these Black Riders brought terror to the hearts of even the bravest peoples of Middle-earth.

Rivendell

In the year 1697 of the Second Age, in the wake of the War of Sauron and the Elves, Master Elrond Half-elven fled Eregion with a remnant of the Gwaith-i-Mírdain. While most of the kingdom of the Elven-smiths of Eriador was destroyed, the surviving High Elves built the refuge of Rivendell in the steep, hidden valley of Imladris in easternmost Eriador at the foot of the Misty Mountains, in the angle of land between the two branches of the Loudwater.

Here was hidden the great House of Elrond. Considered the 'Last Homely House East of the Sea', it was a house of wisdom, great learning and a refuge of kindness for all Elves and Men of goodwill. It was here that Bilbo Baggins found refuge, as later did the Fellowship of the Ring. The house and valley were guarded by Elven enchantments that caused the rivers on either side to rise up and repel invaders. Rivendell survived all the wars of the Second and Third Ages, and besides being an Elven refuge, it was also a refuge for the Dúnedain, and particularly the Chieftains of the North Kingdom. After the War of the Ring, Elrond left Rivendell for the Undying Lands, but Elrohir, Elladan and Celeborn remained there with many other Elves until that time in the

Fourth Age when the last Elven ship departed from the Grey Havens.

River Anduin

In the Third and Fourth Ages of the Sun, the Anduin was the largest and longest river on Middle-earth. Its name is Elvish for 'great river' and it was often simply called The Great River. Its major tributaries were Celebrant, Gladden, Entwash, Limlight, Morgulduin, Erui, Poros and Sirith. The Anduin lands, stretching from its source in the Grey Mountains in the far north to its delta which drained into the Bay of Belfalas in the south, were the lands most hotly contested on Middle-earth during the War of the Ring.

River-women

In the histories and writings of Middle-earth, mention is made of the River-women. Whether, like Ossë and Uinen, these were Maiar of Ulmo, Lord of the Waters, or whether they were spirits who came into the World like Ents, is not told; but it is certain they were chiefly concerned with the Kelvar and Olvar of the World.

The 'Red Book of Westmarch' tells how the River-woman of the Withywindle had a daughter named Goldberry, who was the wife of Tom Bombadil. This River-daughter was golden-haired and bright as an Elf-maiden. Her garments were often silver and green, and flowers continuously blossomed in the spring of her light and laughter.

RIVER ANDUIN The largest and longest river on Middle-earth. Its name is Elvish for 'great river'.

GOLDBERRY This River-daughter was golden-haired and bright as an Elf-maiden.

Roäc the Raven

Raven lord of Erebor. The son of Carc, he was born in the year 2788 of the Third Age. Roäc was 153 years old and rather feather-bald when he helped out the Dwarves of Thorin and Company. It was Roäc who told Thorin of the death of Smaug the Golden Dragon, and it was he who sent his Ravens to the Dwarves of the Iron Hills to recruit them for the Battle of Five Armies.

Rógin

In the language of the Rohirrim horsemen, Rógin was the name given to those primitive tribal people of the Druadan Forest who were more commonly called the Wildmen or the Woses.

Rohan

The kingdom of Rohan, meaning 'horse land', was founded in 2510 of the Third Age of the Sun after the Battle of the Field of Celebrant. During this battle a wandering race of golden-haired horsemen called the Éothéod came to the rescue of the Men of Gondor and turned the tide of battle. In gratitude, they were given Gondor's entire province of Calenardhon as an independent yet allied nation. Thereafter, the Éothéod called themselves the Rohirrim or 'horse-lords' and made Rohan (or Riddermark) their home. Rohan largely consisted of the wide grasslands, horse plains and farmlands bordered by the River Anduin in the east, the White Horn Mountains in the south, the Misty Mountains and the Fangorn Forest in the north. It was divided into five main regions: Eastfold, Westfold, East Emnet, West Emnet and the Wold. The Entwash and the Snowbourn were the main tributaries of the Anduin River that drained its lands. Rohan's capital was the city of Edoras where Meduseld, the Golden Hall of the king was found. Although Edoras was fortified, it was not easily defended. In time of war, the Rohirrim took refuge in the great fortresses of Helm's Deep and Dunharrow, high up in the White Horn Mountains. This happened during the Dunlending Invasion of 2758 and again during the War of the Ring and the decisive Battle of Hornburg. After the Rohirrim's critical role in the Battle of Pelennor Fields and the defeat of the Ring Lord; Rohan, with the Reunited Kingdom of Gondor and Arnor, prospered long and well into the Fourth Age.

Roheryn

Horse of Aragorn II. During the War of the Ring, Roheryn carried Aragorn into many battles. A shaggy, but strong and proud horse, he was the gift of the Elven princess Arwen to her betrothed future king. Roheryn means 'horse of the lady'. During the War he served Aragorn in the Battle of Hornburg, through the Paths of the Dead into the Battle of Pelennor Fields, and right up to that final cataclysm before the Black Gates of Mordor.

Rohirrim

In the year 2510 of the Third Age of the Sun, a host of golden-haired horsemen came to the Battle of the Field of Celebrant to rescue the routed army of Gondor from the Balchoth and Orc hordes. These were the Éothéod whom the Men of Gondor later named the Rohirrim, the 'Horse-lords'. They were Northmen who inhabited the Vales of Anduin, and they were renowned as warriors and Horse-masters.

King Eorl the Young was most praised of their people, for he first tamed the Mearas, the noblest and fairest Horses of Middle-earth, which were said to be descended from Nahar, Oromë the Vala's steed. And, as is told in the 'Book of Kings', it was Eorl the Young who had brought his warriors to the Battle of the Field of Celebrant. At the desire of the Men of Gondor, Eorl made a kingdom in the province of Calenardhon, which was renamed Rohan and the Mark. And he was made the first of the kings of Rohan who for five centuries of the Third Age ruled the Mark.

Yet the Rohirrim were often called to war, to defend both Gondor and Rohan, for they were bordered by many enemies. The Rohirrim were constantly prepared for battle and always wore silver corselets and bright mail. They were armed with spears and with long swords that were set with green gems. Their hair was braided in long golden plaits, and they wore silver helmets with flowing horsetail manes. They carried green shields emblazoned with a golden Sun and green banners adorned with a white Horse. So armed, and mounted on steeds which were white and grey, the blue-eyed Rohirrim advanced against Easterlings, Dunlendings, Haradrim, Uruk-hai and Orcs.

On the rolling hills near the White Mountains were built the royal courts of Edoras in which was Meduseld, the feast hall of Rohan's kings, which was roofed with gold. The histories of the nine kings of the Mark are chronicled in the 'Annals of the Kings and Rulers'. After Eorl the Young, the king of the greatest fame was Helm Hammerhand, the last of the First Line of kings. For though in his time Rohan suffered disaster by Dunlending invasions, famine and the bitter cold that came in the Long Winter of the year 2759, this king's valour and strength were so great that his name alone brought terror to his enemies. For it is said Helm walked through blizzards of snow like a huge Troll in the night. He stalked his foes without weapons and slew them with the strength of his bare hands alone. And though he died before the Long Winter ended, the Dunlendings claimed his wraith remained in that place to haunt them and all enemies of the Rohirrim for many years thereafter.

The tale of the War of the Ring tells how Théoden, the last of the Second Line of kings, fell under the power of the Wizard Saruman. But with the aid of Gandalf, Théoden threw off that enchantment and led his warriors to victory at the Battles of Hornburg and of Pelennor Fields against the Dark Powers. And though he was an old man, it is told how he slew a king of Harad on the Pelennor Fields and was granted a warrior's death there also, for he in turn was slain by the terrible Witch-king of Morgul.

So the lordship of the Rohirrim passed to Théoden's sister's son, who was named Éomer. He was counted among the greatest kings of the Mark, for with the Men of Gondor he made firm the old alliance. After the War of the Ring he often rode out to subdue the peoples of the East and South, and the Rohirrim had victory and their children lived in peace in the Fourth Age of the Sun.

Yet in the War of the Ring there was one other of the Rohirrim who won the greatest fame. This was Éowyn, the fair sister of Éomer. For though she was slender and tall she was filled with strength and was wise in the use of weapons of war. As a warrior of Rohan she came to the Battle of Pelennor Fields, and over Théoden, the fallen king, she stood against the Witch-king of Morgul. She then achieved a deed that in four thousand years of terror the mightiest warriors of all Middle-earth could not, for it had been foretold that the Witch-king could not be slain by the hand of Man. So Éowyn revealed that she was not a Man but a shield-maiden, and with her sword she slew the Winged Beast that was the wraith's steed. Then with the aid of the Hobbit, Meriadoc Brandybuck, she slew the Witch-king himself.

S

Samwise Gamgee

Hobbit of the Shire. Samwise Gamgee was born in 2980 of the Third Age and became a gardener at Bag End. A faithful servant of first Bilbo, then Frodo Baggins, Sam travelled with the Ringbearer to Rivendell, where he became a member of the Fellowship of the Ring. Samwise was the only one to remain with the Ringbearer through the entire quest. On numerous occasions Sam saved Frodo's life in many perilous encounters. Most remarkable of all, was Sam's fight with Shelob the Giant Spider. Using the Phial of Galadriel and the Elf blade Sting, he blinded and mortally wounded the monster. He then helped his weakened master to enter Mordor and reach the fires of Mount Doom where the One Ring was finally destroyed. When Frodo sailed to the Undying Lands, Samwise inherited Bag End, and became a highly famous and respected figure in the Shire. He married Rose Cotton and sired thirteen children. He was elected Mayor of the Shire seven times. After the death of his wife in the eighty-second year of the Fourth Age, Samwise sailed to the Undying Lands to rejoin his friend and master, Frodo Baggins.

Saruman

Istari, Wizard of Isengard. Saruman the White was the head of the Istari, the Order of Wizards, who came to Middle-earth about the year 1000 in the Third Age of the Sun. In the Undying Lands he was Curumno, a Maia spirit of Aulë the Smith. When he first appeared he wore white robes, had raven hair and spoke with a voice both wise and fair. Called Curunír, meaning 'man of skill' by the Elves, he wandered Middle-earth seeking to overcome the Dark Lord. But after a time he grew proud and wished to have power for himself. In the year 2759, Saruman entered Isengard, and the tower of Orthanc, and summoned Orcs, Half-orcs, Uruk-hai and Dunlendings under a black banner marked with a white hand. He became ensnared in the Ring Lord's web and unwittingly became his servant. Yet, in the War of the Rings, Saruman's power was annihilated by a combination of the Ent's March on Isengard, and the Rohirrim in the Battle of Hornburg. Finally, his staff was broken and his sorcerous power was taken from him by Gandalf. So low did Saruman fall that in defeat he looked for petty vengeance in the Shire. There, in a pathetic last bid for dominion, Saruman was bested by the Hobbits, then slain by his own lowly servant, Gríma Wormtongue.

Sauron

Maia, Lord of the Rings. Once a Maia spirit of Aulë the Smith, Sauron, meaning 'the abhorred', became the chief lieutenant of Melkor, the Dark Lord. In the Ages of Darkness, while Melkor ruled in Utumno, and in the Ages of Stars while Melkor was chained by the Valar, Sauron ruled the evil realm of Angband. During the Wars of Beleriand, Sauron served his master until Melkor was cast into the Void, at the end of the First Age of the Sun. Sauron reappeared on Middle-earth during the fifth century of the Second Age as Annatar, 'giver of gifts'. In 1500 he seduced the Elven-smiths into forging the Rings of Power. Then he made himself Lord of the Rings by forging the One Ring. In the War of Sauron and the Elves, from 1693 to 1700, Sauron laid waste to Eregion and was only stopped from annihilating the Elves by the arrival of the Númenóreans. For the next 1500 years, Sauron built up the power of Mordor and brought the Men in the East and

ANNATAR 'Giver of gifts'.

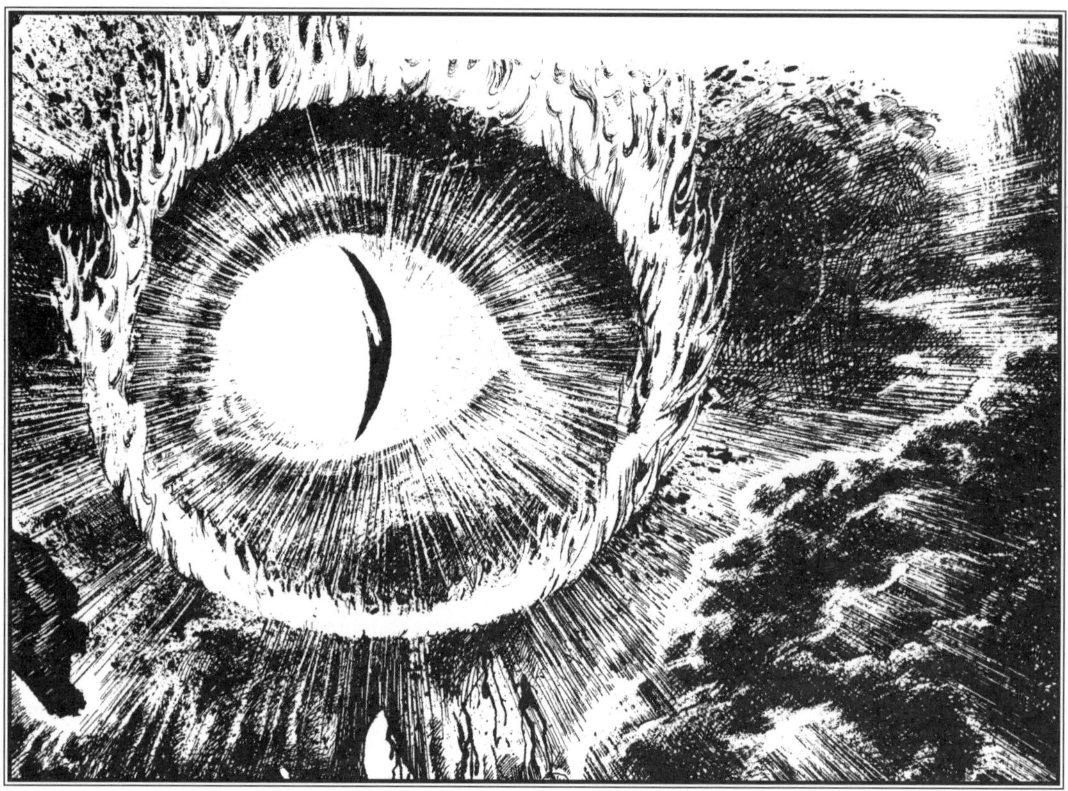

the South under his dominion. Finally, the Númenóreans came to make war on him in 3262, but so great was their power that Sauron surrendered to them. Unable to beat them militarily, he managed to corrupt them. In this he was so successful that he brought about the total destruction of Númenor. In that cataclysm, Sauron's fair form was destroyed. Yet his spirit fled to Mordor, and with the One Ring made himself into the Dark Lord – a fearsome warrior with black armour on burnt black skin, and terrible, raging eyes. However, even this form was destroyed at the end of the Second Age, after war with the Last Alliance of Elves and Men, when the One Ring was cut from his hand. Yet, because the One Ring had not been destroyed, Sauron's spirit was able to rise again. In the year 1000 of the Third Age, he manifested himself in the form of one great, lidless Eye. It was like the eye of a huge cat, but filled with hate, wreathed with flame and ringed in darkness. For nearly two thousand years, Sauron hid himself in Mirkwood and was known only as the Necromancer of Dol Guldur, while he sent Ringwraiths, Orcs and barbarian kings against the Dúnedain and their allies. In 2941, Sauron re-entered Mordor and began to rebuild the Dark Tower. Unfortunately for Sauron, this was the same year that the One Ring came into the possession of the Hobbit, Bilbo Baggins. Even less fortunately for Sauron, in the year 3018, just months before he launched the War of the Ring, Frodo Baggins undertook the Quest of

SAURON The evil Lord of the Rings who ruled from his Dark Tower in Mordor. By the Third Age Sauron was the very embodiment of evil and manifested his being in the form of a lidless Eye wreathed with flames.

the Ring, which resulted in the destruction of the One Ring in the fires of Mount Doom. Once more, and finally, Sauron was swept into the shadows. Never again did his spirit arise.

Scatha the Worm

Dragon of Grey Mountains. Scatha the Worm was a Dragon who in the second millennium of the Third Age of the Sun led his brood of Cold-drakes into the gold-rich kingdom of the Dwarves in the Grey Mountains. There they slaughtered the Dwarves and took their hoards of gold. In time, Prince Fram, son of Frumgar of the Éothéod entered the Grey Mountains, slew Scatha the worm and took his hoard.

Sea-elves

Of all the Elves, the Third Kindred, the Teleri, most loved the seas of Ulmo the Ocean Lord and lived longest on the shores of Belegaer, the Sea of the West. They were wisest in its lore and so were named the Sea-elves. They were the first people to build ships, for they were taught by Ossë, a Maia of the turbulent waves. His spouse was Uinen, Lady of the Calms, and together they taught the Sea-elves about the life in the sea: its fishes and its grottoes and gardens, and the wealth of its precious gem stones and pearls.

And so the Sea-elves sailed on the sea in the fairest ships, which were white and shaped like the great Swans of Ulmo that once drew them to the shores of Eldamar. And in the Undying Lands they sail and sing with voices like the rippling waves, for they know the language of the sea, a language which is subtle beyond the reckoning of the wisest of the races of Men.

Secondborn

Before the World was made, in that dimension before Time began, it had been foretold that Ilúvatar alone would call forth two great peoples out of the World to Be. The Firstborn of Ilúvatar was the immortal race of the Elves who arose with the Rekindling of the Stars. Those who were named the Secondborn, the mortal race of Men, came into being when Arien the Sun first shone on Middle-earth. In the Quenya tongue Secondborn translates as 'Atani' and in the Sindarin as 'Edain'; and these were the names by which the first Men to enter the lands of Beleriand were known.

Seregon

In ancient Beleriand was once a stony hill called Amon Rûdh, the 'bald hill', wherein were cut the caverns of the last of the Petty-dwarves. Upon that hill nothing would grow except the hardy Seregon plant. In Elvish its name means 'blood-stone', for when the plant blossoms with its dark red flower the stone summit appears to be covered in blood. This vision proved to be prophetic, for the outlaws of Túrin Turambar were slaughtered upon the summit, and the last of the Petty-dwarves put to death in the caverns below.

Shadow Host

In the War of the Ring there was a great battle before the ancient port of Pelargir when the ships of the Corsairs of Umbar were conquered by phantom warriors. These warriors were the Dead Men of Dunharrow, ghosts who through the long years of the Third Age had lingered on Earth because of a broken oath. To fulfil that oath and become released from limbo, this Shadow Host led by Aragorn, son of Arathorn, came to battle against the Corsairs, enemy of the Dúnedain. Once victory was assured the Shadow Host vanished from Earth for ever.

Shadowfax

Meara, Horse of Rohan. Greatest of the Mearas 'horse-princes' of Rohan at the time of the War of the Rings, Shadowfax was tamed and ridden without bridle or saddle by Gandalf the Wizard. Called Shadowfax because of his silver-grey coat, he was the only horse who could outrun the phantom black Horses and Winged Beasts of the Ringwraiths. He carried Gandalf the White to the defence of the Tower of Gondor and into the last battle before the Black Gates of Mordor.

Shadowy Mountains

In the histories of Middle-earth there are two mountain ranges which are called the Shadowy Mountains. One was in the north-west of Beleriand in the First Age and by the Elves was called the Ered Wethrin, the 'mountains of shadow'. They formed a natural defensive border around the Noldor kingdoms of Hithlum. The second Shadowy Mountain range was so-named in the Second Age and formed the thousand-mile border of western and southern Mordor. Known by the Elves as Ephel Dúath, the 'fence of dark shadow', they formed two sides of the great horseshoe of mountains that were Mordor's primary defence. The Shadowy Mountains of Mordor appear to have been virtually unclimbable and had only two known passes, Cirith-Gorgor and Cirith Ungol.

Shagrat

Uruk-hai of Cirith Ungol. During the War of the Ring, Shagrat was the Captain of the Orcs of the Tower of the Spider's Pass.

His Orc band became involved in a brief, bloody battle with a Morgul Orc band, over possession of Frodo Baggins's mithril mail coat. Although grievously wounded, Shagrat managed to keep the mail coat and take it to his master, Sauron the Ring Lord.

Shelob

Spider of Cirith Ungol. Shelob was the largest and nastiest of the Great Spiders to survive the destruction of Beleriand. Through the Second and Third Ages, Shelob the Great and her lesser offspring lived in the Mountains of Mordor and forests of Mirkwood. By the end of the Third Age, her offspring had taken over large parts of Mirkwood, while Shelob largely kept to her den in Cirith Ungol, where she fed on anyone of any race who attempted to enter Mordor via that pass through the mountains. In the year 3000 she captured Gollum, but released him so he might bring her more victims. In 3019 Gollum brought Frodo Baggins and Samwise Gamgee to her lair. Shelob paralysed Frodo the Ringbearer, and would have consumed him but for Samwise who first blinded Shelob with the light of the Phial of Galadriel, then severely wounded her with an Elf blade. She appears to have crept away to die in her lair.

Shire

The green and pleasant land of the Shire in Eriador – just west of the Brandywine River and east of the Far Downs – had been the homeland of the Halfling people called the Hobbits since the seventeenth century of the Third Age of the Sun. Once a part of the kingdom of Arnor that through centuries of war had become deserted, the Shire was given over to the Hobbits in 1601 by decree of the Dúnedain king Argeleb II of Arthedain.

The Shire itself was divided into four primary areas, called the Four Farthings; later, in 2340, the Hobbit family called the Oldbucks crossed the Brandywine River and settled in what became called Buckland. In the Fourth Age, Buckland, along with the lands of Westmarch from the Far Downs to the Tower

SHADOWFAX He was the only horse who could outrun the phantom black Horses and Winged Beasts of the Ringwraiths.

2018

Hills, was officially added to the Free Lands of the Shire. The humble ways of the Hobbits were well suited to those fertile lands and through their modest farms and honest labour they prospered. The Shire villages and towns of huts and Hobbit holes grew: Hobbiton, Tuckborough, Michel Delving, Oatbarton, Frogmorton and a dozen others. It appears that aside from a few natural disasters and a single Orc raid in 2747, the Shire was an extraordinarily peaceful land, largely unaware of the world about it. It managed to escape most of the conflicts of the Third Age until the time of the War of the Ring, when this sleepy land was suddenly caught up in events. For here lived Bilbo Baggins, who joined the Quest of the Lonely Mountain, and on that adventure acquired a magic Ring. This chance discovery drew Bilbo, his heir Frodo Baggins and all the Hobbits of the Shire into the greatest drama of that age. So it was that the Hobbits, the meekest and least of all the peoples of Middle-earth, came to hold the fate of all the World in their hands.

Silvan Elves

Those Elves who undertook the Great Journey were the Teleri. Of this kindred were those called the Nandor, 'those who turn back', who stopped their westward march at the Anduin River and went no further. Of these Nandor, there were some who settled in Greenwood and Lothlórien. These were named Silvan Elves, for most of them lived in forests: they were a tribal people who built no cities and had no kings.

In the years that followed the First Age of the Sun, however, the numbers and lands of these Noldorin and Sindarin Elves had dwindled and to swell their kingdoms these High Elves took Silvan Elves as their subjects. In this way

the Silvan Elves learned much of the High Elven language and culture, and many of the skills that had come from the Undying Lands. For a time the Silvan Elves grew strong and prosperous under these lords. The greatest power and beauty were to be found in the Silvan Elves whom Celeborn and Galadriel ruled in the Golden Wood of Lothlórien. For Celeborn, kinsman of Thingol, was counted among the greatest lords of the Sindar, and Galadriel was the daughter of the High King of the Noldor, who had stayed in the Undying Lands; thus, she was noblest of the Elves who stayed in Middle-earth. The power of Celeborn and Galadriel over the Golden Wood held evil powers at bay, and the Silvan Elves remained prosperous through the troubles of the Third Age though thrice attacked. These Elves were the Galadhrim, 'tree-people', and not until Queen Galadriel finally went to the Undying Lands did the light and glory of the Golden Wood fade.

It is told in the Elvish writings how in Greenwood the Great (which was later named Mirkwood) through the Second, Third and Fourth Ages of the Sun there was the Woodland Kingdom of the Sindar Lord Thranduil. The concealed city of the Silvan Elves of Thranduil was beautiful and magical, for it was the diminished image of the ancient Sindar realm of Menegroth – once the fairest city of Middle-earth. But a part of its beauty had lived on and withstood the dark invasions of the Third Age, even the Battle under the Trees during the War of the Ring. It is told that in the Fourth Age, the son of the king took part of the Silvan Elves of this realm to the woodlands of Ithilien in Gondor. This prince was named Legolas and he became lord of the Elves in Ithilien. For a time these people also prospered, for this was the Elf who had won fame in the War of the Ring and who with his great friend Gimli the Dwarf had fought in the battles of the Hornburg, Pelargir and Pelennor Fields. Indeed, as one of the Fellowship of the Ring, his bright Elvish eyes, his forester's knowledge and his keen archery were much needed in the Quest. And though Legolas ruled his new realm for many years in the Fourth Age, after a time, with Gimli, he took an Elven-ship to the Undying Lands.

Simbelmynë

Near Edoras, the Golden Hall of the kings of the Mark, lay the great barrow graves of the kings who for the last five hundred years of the Third Age of the Sun had ruled Rohan. By the end of the Third Age the graves were laid in two rows: one of nine for those of the First Line; the other of eight for those of the Second Line. On these graves, like glittering snow, grew the white flowers called Simbelmynë, which in common speech of Men is 'Evermind' and by the Elves was known as Uilos. They blossomed in all seasons, like the bright eyes of Elves, glinting always with starlight.

Simbelmynë grew whitest and thickest on the grave of Helm Hammerhand, the ninth king of the First Line, who during the Siege of the Hornburg went alone among his foes, the Dunlendings. And Simbelmynë reminds these foes of him who was the fiercest king of the Mark. Through the famine of the Fell Winter Helm Hammerhand had sounded his mighty horn and like a snow-troll hunted his foes and slew them. And though he perished at that time, his wraith was said still to walk the land and his horn could be heard in the Helm's Deep.

SHIRE The Shire was given over to the Hobbits in 1601 by decree of the Dúnedain king Argeleb II of Arthedain.

Sindar

How the Grey-elves, who are called the Sindar, came to be a separate race, is told in the tale of the Journey of the Elves. In the beginning they were of the Third Kindred, the Teleri, and their king was the High King of all Teleri. In those first years he was named Elwë Singollo and he was the tallest of Elves. His hair was silver and he alone of the Teleri (with the Noldor Lord Finwë and the Vanyar Lord Ingwë) was taken by Oromë, the Horseman of the Valar, to the Undying Lands to experience the Light of the Trees of the Valar. When Elwë Singollo was brought back to his people to tell them what awaited the Elves in the Undying Lands no one was more eager to reach the Light than he. The Teleri were largest of the hosts that went to the West but because they were so numerous they were always farthest behind on the long road. Many of the Teleri were lost on that Journey, but Elwë always urged them on, until they came at last to Beleriand beyond the Blue Mountains. In Beleriand for a time they made a camp near the River Gelion in a wood. In this place, according to Elven-lore, Elwë Singollo entered the Wood of Nan Elmoth and fell under a timeless spell. His people searched for him, but as years passed many gave up hope and gave the kingship to Olwë, his brother, and they resumed their Journey to the West. But many others would have no other king and would not leave that place. So these people remained in Beleriand and called themselves the Eglath, the 'forsaken', and thereafter they were divided from the Teleri kindred. In time, the Eglath had their reward, for Elwë Singollo returned from the Wood of Nan Elmoth but the great change that had occurred in him amazed his people. With him came the source of his enchantment, Melian the Maia, Elwë's queen and wife. The light of her face was brilliant and lovely, and the Eglath worshipped her and wept in joy at the return of their king.

The king was changed in other ways, for he wished no longer to go to the West but to stay in the Forest of Beleriand and draw about him his people and make a kingdom there. The light on the face of Melian was to him more fair than that of the Trees. So a new kingdom was made; its people were no longer called the Eglath but the Sindar, the 'Grey-elves', and the Elves of the Twilight.

In the Ages of Stars the Sindar became the greatest of the Elvish people in Mortal Lands and all the lands of Beleriand belonged to them. They found a remnant of the Teleri, called the Falathrim, living by the sea and these people, under their lord Círdan, welcomed the returned king and swore allegiance to him. So it was too with a remnant of the Nandor who had come to Beleriand (and were later named the Green-elves and Laiquendi); these people also accepted Elwë as their king. In time, a new Elvish tongue arose among the Sindar and in that Sindarin language their king was no longer Elwë Singollo, but Elu Thingol, 'King Greymantle'.

In the Ages of Starlight, it is told, a strange people who called themselves Khazâd came out of the Blue Mountains; the Elves called them Naugrim, or the 'stunted people'. They were Dwarves, who came in peace to trade with the Elves of Beleriand. There was great prosperity between the two peoples and they learned many crafts from each other. With the help of the Dwarves the greatest Elven city of Middle-earth was built, called Menegroth, the 'thousand caves'. Though it was a city within a mountain, it was described as a beech forest in which gold lanterns shone, birds sang, beasts wandered and silver fountains ran. It was always light there and throughout the forests around Menegroth, for this Sindarin kingdom was all-powerful, being ruled by a combination of Elf and Maia. From the union of Elu Thingol and Melian came forth a daughter who was called Lúthien, and the tales say she was the fairest creature ever to enter the World.

But the Ages of peace beneath the Stars drew to an end; war broke out in Valinor and the Trees of Valar were destroyed. Melian, however, was a wise queen, gifted with fore-knowledge, and she chose to take the Sindar away from the evil that was to befall the land about them. She cast a powerful spell and wove an enchantment in the Great Forest of Doriath around Menegroth, so that the Sindarin realm became a hidden kingdom. This enchantment was stronger than any citadel's high walls and was named the Girdle of Melian, and no evil could break that spell from without, and all evil was lost before it could enter.

So, though the Noldor, pursuing Morgoth, came out of the Undying Lands and, in Beleriand, the War of the Jewels raged, for the most part the Sindar were not at risk. Nor did they choose to deal with or aid these Kinslayers, for they had heard of the Noldorin deeds in the Undying Lands and how the Noldor had slain their kindred and stolen the ships of the Teleri of Alqualondë.

But as is told in the tale of Lúthien and Beren, great evil came in unexpected ways from within the kingdom. For of the race of Men, one named Beren came to Thingol and asked for the hand of Lúthien. Thingol looked on mortals with disdain and was tempted to put him to death, but rather than slay him he set Beren an impossible task. As a bride-price Beren was to cut a Silmaril from Morgoth's Iron Crown and bring it to Thingol. This was the Quest of the Silmaril, which brought so much evil to the Sindar. This Quest drew the Sindar into the Doom of the Noldor and the curse that lay on the Silmarils.

In a deed beyond belief, Beren, with the help of Lúthien and the Wolfhound Huan, completed his task, but he incurred not only the wrath of Morgoth but also that of the Dwarves and the Noldor. For, desiring the Silmaril, the Dwarf workmen who lived within the Hidden Realm and who had laboured for Thingol, now murdered him and stole the jewel. But they could not escape and were themselves killed. On the death of Thingol, Melian veiled her power and, weeping, left Middle-earth for ever. In that moment the ring of enchantment fell from the Hidden Realm in Doriath.

Now that a barrier no longer guarded it, the Dwarves of Belegost, and the Noldor sons of Fëanor came to the citadel of Menegroth and laid it waste. So the great kingdom was gone for ever, though a few of its lords survived.

In the Second Age of the Sun some of these Sindar lords, with many of the Noldor, took ships to Tol Eressëa and built the city and haven of Avallónë. But there were other Sindar lords who remained in the remnant of Beleriand called Lindon. As the years passed some sons of the Sindar lords left Lindon for the lands beyond the Misty Mountains, where they made new kingdoms among the Silvan Elves. Two of the most famous were Thranduil, who went to Greenwood the Great and there made the Woodland Realm, and Celeborn, the kinsman of Thingol, who with the Noldor princess Galadriel made the kingdom of Lothlórien, the Golden Wood. Then too some Sindar lords settled in Rivendell with Elrond and in the Grey Havens with Círdan the Shipwright. In the War of the Ring the most famous Elf was Legolas, the son of Thranduil. Legolas was one of the nine heroes of the Fellowship of the Ring and after the War of the Ring he founded one last woodland Elf-colony in the fair forests of Ithilien in Gondor.

Finally, in the Fourth Age of the Sun, all the Eldar powers were fading from the World, and with the other Elves the last of the Sindar sailed from the Grey Havens to the Undying Lands.

Sirion River

The most important river system in Beleriand was that of the Sirion, whose delta emptied into the Bay of Balar. The Sirion and its many tributaries drained all of central Beleriand south of the Mountains of Shadow and the Mountains of Terror. Its major tributaries were the Narog and Ginglith in the realm of Nargothrond and the Aros, Celon, Esgalduin, Mindeb, Teiglin and Maduin in Doriath. In its northernmost reaches was the important fortified island of Tol Sirion which guarded the Sirion Pass. A stone bridge crossed its tributary, the Esgalduin in central Doriath, and entered the Thousand Caves of Menegroth, that wonderful hidden city of the Grey Elves, while the canyon and caverns of the Narog tributary was where the Noldor Elves of Finrod built their city of Nargothrond. The Sirion is believed to have come into being in the confusion and conflict of the War of Powers at the end of the First Age of Stars, when the Valar destroyed Utumno. It was obliterated at the end of the First Age of the Sun and the War of Wrath when the Valar and Eldar destroyed the Angband and all of Beleriand sank into the sea.

Skinbark

Ent of Fangorn Forest. Skinbark was one of the three oldest surviving Ents, or 'Tree-herds', surviving at the time of the War of the Rings. Skinbark was called Fladrif by the Elves and most resembled a birch tree in appearance. At the time of Saruman's rise to power, Skinbark lived just west of Isengard, where he was attacked and wounded by Orcs. He fled to the highest hills of the Fangorn Forest and remained there, refusing to come down even during the March of the Ents on Isengard.

Smaug the Golden

Dragon of Erebor. Smaug was the greatest Dragon of the Third Age. A huge golden-red Fire-drake, Smaug had vast bat-like wings and a coat of impenetrable iron scales. His one vulnerable part, his belly, was protected by a waistcoat of gemstones which became embedded there from centuries of laying on jewelled treasure hoards. Although his beginnings are obscure, he is known to have lived in the Grey Mountains before he came, in the year 2770, to Erebor. There he burned and sacked Dale before he entered the Kingdom under the Mountain, where he slaughtered or drove out the Dwarves. For two centuries he contentedly lay on his hoard within Erebor. Then in 2941, his slumbers were disturbed by the theft of a part of his treasure from Thorin and Company. In a rage, he attacked the Lake Men of Esgaroth and was killed by a shot with a black arrow from Bard the Bowman which pierced the one spot on his belly not covered by his gemstone armour.

Snaga

Among those evil beings that in the histories of Middle-earth are named Orcs, there were many breeds, each it seemed being made to suit some particular evil. The most common breed was that which in Black Speech was called Snaga, meaning 'slaves'. Orcs, being creatures filled with hatred, were also self-contemptuous, for they were indeed a race of slaves and were thralls to the Dark Powers who directed them. Snaga also appears to have been the name of one particular Orc of Cirith Ungol. This Orc was one of the Orc guardsmen of the Tower of the Spider Pass who fought under the Uruk captain, Shagrat, against the Morgul Orcs for possession of Frodo Baggins' mithril mail coat. He survived that battle, only to die by breaking his neck during a struggle with Samwise Gamgee.

Snowmane

Meara, Horse of Rohan. During the War of the Ring, Snowmane was the mount of King Théoden, King of Rohan. He carried his master into the Battle of Hornburg. At the Battle of Pelennor Fields, both were slain by the Witch-king.

Snowmen

In the northern land of Forochel, in the Third Age of the Sun, there lived a primitive people who were descendants of the ancient Forodwaith. In Sindarin these were the Lossoth, but in the common western tongue they were called the Snowmen of Forochel. They were not a strong people and they chose to live on the shore of a great icy bay so that they might be beyond the reach of the more war-like folk of the South. They were a wary people, but wise in the ways of ice and snow and able to withstand the harshness of the wastes. They hunted where other folk could find no game; they built warm homes of snow where others would perish of terrible cold; and they travelled swiftly over ice with skates of bone and sledges where others would flounder and make no passage at all. Indeed, they were undisputed masters of this frozen land of their choice.

SMAUG THE GOLDEN The great golden-red, winged, fire-breathing Dragon of Erebor. In 2941 of the Third Age, Smaug was disturbed by Thorin and Company, and slain by the hero Bard The Bowman.

Southrons

A part of the histories of the Westlands is given to the fierce people who, in the Second and Third Ages of the Sun, came from the hot deserts and forests of the Sunlands, which lay in the South of Middle-earth. These people were ruled by many kings and lords, until in time Sauron the Maia corrupted them and called them to war. The Dúnedain named them Southrons, though more often they were called the Haradrim.

The Southrons were brown- and black-skinned Men who came forth fiercely in war, ornamented with much gold. Their banner was a black serpent on a scarlet ground. Their armour was of bronze, their robes crimson, and they carried spears and scimitars. They came on foot, in the ships on the sea, on Horses and even on the backs of the mighty war beasts that are named Mûmakil.

Speakers

The Elves were conceived in the Music of the Ainur and were the first race to give voice to the music and make song. They were also the first to use speech in Arda, and it is said that their speech was as bright and subtle as starlight on running water. For their language was not just the first but also the fairest tongue that ever was conceived. The Elves therefore called themselves the Speakers, which in that first Elven tongue was the 'Quendi'. All living beings who could learn such skills were taught the arts of language from these first Elves.

Spiders

Among the foulest beings that ever inhabited Arda were the Giant Spiders. They were dark and filled with envy, greed and the poison of malice. Greatest of the giant beings that took Spider form was Ungoliant, a mighty and evil spirit that entered the World before the Trees of Valar were made. In the waste land of Avathar, between the Pelóri Mountains and the dull cold sea of the South, Ungoliant lived alone for a long while. She was dreadful and vile, and possessed of a web of darkness, called the Unlight of Ungoliant, that even the eyes of Manwë could not penetrate.

The Great Spider Ungoliant was the most infamous creature, for she came with Melkor to Valinor and destroyed the Trees of the Valar. And, as she devoured the Light of the Trees, Ungoliant tried to take even Melkor as her prey. Had not the demons of fire called Balrogs come and lashed her with their whips of flame, she might have devoured the Lord of Darkness himself.

But come the Balrogs did, and they drove Ungoliant from the North. And so this heart of darkness came into Beleriand and she entered that place called Nan Dungortheb, the 'valley of dreadful death', where other monsters of her race lived. Though not so vast nor so powerful as Ungoliant, these Spiders were none the less immensely strong, for Melkor had bred them long ago among the evil monsters that came forth before the Light of the Trees was made. Ungoliant now bred with them, and few Elves or Men ever dared to enter that valley.

Yet perhaps Ungoliant was too vast an evil for the World to hold. In time she travelled beyond Beleriand to the south lands, pursuing whatever she could consume, for her gluttony was a fearful thing, and it is said that in her ravening hunger she finally consumed herself in the deserts of the South. In Nan Dungortheb her many daughters lived all the years of the First Age of the Sun, but, when the land was broken in the War of Wrath, it is said few could save themselves from the rushing waters.

But, among the few, one great daughter called Shelob and some of the lesser Spiders crossed the Blue Mountains and found shelter in the Shadowy Mountains, which walled the realm of Mordor. In the mountain passes of this evil place the Spiders grew strong again, and in the Third Age of the Sun they came into the forest of Greenwood the Great. This they made evil with the ambush of their webs and so Greenwood went dark and was re-named Mirkwood. Though the Spiders of Mirkwood were but small forms compared to their great ancestors, they were large in number and wise in their evil craft of entrapment. They spoke both Black Speech and the common tongue of Men, but in the Orkish fashion, full of evil words and slurring rage.

After the First Age of the Sun only Shelob the Great approached the majesty of Ungoliant; she inhabited the place called Cirith Ungol, the 'Spider's Pass', in the Shadowy Mountains. For two Ages she lived in this pass, and though many a Dúnedain and Elvish warrior came to her realm, none could stand before her; she devoured them all. Like her great mother she spun black webs and vomited darkness from her belly. She was armed with venom from her great beak and horns, and she had a long claw of iron on each of her many gnarled and jointed legs. Her bloated body was black and thick-skinned. There was no vulnerable place on the beast except the great, globed cluster of her eyes. Her vast form was black and stained, with hair-like spikes of steel and an underbelly paled with streaks of green slime and luminous with her septic poisons. Vast and strong as she was, Shelob's long life ended before the Third Age was gone. She met her end at the unexpected hand of the Hobbit, Samwise Gamgee, the least of all her challengers. For the Hobbit put out one of Shelob's great eyes, and by her own act Shelob impaled herself upon his Elven-blade. Before the end of the Third Age, the greater part of the Great Spiders had also disappeared from the World, for after the mortal wounding of Shelob, Mordor and

Dol Guldur were destroyed and the Spiders of the Shadowy Mountains and even the Spiders infesting the gloomy Mirkwood perished.

SHELOB The giant spider who guarded the pass of Cirith Ungol. Shelob's reign of terror ended in the year 3019 of the Third Age when she was mortally wounded by the most unlikely hero, Samwise Gamgee, the Hobbit.

Stoors

Along of the three Hobbit strains, those named Stoors knew the arts of boating, fishing and swimming. They were lovers of flat river lands and were most friendly with Men. The Harfoots thought the Stoors a queer folk. Last of the Hobbits to settle in the Shire, the Stoors had attained a Mannish appearance in the eyes of the Harfoots, for they were heavier and broader than the other strains, and, unlike other Hobbits, they were able to grow beards.

Swans

It is told in the tale of the Great Journey of the Elves how the Teleri were brought at last to Eldamar by the Swans of Ulmo after long exile on Tol Eressëa, the Lonely Isle.

Ossë the Maia had come to the Teleri and taught them how to build a great fleet that could carry all their Kindred. Once the ships were made the Swans of Ulmo, Lord of the Waters, came out of the West. These brilliant creatures were foam white and they circled in great broken rings round the ships of the Elves. The feathered glory of these birds was nearly equal to the size and strength of the Eagles of Manwë. By many long ropes, the Swans drew the great fleet of Elven-ships to Eldamar. Then, vast and stately, as if unaware of their mission and hearing some wild call, they departed. But before those indifferent beaks let drop the towing lines, that white rush engendered in the hearts of Elves a knowledge of the winds that play on the seas and a mastery of their white ships that sail on them. It is said that when these Elves listen to the sea on the Shore they hear those great wings beating still.

After that time the Teleri were named Sea-elves, because of the wisdom that they gained from the great Swans. In that place to which the Swans of Ulmo had brought them, the Teleri made a city named Alqualondë, the 'haven of Swans'. There they made the finest ships of Arda, even more cunningly fashioned than those first ones, and they built them in the forms of the Swans of Ulmo with vast, white wings and beaks of jet and gold.

Swarthy Men

In the First Age of the Sun those Men who came after the Edain to Beleriand were named Easterlings. However, some called them Swarthy Men, for they were shorter, broader and darker of hair and eye than the Edain. Mostly there were a less worthy people, and they betrayed the Elves to their enemies.

But, in the Third Age, Swarthy Men was a name given to the tall, brown-skinned Haradrim, who many times made war on the Men of Gondor. They were fierce Men dressed in crimson and gold. On foot, on Horse and on the mighty Mûmakil they went into battle with scimitar, bow and spear.

Swertings

In the last centuries of the Third Age of the Sun, rumours and tales reached the peaceful lands of the Shire about the wars between the men of Gondor and the fierce warrior people far to the south who were named the Haradrim. In the dialect of the Shire the Haradrim people were called Swertings.

STOOR The Harfoots thought the Stoors a queer folk.

T

Taniquelassë

Among the many beautiful, fragrant evergreen trees that the Elves of Tol Eressëa brought as a gift and a blessing to Númenor was one called Taniquelassë. The flower, the leaf and the bark were much prized by the Númenóreans for their sweet scent. Its name suggests that the tree had its origins on the slopes of Taniquetil, the Sacred Mountain of Manwë and the highest mountain in the Undying Lands.

Taniquetil

The highest mountain in Arda was Taniquetil in the eastern Pelóri Mountains in the Undying Lands. Taniquetil means 'high white peak' and upon its summit was built Ilmarin, the mansions of the king and queen of the Valar, Manwë and Varda. From his throne on Taniquetil's summit, Manwë could see over all the lands of Arda. The Vanyar Fair Elves live on its slopes and call it Oiolossë, meaning 'snow everwhite' because it is always covered in snow. The Olympus of Arda it is also known by many other names: the White Mountain, Mount Everwhite, Amon Uilos and the Holy Mountain.

Tareldar

Those of the Elven people who heeded the summons of the Valar, departed to the West and looked on the Blessed Realm in the days of the Light of the Trees, were in the Quenya tongue called Tareldar or High Elves. They were a great people who thrived and built Elven cities and kingdoms the like of which had never been seen in Middle-earth, and never will be again, for the Tareldar were clear-sighted and keen-eyed beyond imagining. To compare them to the Moriquendi would be to compare diamonds to coal.

Tarks

In the Westron dialect there were many words taken from Elvish that were twisted in Orkish use. One of these was the Quenya word 'tarkil', meaning the Dúnedain. In the Orc usage this became Tark, a word of contempt for the Gondor Men.

Tasarion

Among the most ancient of trees were those that the first Elves called the Tasarion. With many other kinds of tree they had come into the World in the Ages of the Lamps at the wish of Yavanna, Queen of the Earth. The Tasarion were strong, long-lived trees that loved to grow most of all by ruins, lakes, marshes and streams. In the Ages of Starlight the greatest forest of these trees on Middle-earth was in the Nan-tasarion, the 'valley of the Tasarion', in Beleriand. And though this forest was destroyed when Beleriand sank beneath the sea, the species of Tasarion survived all the changes of the World, and even the great invasions by the race of Men. For the Tasarion are the trees Men now call the Willow.

Telcontari

At the end of the War of the Rings a new line of kings was established to rule over the realms of Arnor and Gondor. The first of this line was Aragorn, son of Arathorn, who became King Elessar of the Reunited Kingdom. He chose Telcontar as the name of his House, for this was the Quenya form of Strider, the name by which he went in his years of exile. His descendants and successors preserved the name of the House that Aragorn had founded, calling themselves the Telcontari.

Teleri

There were three Kindred of Elves who in the years of Stars undertook the Great Journey from the East of Middle-earth to the Undying Lands. The first two were named the Vanyar and the Noldor, and they were the first of the Elvenhost to reach the Undying Lands beyond the Great Sea. The people of the Third Kindred were the Teleri; their destiny differed from the first two Kindred, for they were the largest in number of the Elven people and so their passage was slowest across the lands of Middle-earth. In the course of the Great Journey the Teleri became a scattered and divided people.

At the Marchlands of the West of Middle-earth the Teleri tarried and stood back in fear of crossing the Great River Anduin and the Misty Mountains. Some Elves broke away and went South into the Vales of Anduin, where they lived for many centuries. These people were named the Nandor, and they took one called Lenwë as their lord.

But the main host of the Teleri continued westwards, over the Misty Mountains and the Blue Mountains, to the land that was later named Beleriand. It was then that the greatest division of the Teleri occurred. They were all encamped in a great forest beyond the River Gelion, when they lost their king, Elwë Singollo, who alone among them had seen the Trees of the Valar in the Undying Lands. Elwë walked into the Forest of Nan Elmoth and there, enchanted, fell under a spell of love for Melian the Maia. In that spell he was held, though years passed and his people searched for him. A part who called themselves the Eglath, the 'forsaken', would go no further without him. They remained faithful to him until, at last, he returned with Melian his bride. The Eglath were renamed the Sindar, the 'Grey-elves', and under this union of Elf and Maia they built the most powerful kingdom of Elves on Middle-earth in the years of Starlight.

But long before King Elwë returned, the larger part of the Teleri had taken his brother Olwë as king and had gone west again to the Great Sea. There they awaited some sign from the Valar that would bring them to the Undying Lands. The Teleri waited a long time on the shores of Middle-earth and grew to love the sea under the Stars. While on the shores they sang songs sad and brave. Of all Elves they were the loveliest of singers, and loved the sea the most. By some they were called the Lindar, the 'singers', and by others the Falmari, the Sea-elves. Hearing the Elven songs, Ossë, the Maia of the waves, came to them and sang to the Teleri of the waves and the sea. They learned much from Ossë of the ways of the sea and their love for the sight and sounds of those turbulent shores of Middle-earth increased.

So it was that, when Ulmo the Ocean Lord came to the Teleri with that rootless island that was his ship, once again some of the kindred forsook the Journey. These were named Falathrim, the 'Elves of the Falas', who, for the love of the shores of Middle-earth, remained. They chose Círdan as their lord, and they settled in the havens of Brithombar and Eglarest. In later years they were the first shipbuilders of Middle-earth.

The greatest part of the Teleri went West with Ulmo, though Ossë pursued them and sang to them and would not let them forget the blessings of the seas. Ulmo, seeing how they so loved the waves, was loath to take them beyond the reach of the sea. So when he came within sight of the Undying Lands he did not take them ashore but anchored the island in the Bay of Eldamar, within sight of the Light and the land of their kindred, though it was beyond their reach. Once again the Journey of the Teleri was stayed, and for an Age they again lived apart from their kindred. Their language changed with their stay on Tol Eressëa, the 'lonely isle'; the sounds of the sea were always on their tongue, and their language was no longer that of the Vanyar and Noldor.

The Valar were, however, displeased with their brother Ulmo, for they wished to bring the Third Kindred to the actual shore of their realm. At their bidding Ulmo relented and he sent Ossë to them once more. Reluctantly, Ossë taught them the art of building ships and, when the ships were built, Ulmo sent to them vast winged Swans, which drew the Teleri finally to Eldamar.

The Teleri were grateful to reach their Journey's end at last and great indeed was the welcome they were given. The Noldor and Vanyar came from the city Tirion upon Túna with many gifts of gemstones and gold. And in time the Teleri came to know the Light of the Trees and the wisdom of the Valarian people.

Under their king Olwë, they built beautiful mansions of pearl, and ships like the Swans of Ulmo, with eyes and beaks of jet and gold. They named their city Alqualondë, which is the 'haven of Swans'. Remaining close to the waves they had learned to love, they walked the shores or sailed on the Bay of Eldamar. The Teleri were a happy people and so they remain; their ships constantly sail out through the arching sea-carved stone gate of their haven and city. They know little of war and strife; their concerns are with the sea, with ships and with singing. These are their chief joys.

War came to them twice, and each time it was unlooked for and unexpected. The first time, according to the 'Aldudénië' – the tale of the Darkening of Valinor – Fëanor, lord of the Noldor, came to the Teleri of Alqualondë, desiring their ships to go to Middle-earth so that he could avenge his father's death and regain the Silmarils from Morgoth. King Olwë denied him his wish, however, and so the fierce Noldor slew many of the Teleri and took their ships. This was the first slaying of Elf by Elf known in Arda. It has always been counted a great evil and has been held against the sons of Fëanor ever since.

Only once more did the Teleri of Alqualondë in any way test themselves in war. This was the War of Wrath when the Valar, the Maiar and the Eldar went to the Great Battle at the end of the First Age of the Sun and defeated the rebel Vala, Melkor, whom the Elves named Morgoth. But even then the Teleri did not fight but only used their ships to carry the Vanyar and Noldor warriors from the Undying Lands across the western sea to Middle-earth. Though they would help the Noldor, they would not die on their behalf on the battle-field for they well remembered the First Kinslaying on the Soil of Eldamar.

The 'Akallabêth' tells that, when Númenor tore open the belly of the World with its Downfall, the Spheres of mortal and immortal lands fell apart. Thereafter, only the ships of the Teleri could ever cross the gap between the Spheres. The fair, white Swan ships of the Teleri are a wonder and a miracle and the mortal World has never since seen their like, though they still sail in the Bay of Eldamar and will do so until the Unmaking of Eä.

Thangorodrim

The huge volcanic mountain that Morgoth raised above his mighty armoury and fortress of Angband after he and Ungoliant destroyed the Trees of the Valar and stole the Silmarils was called Thangorodrim. This terrible, three-peaked mountain of slag and volcanic rock constantly belched out poisonous smoke and fumes. Its name means 'mountains of oppression' and deep within its bowels, Morgoth devised and gathered many monsters and evil beings. However, Thangorodrim did not survive the First Age of the Sun, for in the Great Battle during the War of Wrath, when Ancalagon the Black, the mightiest of the Winged Dragons was slain, he fell from the sky and broke open Thangorodrim.

THÉODEN Théoden won a warrior's death by daring to stand against the Witch-king of Angmar.

Théoden

Northman, king of Rohan. Born in 2948 of the Third Age, Théoden, son of Thengel, became the seventeenth king of Rohan in 2980. In the beginning he was a good and strong king, but near the end of his reign he fell under the influence of Gríma Wormtongue, who secretly was a servant of the evil Wizard Saruman. However, in 3019, Gandalf healed him from the evil spells of Saruman. Théoden mounted his steed, Snowmane, and led the Horsemen of Rohan onto the battlegrounds of Hornburg and Pelennor Fields. Upon Pelennor, after overthrowing the Haradrim, Théoden won a warrior's death by daring to stand against the Witch-king of Angmar.

Thingol

Elven king of Doriath. Born by the Waters of Awakening at the beginning of the Ages of the Stars, Elwë Singollo – who later became King Thingol – was the High King of the Teleri Elves. He was the tallest of the Elves and had silver hair, and led his people on the Great Journey. This he did as far as Beleriand, where he met Melian the Maia and fell into a trance of love for many years. By the time he reappeared, most of the Teleri had taken his brother, Olwë, as their new king and completed the journey. Those who remained behind became the Sindar or Grey-elves. With their transformed King Thingol, meaning 'King Grey-mantle', and their Queen Melian the Maia, they built the forest kingdom of Doriath and the mansions of Menegroth. Thingol ruled a peaceful kingdom through all the Ages of the Stars, and Melian gave birth to the incomparable Princess Lúthien. Even during the war-torn First Age of the Sun, Doriath appeared to be safe because a spell called the Girdle of Melian protected it. However, in the fifth century, Thingol's daughter met and fell in love with the mortal hero, Beren. Not wishing to lose his daughter to a mortal, Thingol sent Beren on the Quest of the Silmaril. The lovers managed to steal a

jewel from Morgoth's crown. However, when Thingol hired the Dwarves of Nogrod to set the Silmaril in the necklace called the Nauglamír, the craftsmen were suddenly overcome by a desire to possess the jewel. They slew Thingol and stole the Silmaril.

Thorin I

Dwarf king of Grey Mountains. Born in the Kingdom under the Mountain in 2035, Thorin was the son of King Thráin I. In 2190, he became Thorin I, the second King under the Mountain. Thirty years later, wishing to find new challenges, Thorin I led his people to the Grey Mountains where he founded and ruled a prosperous new kingdom until his death in 2289.

Thorin II

Dwarf king-in-exile. Born in 2746 of the Third Age in the Kingdom under the Mountain, Thorin was the grandson of King Thrór. In 2770, all the Dwarves of Erebor were driven out by Smaug the Dragon. In 2790, his grandfather was slain, and his father, King Thráin II, led his people into the War of the Dwarves and the Orcs. At this time he became known as Thorin Oakenshield because, when disarmed during the Battle of Azanulbizar, he used an oak bough as a weapon. After the war, Thorin Oakenshield remained in the Blue Mountains and in 2845, he became Thorin II, king-in-exile. Nearly a century later, in 2941, he formed the expedition of Thorin and Company and went on the Quest of the Lonely Mountain. The adventure finally resulted in the death of Smaug the Dragon and the re-establishment of the Dwarf Kingdom under the Mountain. However, in the fight to keep possession of what the company had won, Thorin Oakenshield was mortally wounded in the Battle of Five Armies, and died shortly after.

THINGOL: Thingol, meaning 'King Grey-mantle', and Queen Melian the Maia, built the forest kingdom of Doriath and the mansions of Menegroth.

Thorin III

Dwarf king of Erebor. Known as Thorin Stonehelm, this son of King Dáin Ironfoot (heir of Thorin II) was born in Erebor in 2866 of the Third Age. He became King under the Mountain in 3019 after his father died defending Erebor during the War of the Ring. A brave warrior, Thorin Stonehelm rallied his people and, with the Men of Dale, broke the siege of Erebor and defeated the Easterling and Orc armies.

Thorondor

Eagle of Encircling Mountains. Thorondor was the king of the Eagles during the First Age of the Sun. With a wingspan measured at thirty fathoms, he appears to have been the largest Eagle ever to have lived. During the Wars of Beleriand, Thorondor rescued the Noldor prince Maedhros from Thangorodrim, brought back the body of King Fingolfin from Angband, and scarred the face of Morgoth with his talons. Beren and Lúthien were also rescued from Angband by the Eagle Lord. For centuries, Thorondor's Eagles guarded the hidden realm of Gondolin from its enemies. However, Thorondor and his Eagles won greatest fame in the Great Battle by destroying the Winged Dragons of Angband. Thorondor, meaning 'high eagle', appears to have returned with the Valar and Maiar to the Undying Lands at the end of the First Age of the Sun.

Thráin I

Dwarf king of Erebor. Thráin I became the first King under the Mountain at Erebor in 1999 of the Third Age of the Sun. Born in Moria in 1934, Thráin was the son of King Náin I. His father ruled Moria for just one year before being slain by the Balrog in 1981. Forced to abandon Moria, Thráin I became king-in-exile. Finally, Thráin I brought his wandering people to Erebor, where he found that great jewel called the Arkenstone, the 'heart of the mountain'. There he founded the Kingdom under the Mountains and prospered until his death in 2190.

Thráin II

Dwarf king-in-exile. Born in the Kingdom under the Mountain in 2644 of the Third Age of the Sun, Thráin was the son of King Thrór. In 2770 Thrór, Thráin and all the Dwarves of Erebor were driven out by Smaug the Dragon. In 2790, King Thrór was murdered by the Orcs of Moria, and Thráin II launched the bloody six-year War of Dwarves and Orcs. It culminated in the slaughter of the Orcs of the Misty Mountains at the Battle of Azalnulbizar, in which Thráin II lost an eye. Still without a kingdom after the war, Thráin II lived for a long time in the Blue Mountains. Finally, however, in 2845 he rather foolishly resolved to return to Erebor with a few companions. Unfortunately, he was taken captive by Sauron in Mirkwood, and had the last of the Dwarf Rings of Power taken from him. In 2850, after five years of imprisonment, Gandalf managed to find him and Thráin gave the Wizard the key to a secret door in Erebor.

Thrushes

The 'Red Book of Westmarch' tells that in the Third Age of the Sun there were many bird races such as Crows and Ravens that possessed languages that Elves, Dwarves or Men might know. But the ancient breed of Thrush that lived in Erebor had an alliance with the Men and Dwarves of that place. The Men of Dale and some of the Lake Men of Esgaroth knew the Thrush language and used these birds as messengers. Thrushes would also approach Dwarves out of friendship, and although the Dwarves did not understand the quick Thrushes' speech, the Thrushes understood Westron, the common daily speech of Dwarves and Men.

These birds were especially long-lived. Legend relates how one very old Thrush of Erebor came to the Dwarves of Thorin Oakenshield and bore a message to Lake Town, to the heir of Dale named Bard the Bowman. Men, Elves and Dwarves had reason indeed to be grateful to this Thrush, for on the strength of its message Bard the Bowman learned of the weakness of the Dragon of Erebor, and with that knowledge slew the beast.

Thuringwethil

Maia and Vampire. Thuringwethil, meaning 'the woman of shadows', was an evil Maia spirit of Melkor, who took on the form of a huge Vampire Bat with iron claws. During the First Age of the Sun, Thuringwethil was one of the many shape-shifting monsters inhabiting Sauron's tower on the Isle of Werewolves in Beleriand. She flew between Sauron and Melkor carrying messages and doing evil deeds. After the overthrow of Sauron and the Werewolves, her power seems to have been destroyed. Her shaping-cloak was taken and was used by Lúthien as a means of entering the realm of Angband.

Tilion

Maia guardian of the Moon. Tilion of the Silver Bow was once a Maia spirit of Oromë the Huntsman. However, after Telperion, the last flower of the silver Tree of the Valar, was placed in a silver vessel to become the Moon, Tilion was chosen as its guiding spirit. Ever since the first rising of the Moon, he has laboured each night to carry the silver vessel and flower through the heavens.

Tindómerel

Fairest of the song birds of Arda was the Tindómerel, the 'twilight daughter', which common Men called the Nightingale. Elves loved this night-singer, which they named Tinúviel, 'maiden of twilight', and told many tales in which nightingales play a part.

Tinúviel

Among the songs and tales of Elves much is made of the night-singing bird that men call the nightingale. Of all birds its song is most loved, for like the Elves themselves it sings by the light of the Stars. This bird has many names: Dúlin ('night-singer'), Tindómerel ('twilight-daughter'), Lómelindë ('dusk-singer') and Tinúviel ('maiden of twilight').

The greatest legends of this bird came from Doriath. For always about the Queen of the Grey-elves, Melian the Maia, were the sweet voices of Nightingales. In time a daughter was born to Melian and King Thingol – the only child born of Elf and Maia in the Circles of the World. She was the most beautiful of Elves, the fairest singer of all her race, and so she was named Lúthien Tinúviel. The 'Lay of Leithian' tells how by the magic of her song she wielded immense power in Arda. But like the short-lived night bird she faded from the World, for she took the mortal Beren, son of Barahir, as her husband, and she herself was made mortal. So, the fairest being in Arda was gone long before the First Age of the Sun was ended.

Many songs recall Lúthien's beauty, and in the 'Tale of Aragorn and Arwen' it is said that in the Third Age of the Sun the dark beauty of Lúthien again found form in Arwen, the daughter of Elrond Half-elven. Arwen was also

THRUSHES Song birds who knew the language of Men and Dwarves. One old Thrush of Erebor became famous as Thorin Oakenshield's messenger. He flew to Lake Town with a message which enabled Bard the Bowman to slay Smaug the Dragon.

known as Tinúviel. Her song was beautiful and, like Lúthien, she married a mortal and chose a mortal life.

Tirion

In the Undying Lands, the Noldor and Vanyar Elves built the first and greatest city in Eldamar. This was Tirion of the white towers and crystal stairs. It was set on the hill of Túna in Calacirya, the Pass of Light. The city was placed so that not only could the Elves live in the light of the Trees and look out on the sea but also, from under the shadow of Túna and the tall towers, could view the glittering stars which shone down on the world beyond the Pelóri Mountains of Valinor. Appropriately, the name Tirion is Elvish for 'watch tower', perhaps referring specifically to the tallest tower which was called Mindon Eldalióva and in which was set a great silver lamp. In the courtyard of this tower was planted Galathilion, the sacred White Tree of the Eldar.

Tol Eressëa

In the first ages of Arda, there was a large island in the middle of the Great Sea of Belegaer that Ulmo the Valarian, Lord of Oceans uprooted and made into a floating island that served him as a vast ship. This was the Ship of Ulmo that transported the Vanyar and Noldor Elves of the Great Journey from Middle-earth to the Undying Lands. Upon departing, however, a portion of the island ran aground just off Beleriand and broke off to become the Isle of Balar. Nonetheless, the Vanyar and Noldor were safely delivered and Ulmo's island returned to Beleriand to transport the Teleri Elves. However, many years had passed since the first passage and in that time the Teleri came to love the sea so greatly that Ossë the Maiar spirit, who is Master of the Waves, persuaded Ulmo not to complete the crossing, but to anchor the isle in the Bay of Eldamar. Although within sight of the Undying Lands and their brethren in Eldamar, for an Age of Starlight the Teleri Sea Elves were separated from their brethren, and during this time the island was given its name, Tol Eressëa, the 'Lonely Island'. It was not until they were taught the craft of ship building that their isolation ended. Thereafter, they were masters of the seas and went where they wished. Some went and built the Teleri city of Alqualondë in Eldamar, and another part remained on Tol Eressëa and its port-city of Avallónë that looked eastward over the sea. These were the Elves who traded with the Númenóreans and brought gifts and knowledge to them during the Second Age of the Sun before the Change of the World, and whose white tower of Avallónë could be glimpsed glittering in the western sea from Númenor's highest peak.

Tol Sirion

In Beleriand during the First Age of the Sun, there was a green island on the northern reach of the Sirion River that controlled the Pass of Sirion. This was called Tol Sirion, and was where the Noldor Prince Finrod built the fortress of Minas Tirith to guard the pass against the forces of Morgoth. It remained secure until the year 457 when it was seized by Sauron and a mighty host of Werewolves. For a decade thereafter, the island was called Tol-in-Gaurhoth, the 'isle of Werewolves'. Within its dungeons were thrown Finrod and Beren, until the coming of Lúthien and Huan the Wolfhound of the Valar. In the ensuing conflict Huan slew Sauron's chief lieutenant Draugluin, the lord and sire of Werewolves, and overcame Sauron himself in Werewolf form. After Huan's victory, the evil powers fled from the island which once again was called Tol Sirion. Finrod was buried here, and it remained a green and peaceful isle until the end of the age and the destruction of Beleriand.

Tom Bombadil

Maia master of Old Forest. Tom Bombadil was the Hobbit name for the powerful and eccentric master of the Old Forest. Called Iarwain Benadar, which means both 'old' and 'without father', by the Elves, he was probably a Maia spirit that came to Middle-earth in the Ages of Starlight. By Dwarves he was called Forn, while Men knew him as Orald. He was a very strange and merry spirit. He was a short, stout Man, with blue eyes, a red face and a brown beard. He wore a blue coat, a tall battered hat with a blue feather, and yellow boots. Always singing or speaking in rhymes, he seemed a nonsensical being, yet within the Old Forest his power was absolute, and no evil was strong enough to touch him. His spouse was Goldberry the River-daughter. Tom Bombadil played a role in the Quest of the Ring by twice rescuing the Hobbits who carried the Ring: first from Old Man Willow in the Old Forest, and later from the Barrow-wights in the Barrow Downs.

Torogs

During the Wars of Beleriand there came forth in the service of Morgoth, the Dark Enemy, a race of Man-eating Giants of great strength. Elves named these creatures Torogs, from which Men later invented the name Trolls. The lore of Middle-earth was filled with tales of this evil but stupid race of Giants who often beset the lone unwary traveller.

Treebeard

Ent of Fangorn Forest. Treebeard, which is 'Fangorn' in Elvish, was the guardian of the Fangorn Forest. He was an Ent, a fourteen foot tall giant 'tree shepherd' who resembled something between an evergreen tree and a man. He had a rough and sturdy trunk, a thatch beard and branch-like arms with smooth seven-fingered hands. At the time of the War of the Ring, he was the oldest of his race still surviving on Middle-earth. Although not generally concerned with the ways of Elves and Men, Treebeard's discussions with the Hobbits, Meriadoc Brandybuck and Peregrin Took, soon roused his long-held resentment towards the Orcs of Isengard. Treebeard persuaded the Ents to march on Isengard. The March of the Ents resulted in the total destruction of its walls and imprisonment of Saruman the Wizard in his own tower. Treebeard also sent those bad-tempered tree-spirits called Huorn in against the Orcs after the Battle of Hornburg.

Trees of the Valar

From the seeds devised by Yavanna, Queen of the Earth, there grew in the Ages of the Lamps the trees of the Great Forests of Arda. Many of these were the same as trees we now know, yet taller in those days and of greater girth. There were trees of oak, alder, rowan, fir, beech (which was called Neldoreth), birch (called Brethil), and holly (which was called Region). But there were others that have now vanished from the World: the red-gold Culumalda of Ithilien and the golden Mallorn, the tallest tree of Middle-earth, which stood in Lothlórien.

Yet the most amazing and beautiful of all the trees that ever grew were the two Trees of the Valar, which appeared after the Ages of the Lamps. After Melkor had destroyed the Lamps of the World, the Valar left Middle-earth and came to the Undying Lands. There they made a second kingdom, which they named Valinor, and Yavanna, Giver of Fruits, sat on the green mound Ezellohar near the western golden gate of Valimar and sang, while the Valar sat on their thrones in the Ring of Doom and Nienna the Weeper silently watered the Earth with her tears. First, it is told, there came forth a Tree of silver and then a Tree of gold; glowing with brilliant Light, they grew as tall as the mountains of Aulë. Telperion was the elder of these Trees and had leaves of dark green and bright silver. On his boughs were multitudes

of silver flowers from which fell silver dew. In praise Telperion was also called Ninquelótë and Silpion. Laurelin, the younger of the Trees of the Valar, was the 'song of gold'. Her leaves were edged with gold yet were pale green; her flowers were like trumpets and golden flames, and from her limbs fell a rain of gold Light. In praise Laurelin was also named Culúrien and Malinalda, the 'golden tree'.

So it was that these two Trees stood in the Undying Lands and lit the lands with silver and gold. From the rhythm of the Light of the Trees of the Valar came the Count of Time, for Time had not before been measured, and so began the days and years of the Trees, which were many long ages – longer far than the years of the Stars of the Sun. The Light of the twin Trees in the Undying Lands was eternal, and those who lived in it were ennobled and filled with immense wisdom.

In their Light the Valar lived in bliss, while Middle-earth was plunged in darkness and Melkor strengthened the power of his kingdom of Utumno and his armoury of Angband. Yet after a time Varda, who made wells beneath the Trees in which the dews of Light fell, took the silver Light of Telperion and climbed the vault of the skies and rekindled the faint stars. She made them more brilliant, and evil servants of Melkor on Middle-earth quailed in fear. For the starlight was now like spears to them, or like daggers of ice, that cut them deep. In this Light of the Stars the Elves came forth. Joyfully were they awakened by that Light.

Though the life of the Trees of the Valar was long, their end was tragic and disastrous. For, it is told, Melkor made a pact with Ungoliant the Great Spider, and they came invisibly in the Unlight of the Spider, and the Trees were lasted with sorcerous flame, and the sap of their lives was drawn out. Their Light was extinguished and they were left but shattered trunks and roots blackened and poisoned. The wells of Light were drained and consumed by the Spider Ungoliant, and a terrible darkness fell on Valinor. So in all the World the Light of the Trees was gone, except in the three jewels called the Silmarils that the Elves of Eldmar had made, in which a little of the Light from the Trees was preserved. But Melkor took these gems too, though he did not destroy them, and it was for these Silmarils that the long disastrous War of the Jewels of all the next Age was fought. Mournfully, the Valar came again to the Trees, and again they sent for Yavanna and Nienna. Over the dead Trees Yavanna sang her green song and Nienna wept tears of endurance beyond hope, and from the charred ruins came a single golden fruit and a single silver flower. These were named Anar the Fire Golden and Isil the Sheen. The 'Narsilion' tells how Aulë the Smith made great lanterns about these radiant lights that they might not fade. Manwë hallowed them, and Varda lifted them into the heavens and set them on a course over all the lands of Arda. Thus, the fragments of the living Light of the Trees of the Valar were brought to the whole World and they were called the Sun and the Moon. Arien the Maia fire spirit carries the Sun, Anar, which is also named Vása, the 'heart of fire'; and Tilion the Maia hunter and bowman carries the Moon, Isil the silver flower, which is also called Rána.

It was not in their Light alone that the Trees remained in the World, for Yavanna made the tree Galathilion in the image of Telperion, though it did not radiate Light. She gave this tree to the Elves of Tirion, who knew it as the White Tree of the Eldar. Many of its seedlings grew and still grow in Eldamar. One of these was Celeborn, which bloomed on Tol Eressëa and brought forth the seedling that Elves gave to the Men of Númenor. This seedling became the tree named Nimloth the Fair, the White Tree of Númenor, which grew in the royal court until King Ar-Pharazôn destroyed it. With that act the Isle of Númenor was doomed. Yet a sapling had already been taken

TREEBEARD **Treebeard persuaded the Ents to march on Isengard.**

from Nimloth by the princes of Andúnië, and before the Downfall of Númenor one prince named Elendil the Tall took this sapling to Middle-earth. His son first planted the fruit of Nimloth in Minas Ithil in Gondor, and until the Fourth Age of the Sun the White Trees of Gondor bloomed. Though three times a White Tree perished in plague or war, a sapling was always found and the line never died out. These White Trees were a living link with the most ancient past of the Undying Lands, and they were a sign of the nobility, the wisdom and the goodness of the Valar come to mortal Men.

Trolls

It is thought that in the First Age of Starlight, in the deep Pits of Angband, Melkor the Enemy bred a race of giant cannibals who were fierce and strong but without intelligence. These black-blooded giants were called Trolls, and for five Ages of Starlight and four Ages of the Sun they committed deeds as evil as their dull wits allowed.

Trolls, it is said, were bred by Melkor because he desired a race as powerful as the giant Ents, the Treeherds. Trolls were twice the height and bulk of the greatest Men, and they had a skin of green scales like armour. As Ents were to the substance of wood, so Trolls were to stone. Though not so strong as Ents who could crush stone, Trolls were rock hard and powerful. Yet in the sorcery of their making there was a fatal flaw: they feared light. The spell of their creation had been cast in darkness and if light did fall on them it was as if that spell were broken and the armour of their skin grew inwards. Their evil, soulless beings were crushed as they became lumps of lifeless stone.

The stupidity of Trolls was so great that many could not be taught speech at all, while others learned the barest rudiments of the Black Speech of Orcs. Though their power was often brought to nought by the quick-witted, in mountain caverns and dark woods Trolls were rightly feared. They desired most a diet of raw flesh. They killed for pleasure, and without reason – save an undirected avarice – hoarded what treasures they took from their victims.

In the Ages of Starlight they wandered Middle-earth freely and with Orcs made travel a great peril. At this time they often went to war alongside Wolves and Orcs and other evil servants of Melkor. But in the First Age of the Sun they were far more wary, for the great light of the Sun was death to them and only in darkness did they go forth in the Wars of Beleriand. It is told in the 'Quenta Silmarillion' that in the Battle of Unnumbered Tears, Trolls in great numbers were the bodyguard of Gothmog, Lord of the Balrogs, and, though they fought neither with craft nor skill, they fought fiercely and knew nothing of fear. Seventy of their number were slain by that one great Edain warrior called Húrin, yet other Trolls came on and at last took him captive.

After the War of Wrath and the First Age of the Sun, many of the Troll race remained on Middle-earth and hid themselves deeply under stone. When Sauron the Maia arose in the Second Age, he took to himself these old servants of his master, Melkor. Sauron also gave the Trolls craftiness of mind born of wickedness, and they became more dangerous than before. Freely and fearlessly, these monsters wandered in dark places of the World.

In the Third Age of the Sun, when Sauron for a second time arose in Mordor, there were still many evil and slow-witted Trolls who haunted Mortal Lands. Some of these were called Stone-trolls; others were Cave-trolls, Hill-trolls, Mountain-trolls and Snow-trolls. Many tales of the Third Age tell of their evil. In the Coldfells north of Rivendell they slew the Dúnedain chieftain Arador.

TROLLS Trolls in great numbers were the bodyguard of Gothmog, Lord of the Balrogs, and, though they fought neither with craft nor skill, they fought fiercely and knew nothing of fear.

In the Trollshaws of Eriador, for centuries, three Trolls fed on village folk of that land. By Troll standards these three Trolls were mental giants, for they spoke and understood the Westron tongue of Men and had an elementary, if faulty, knowledge of arithmetic. None the less, by quickness of wit, the Wizard Gandalf was able to turn them to stone. In Moria the Balrog commanded many huge Cave-trolls.

Yet it is said Sauron was not yet pleased with the evil of these servants and sought to put their great strength to better use. So it was that, towards the end of the Third Age, Sauron bred Trolls of great cunning and agility who could endure the Sun as long as Sauron's will was with them. These he called the Olog-hai, and they were great beasts with the reasoning intelligence of evil Men. Armed with fangs and rending claws and stone-scaled as others of the Troll race, they also carried black shields, round and huge, and swung mighty hammers that crushed the helmets of foes. So, in the Mountains of Mordor and the forests about Dol Guldur in Mirkwood where the Olog-hai were sent to war by Sauron, a great evil was loosed upon Sauron's foes.

In the War of the Ring on Pelennor Fields and before the Black Gate of Mordor, the terror of these savage beings caused terrible destruction. Yet they were held by a mighty spell, and, when the Ring was unmade and Sauron went into the shadows, the spell was broken. The Olog-hai drifted as if their senses were taken from them; they were like mute cattle wandering dark fields and for all their great strength they were scattered and slain.

Trollshaws

In Eriador, during the last thousand years of the Third Age, the forest that stood just north of the Great East Road and east of the Elf-kingdom of Rivendell was called the Trollshaws. It had once been a civilized part of Arnor, and the ruins of Dúnedain castles were there, but since the wars with the Witch-king of Angmar the forest had become the domain of Trolls who loved nothing better than feasting upon unwary travellers. The Trollshaws was the home of three trolls: Bert, Tom and William Huggins, who were turned to stone by Gandalf during the Quest of Erebor.

Tulkas

Vala called 'the Wrestler'. Tulkas was the Hercules of the Valar. Last of the Ainur to enter Arda, he came to fight Melkor in the First War. Even-tempered and slow to anger, Tulkas loved testing his strength against others. He was youthful and handsome with golden hair and beard. Sometimes called Tulkas the Strong, and Tulkas Astaldo, meaning 'valiant', his spouse was Nessa the Dancer. During the War of Powers, Tulkas captured Melkor.

Tuor

Edain of Dor-lómin. Tuor was born in 473 of the First Age of the Sun, just before the Battle of Unnumbered Tears, in which his father Huor was slain and his uncle, Húrin, was captured. Tuor was raised by Sindar Elves in the caves of Androth until he was sixteen, when he was captured and made the slave of Lorgan the Easterling. He later escaped and for four years lived as an outlaw. In 496, Tuor entered the hidden realm of Gondolin in order to deliver to King Turgon Ulmo the Ocean Lord's warning of Gondolin's imminent destruction. Turgon, however, refused to go, and Tuor also remained and married the Elven princess, Idril. The couple had a single child, Eärendil. In 511, Gondolin was sacked. Tuor, Idril and Eärendil, with the survivors of Gondolin, escaped to the Havens of Sirion. Some years later, Tuor sailed with Idril to live in Eldamar.

Turgon

Elven king of Gondolin. Born during the Ages of Stars in Eldamar, Turgon was the second son of Fingolfin of the Noldor. After the destruction of the Trees of Light, Turgon was among the Noldor who pursued Morgoth and the Silmarils to Middle-earth. In Beleriand, Turgon claimed Nevrast as his realm. However, in the year 51 of the First Age of the Sun, Ulmo the Vala showed Turgon the hidden valley of Tumladen within the Encircling Mountains. There he built a city of white stone and called it Gondolin. It was completed in 104, and Turgon ruled his hidden kingdom for five centuries. In 473, he led the Gondolindrim into the Battle of Unnumbered Tears. Only the sacrifice of the rear guard of the Edain averted total disaster. In 496, Ulmo sent the Edain hero Tuor to warn Turgon, but he refused to flee. After years of spying in 511, Morgoth finally discovered Gondolin's location and sent his armies to destroy it. Turgon, with his sword Glamdring in his hand, died fighting in defence of his beloved city.

Túrin Turambar

Edain of Dor-lómin and Dragon-slayer. Túrin was born in 465 of the First Age, the son of Húrin and Morwen. After the disaster of the Battle of Unnumbered Tears in 473, Túrin was sent to be raised by the Grey-Elf king Thingol in Doriath. From 482, Túrin, with his mentor, the Sindar warrior Beleg Strongbow, fought the minions of Morgoth in the marches of Doriath and beyond. In 486 he adopted the name Neithan and went into exile. After capturing the Petty-dwarf, Mîm, he and his outlaw band made the caves beneath Amon Rûdh the centre of their operations. During this time, he was called Gorthol Dragon-helm. From 488 to 496, Túrin lived in Nargothrond and was called Mormegil the Black Sword. After fighting in the disastrous Battle of Tumhalad, Túrin returned to Nargothrond where Glaurung the Dragon bound him with a spell and an evil curse. For the next three years, calling himself Turambar ('master of doom'), he lived among the Haladin, and in 500 married the maid, Níniel. In 501, Glaurung entered Brethil and Túrin ambushed and slew him with his sword, Gurthang. However, before dying, the Dragon revealed to Túrin that his wife Níniel was, in fact, his long lost sister, Nienor. Realizing he had married his own sister, Túrin killed himself.

Turtle-fish

In the lore of Hobbits there is the tale of a great Turtle-fish that is called the Fastitocalon. Whether the tale grew from the sighting of a leviathan upon the sea or was the product of Hobbit fancy cannot now be discovered, for no other race upon Arda ever makes mention of this mighty creature.

THE TROLLSHAWS The home of three trolls: Bert, Tom and William Huggins, who were turned to stone by Gandalf during the Quest of Erebor.

U

Uglúk

Uruk-hai of Isengard. During the War of the Ring, Uglúk was the captain of the quarrelsome Orc band that captured the Hobbits, Meriadoc Brandybuck and Peregrin Took, in Rohan. Shortly after the band was slaughtered by the Horsemen of Rohan. Uglúk's rank was probably due to the fact that he was larger, stronger and nastier than ordinary Orcs. Uglúk was slain by Éomer, the Marshal of Riddermark.

Uilos

On Middle-earth there was an eternally blossoming flower called Uilos, meaning 'white' in Elvish. It was a star-like flower and appeared in great abundance on burial mounds. By Men it was called Simbelmynë or Evermind in Westron.

Uinen

Maia sea spirit. Uinen, the Lady of the Calms, was the wife of Ossë, the Lord of the Waves. Both served Ulmo the Ocean Lord who was master of water in all its forms. Uinen was as loved by those who went on the sea as Ossë was feared. Sailors prayed to Uinen that she might grant them safe passage.

Úlairi

The long histories of the Rings of Power tell how after the War of Sauron and the Elves there arose nine wraiths in the lands of Middle-earth. These were the Úlairi, who were called the Nazgûl in Black Speech and whom Men knew as the Ringwraiths. Once great lords among Men, the Úlairi succumbed to the temptation of the sorcerous Rings and in time became slaves of the Dark Lord Sauron. The tale of their destruction of the realms of Elves and Men is long and terrible.

Ulmo

Vala Ocean Lord. Ulmo, meaning 'Lord of the Waters', commands the movement of all water on Middle-earth: from its seas, lakes and rivers to its rainfalls, mists and dews. During the Ages of Stars, Ulmo helped bring the Elves to the Undying Lands, and he often instructed the Elves in music and the ways of the sea. Ulmo did not often manifest himself but when he did it was usually as a gigantic sea king rising from the waters in a wave-crested helmet and mail armour of silver and emerald. His voice is deep and strong, and when he blows his white sea-shell horns, the Ulumúri, the seas reverberate with their sound.

Úmanyar

Of all those newly arisen Elven people who in the years of Starlight chose to heed the summons of the Valar and leave Middle-earth to come to the Undying Lands, only a part completed the Great Journey. Those who reached the Undying Lands, the continent of Aman, were named Amanyar, while those who were lost on the way, and broke away from the main hosts were named the Úmanyar, 'those not of Aman'. The main divisions of the Úmanyar were called Nandor, Laiquendi, Falathrim and Sindar, but there were also many smaller tribes and families amongst those lost on that long road of many perils.

ULMO Ulmo did not often manifest himself but when he did it was usually as a gigantic sea king rising from the waters.

Umbar

The greatest coastal port in Harad, the southlands of Middle-earth, during the Second and Third Ages of the Sun was called Umbar. The name Umbar referred to the city, port, fortress, cape and surrounding coastal lands. It was a large natural harbour which by the second millennium of the Second Age had become the Númenóreans' chief port in Middle-earth. In the year 3261 of the Second Age, the Númenóreans raised a mighty fleet which landed in Umbar to contest Sauron's power, but after the destruction of Númenor those of that race in Umbar fell under Sauron's power. These people became known as the Black Númenóreans and they often led the powerful fleets of Umbar against the Dúnedain of Gondor, particularly those in the rival port of Pelargir. In the tenth century of the Third Age, kings of Gondor attacked Umbar and broke the sea power of the Black Númenóreans and took possession of port, city and territories. Umbar became a part of the kingdom of Gondor until the civil war and revolt in 1448, when rebel forces and Haradrim allies took possession of the port and separated from Gondor. In 1810, Gondor briefly captured the port and city, but it was soon regained by the Haradrim. Once again the black ships, or dromonds, of Umbar were on the waters raiding the coast, and these people who were called the Corsairs of Umbar became the terror of the seas. In anticipation of the rising power of Sauron, in 2980, Aragorn II (under the name of Thorongil) led a raiding party into Umbar's port and burned a large part of its fleet. During the War of the Ring itself, the Corsairs attacked Pelargir, but were devastatingly defeated by Aragorn and the Dead Men of Dunharrow. The Corsairs were forced to sue for peace and, during the Fourth Age of the Sun, Umbar was controlled by the Dúnedain kings of the Reunited Kingdom of Arnor and Gondor.

UMBAR The name Umbar referred to the city, port, fortress, cape and surrounding coastal lands.

Undying Lands

The vast continent of Aman in the far west of Arda was most often called the Undying Lands. As this was the land of the immortal Valar, Maiar and Eldar, the name appears to be appropriate enough. It was primarily made up of two realms: Valinor, the home of the Valar and Maiar with its capital of Valinor, and Eldamar, the home of the Vanyar, Noldor and Teleri Elves with their capitals of Tirion and Alqualondë. After the Change of the World, the Undying Lands were taken to a place beyond mortal reckoning. Thereafter, they could only be reached by sailing in the magical white ships of the Elves along the 'Straight Road' that takes them out beyond the Spheres of the World.

Ungoliant

Spider of Avathar. Ungoliant was the monstrous and gigantic Spider that lived in Avathar, an uninhabited wasteland between the Pelóri Mountains of Valinor and the cold sea of the south. Probably a corrupted Maia spirit in her beginning, Ungoliant was the vilest creature ever to exist in Arda. She possessed the power to weave a web of darkness, called the Unlight of Ungoliant. At Melkor's bidding, Ungoliant poisoned and destroyed the Trees of the Valar. Then Melkor and Ungoliant fled to Middle-earth, where they fell to fighting one another over the Silmarils. So great was Ungoliant's evil power that Melkor himself might have been overcome had his legion of Balrogs not driven her off. Ungoliant fled to the Valley of Death at the foot of the Mountains of Terror in Beleriand where she bred with the spider-like creatures there, and created a monstrous brood of giant Spiders. Later, Ungoliant wandered south into the deserts of Harad, where – finding nothing else to eat – she consumed herself.

Uruk-hai

In the year 2475 of the Third Age a new breed of Orkish soldiery came out of Mordor. These were called the Uruk-hai. They were black-skinned, black-blooded and lynx-eyed, nearly as tall as Men and unafraid of light. The Uruk-hai were of greater strength and endurance than the lesser Orcs, and more formidable in battle. They wore black armour and black mail; they wielded long swords and spears and carried shields emblazoned with the Red Eye of Mordor.

As the spawning of lesser Orcs was counted among the greatest evils of Melkor, so was the breeding of Uruk-hai numbered among Sauron's most terrible deeds. By what method Sauron bred these beings is not known, but they proved to be well suited to his evil purpose. Their numbers multiplied and they went among all the lesser Orcs and often became their captains or formed legions of their own, for the Uruk-hai were proud of their fighting prowess and disdainful of the lesser servants of Sauron.

When the Uruk-hai multitude came unexpectedly on the Men of Gondor with spear and sword, they drove the Men before them and stormed Osgiliath, set torches to it, and broke its stone bridge. Thus, the Uruk-hai laid waste the greatest city of Gondor.

This, however, was but the beginning of the work of the Uruk-hai, for these great Orcs were valued by the Dark Powers and they fell to evil deeds with a passion. Throughout the War of the Ring the Uruk-hai were among the forces that came from Morgul and Mordor. And under the banner of the White Hand of Saruman they came in vast numbers out of Isengard into the battle of the Hornburg. Yet, with the end of the War and the fall of Mordor, the Uruk-hai were as straw before fire, for with Sauron gone they, with the lesser Orcs and other evil beasts, wandered masterless and were slain or driven into hiding in deep caverns where they might only feed on one another, or die.

Uruks

In the Third Age of the Sun there came out of Mordor a terrible race of giant Orcs. In Black Speech they were named the Uruk-hai, but they were commonly called Uruks. They were as tall as Men with all the evil traits of Orcs, yet they were stronger and unafraid of light.

Urulóki

The Urulóki Fire-drakes that came forth in the First Age of the Sun from the Pits of Angband were part of the great race of Dragons. These Urulóki, or 'hot serpents', were fanged and taloned, dreadful in mind and deed, and filled with breath of flame and sulphur. The first of their kind was Glaurung, Father of Dragons, but he had many offspring who in turn produced many broods. Of all creatures they were the greatest despair of Men and Elves, and the bane of Dwarves.

Utumno

In the northeast of Middle-earth during the Ages of the Lamps, Melkor the Vala built a mighty fortress ringed with mountains, called Utumno. Here he plotted against the other Valar and gathered rebel Maiar spirits and monsters, like the Balrogs, the Werewolves and the Great Spiders. After Melkor destroyed the Lamps of the Valar, Utumno's empire on Middle-earth expanded through the Ages of Darkness that followed. However, conflict with the other Valar was again inevitable after the Rekindling of the Stars and the coming of the Elves. After a history of prolonged destruction the Valar at last made war on Utumno at the end of the First Age of the Stars. This was the War of Powers, and at the end of that war its master Melkor was captured and put in chains.

URUK-HAI Race of Super-Orc bred in Mordor by Sauron in the twenty-fifth century of the Third Age. Besides being larger, stronger and even more vile than the lesser Orcs, they had the advantage of being unafraid of light.

V

Vairë

Vala called 'the Weaver'. Ainur spirit of the Timeless Halls that entered Arda and became one of the Valar, Vairë is the wife of Mandos, the Doomsman. She is the weaver of fate, for she weaves the tapestries which hang on the walls of House of the Dead and tell the tale of the world to the end of Time.

Valar

When Eä, the 'World that Is', was given substance, there came into it a part of the first race, the Ainur, the 'holy ones'. In the Timeless Halls they had been beings of pure spirit who the 'Valaquenta' records entered the World and, taking earthly form, became divided into two peoples. The people that were less powerful were numerous and their tale is recounted in the name of the Maiar; the greater powers were fifteen in number and they are here accounted as the Valar, the Powers of Arda.

It is told in the ancient books that, when the Valar and Maiar came and first shaped the rough form of the World, they strove to make the perfect beauty that they had perceived in the Vision. Yet in this there was strife among the Valar and war marred their work. But at last the first kingdom of the Valar called Almaren, was made on an isle in the middle of the vast lake in Middle-earth, and all the World was lit by two brilliant Lamps that stood to the North and South. Thus began the Ages of the Lamps. Yet one of the Valar revolted and broke the Great Lamps of the Valar and destroyed the Isle of Almaren and its enchanted gardens.

So the Valar left Middle-earth and went West to the Continent of Aman where they placed the Pelóri Mountains about them and made their second kingdom of gardens and mansions more fair than the first. This kingdom was called Valinor and its city of domes, bells and great halls was named Valimar. At this time the Trees of the Valar, which gave Eternal Light, golden and silver, were made and all of Aman was lit within the borders of the Pelóri Mountains; the kingdom was a miracle of beauty.

First of the Valar is Manwë, who lives on Taniquetil, the highest mountain of Arda. He is the Wind Lord and the First King. All of Arda is his domain, but his chief love is the element of the air and so he is called Súlimo, 'lord of the breath of Arda'. He sits on a burnished throne clothed in azure robes, the Sceptre of Sapphire in his hand. Like sapphire too are Manwë's eyes, but even more bright, and as fearsome as lightning. Manwë sees all the World beneath the skies. The turbulence of the air is his mind's workings; his wrath is the thunderstorm that rocks the Earth and breaks even the mountain towers. All the birds of the air are his, the Eagles above all others. His is the Breath of the Earth and the Breath of the peoples of Arda. Speech and sound itself are thus parts of his element, and the arts he loves above all others are poetry and song.

Within the domed halls of Ilmarin, the 'mansion of the high airs' which Manwë made on Taniquetil, there also resides the queen of the Valar. She is Varda, the Lady of the Stars, fairest of all the Valar for the light of Ilúvatar is still on her. She is a spirit of light that is like a fountain of diamonds. It was Varda who made the Stars, and so Elves call her Elentári and Elbereth, the 'Star queen'. Her name is a talisman to all those who would have light dispel darkness. It was Varda who filled the Lamps Illuin and Ormal with the Light that lit all the World, and later too she took the dew of the Trees of the Valar and made the Stars brighter still. She made the forms of the Stars that are known as the constellations: the Butterfly Wilwarin, the Swordsman Menelmacar, the Sickle Valacirca,

the Eagle Soronúmë and many others. In these forms may be read the fate of all the peoples of the World.

It is said that Elves love Varda above all others, for it was her stars that called them into the World, and part of her early light is for ever held in their eyes. For this deed they named her Tintallë and Gilthoniel, the 'Kindler', and for ever they sing to her by starlight and call her the Exalted and the Lofty.

Next of the Valar is Ulmo, whose element is Water. He is the Ocean Lord, whom all mariners know and Dwarves and Orcs fear. Most often he is vast and formless in his deep watery World, but his arising is like a high tidal wave come to shore; his helmet is wave-crested and his mail is emerald and brilliant silver. He raises the Ulumúri, the great white horns of shell, to his lips and blows deep and long. When he speaks his voice too is deep as the sounding depth of the sea. Yet his form is not always fearful, nor indeed does he always appear as the Ocean Lord. For his is water in all its forms, from the spring rains and the fountains, to the rush of brooks and streams, to the sinuous currents of rivers. His voice, as well, may be gentle and sweet, beautiful and sorrowful. Yet, subtle or fierce, Ulmo moves over all the World and all that waters may learn by bank and shore comes finally to this lord.

Nourisher of all the World is Yavanna, for her name means 'giver of fruits'; she is also Kementári, 'Queen of the Earth'. She takes many forms but often stands as tall as the most elegant cypress, green-robed and lit with a golden dew. All those who love the fruits of the Earth love Yavanna and worship her. She is the force that through the green fuse drives the flowers, and the first seeds of all the Olvar were devised and planted by her. She is the protectress of all the fleet-footed Kelvar of woodland and field. It was Yavanna who brought forth the mighty forests of Arda, and she who, during the Ages of Darkness, protected life in the lands of Middle-earth with the Sleep of Yavanna – a great enchantment cast over Mortal Lands. The greatest of her

TREES OF THE VALAR **Varda took the dew of the Trees of the Valar and made the Stars brighter still.**

works was the making of the Trees of the Valar, and, after their destruction, it was she who coaxed from their charred stalks a single flower and a single fruit, from which the Moon and Sun were made.

Spouse of Yavanna, with whom she shares the element of Earth, yet more deeply, is Aulë the Smith, Maker of Mountains, master of all crafts, deviser of metals and gemstones. He is named Mahal, the 'maker', by Dwarves, for he is the power that fashioned these people from earth and stone. Imperfect though they were, the Dwarves were strong and stubborn as the stones themselves and loved all things that concerned their lord. Aulë was also friend and tutor of the Noldorin Elves, who first cut out the gemstones and excelled in building towers and cities of bright stone. They came often to his mansions, cut deep in the mountain roots of Valinor, and learned many of his skills. The greatest of his deeds was the vast work that he undertook in the earliest Ages, when he shaped the forms of the Earth itself.

Deeper still than Aulë's mansions are the Halls of Mandos, which are on the western shore where the waves of Ekkaia, the Encircling Sea, wash the Undying Lands. This is the House of the Dead where the Vala Námo lives, who by all, after his mansion, is called Mandos, the Speaker of Doom. A master of spirits is the Doomsman and, of the Valar, most aware of the Will of Ilúvatar. He is unbending and unmoved by pity, for he knows all the fates that were declared in the Music. In the lore of Elves, the spirits of slain Elves are called to the Lord of the Dead and they inhabit his mansion in the place called the Halls of Awaiting.

Near Mandos on the west shore of Valinor lives his sister, Nienna the Weeper. She is the cloaked woman in mourning, but she is not Despair, even though Grief is her domain; tears flow from her ceaselessly and her house looks out upon the Walls of the Night. Instead, she is Pity and Suffering that brings wisdom and endurance beyond hope; from the waters of her tears much is born that is unlooked for, yet it is often that which sustains life. So it was that the tears of Nienna and the skill of Yavanna brought forth Isil the flower of the Moon and Anar the fruit of the Sun from the ruin of the Trees of the Valar, and from such grief the Light of the World was born, both by day and by night.

In the southern lands of Valinor are the beautiful Woods of Oromë, where Oromë, Tamer of Beasts and the Huntsman, resides. All nations of horsemen love him as well as those who live by hunting and those who are herdsmen and foresters. Oromë is fearsome when hunting and his wrath in battle is dreadful. With spear and bow, the Huntsman rides out on his steed Nahar, a beast white and silver with hooves of gold that shake the Earth. When Oromë blows his great hunting horn Valaróma, all evil creatures flee before him, the mountains and woods echo with sound and in his train come hunting hounds and Maiar and Eldar huntsmen on furious Horses. Most often this huntsman is called Oromë the 'horn-blower', which is Araw to the Men of Gondor and Béma in Westron; to Elves he is Aldaron in Quenya and Tauron in Sindarin, which mean 'forest lord'.

Now these are the eight Valar who are called the Aratar, the mightiest of the powers who dwell in the Sphere of the World. Yet there are six more Valar, and one more after them who fell into evil ways and thus is counted last.

Those who desire eternal youth worship Vána, wife of Oromë and younger sister of Yavanna. Vána the Ever-young is her name; she has gardens of golden flowers and her chief delights are bird song and flower blossom.

Nessa the Dancer is named next; she is Oromë's sister. She loves the fleet woodland creatures and they come to her, for the beautiful Nessa is herself a wild spirit who dances unceasingly on the green and never-fading grasses of Valinor.

The husband of Nessa is Tulkas the Strong, who entered Arda last of the Valar. He is called the Wrestler and also Astaldo, the 'valiant'. He is the strongest of all the Valar, quick and tireless, gold-haired and gold-bearded; even in war he carries no weapon for his naked strength and great heart overwhelm all enemies.

Brother to Mandos is Lórien, the Dream Master. Like Mandos, Lórien is named after the place of his dwelling, for Lórien is the fairest garden within Arda. His true name is Irmo, but to all he is Lórien, King of Dream and Vision.

Within the fair gardens of Lórien is the Lake Lórellin in which there is an island filled with tall trees and gentle mists. Here Estë the Healer, the gentle one, lives. Her mantle is grey, and rest is what she grants. She is praised by all, but her true gifts are most desired by those whose suffering is great.

The Vala named Vairë is the wife of Mandos, and she is called the Weaver. Within her husband's halls she tirelessly weaves on a loom the tapestries of history and fate long before those events are come in the course of Time.

Last of the Valar is he who in the beginning was mightiest of the Ainur. He was named Melkor, 'He who arises in Might'. He owned in part the powers of all the Valar, but chiefly his realm was Darkness and Cold. He moved over Arda like a black cloud that was dreadful to behold, like the World's nightmare come into daylight. All evil that was and is in the World had its beginning in Melkor, for he revolted against Ilúvatar in the Timeless Halls and came to Arda in anger, wishing to make his own kingdom. He brought corruption into the World, and with him came a part of the Maiar twisted by his malice. He made his fortress, Utumno, and his armoury, Angband, deep under the mountain roots of Middle-earth. In Arda he waged five great wars against the Valar and put out the fairest lights of the World by destroying both the Great Lamps and the Trees of the Valar.

In the beginning Melkor appeared in forms both fair and evil: his wiles were many and even Manwë the First King was deceived. Yet after the Darkening of Valinor, he always assumed his evil form and the Elves called him Morgoth, the 'dark enemy of the World'. This warrior king was like a great tower, iron-crowned, with black armour and a shield black, vast and blank. His countenance was evil, for the fire of malice was in his eyes and his face was twisted with rage and scarred by the claws of Thorondor the Eagle lord and the knife of Beren the Edain. He bore eight other wounds and his hands were burned from the fire of the Silmarils, so he was perpetually in pain. Grond the mace, called the Hammer of the Underworld, was his chief weapon and it sounded like thunder and split the Earth with its force. Yet, in the War of Wrath, all this power was destroyed, though Melkor summoned Dragons, Balrogs, Orcs, Trolls and every other evil being to his aid. This war was the end of him, and, though much of his evil and some of his servants remained, he alone of the Valar was driven from the Spheres of the World and now dwells for ever in the Void.

Valaraukar

Of the Maiar, the servants of the Valar, there were many who were of the element of fire. Melkor came among these fire spirits in the earliest days and corrupted many of them, turning them against Ilúvatar and the Valar. From brilliant beings they were transformed to demons that burned with hate: they were hulking monsters robed in darkness and they carried whips of flames. Feared by all, these corrupted Maiar were named Valaraukar, 'scourges of fire', but more commonly in Middle-earth they were known as the Balrogs, the 'demons of might'. It is under that name the history is told of their evil deeds in Mortal Lands of Arda.

VALINOR The mansions of Manwë were built upon Taniquetil, the tallest mountain of Arda.

Valimar

In the centre of Valinor in the Undying Lands was the city of the Valar and the Maiar. It was called Valimar, the 'home of the Vala' and was filled with white stone mansions, silver domes and golden spires. The city was famous for the celestial music of its many gold and silver bells. Before its white walls and golden gate of Valinor was Máhanaxar, the Ring of Doom, where the thrones of the Valar were set in a great council circle. And there, too, for many ages, was the fair Green Mound of Ezellohar upon which grew the Trees of the Valar.

Valinor

The first realm of the Valar and Maiar within the World was Almarin. Their second realm was Valinor, the 'land of the Valar' on the vast western continent of Aman. Protected on three sides by the huge Pelóri Mountains, and bounded by the sea of Ekkaia on the west, the Valar and Maiar built the city of Valimar and planted the Trees of Light by which all their domain as far as the Pelóri Mountains was lit. After the destruction of the Trees of Light, the Valar then created the Sun and the Moon which they set in the heavens and which lighted all the World. Valinor is dominated by the massive mansions and territories of the Valar and their attendant Maiar. Most impressive is Ilmarin, the mansions of Manwë the Wind Lord and Varda the Star Queen on the peak of Taniquetil, the tallest mountain on Arda. After the destruction of Númenor and the Change of the World in the Second Age of the Sun, Valinor, along with the rest of the Undying Lands, could not be reached by those coming from mortal lands, except by the magical boats of the Elves which could sail the Straight Road beyond the Spheres of the World.

Vampires

Whether it was from bird or beast that Melkor bred the evil bloodsucking Bat of Middle-earth, no tale tells. But in the First Age of the Sun, it is told how, in this winged form – made large and armed with talons of steel – Vampire spirits came into the service of Melkor the Dark Enemy.

In the Quest of the Silmaril, Thuringwethil, the 'woman of secret shadow', was a mighty Vampire and was the chief messenger to travel between Angband and Tol-in-Gaurhoth, where Sauron ruled the Werewolf regions. When Tol-in-Gaurhoth fell, Sauron himself took on Vampire shape and fled. Once the sorcerous power of Sauron was broken, many evil enchantments were also shattered. The shaping-cloak that gave Thuringwethil the power to take Bat-shape fell from her, and the Vampire's dread spirit fled.

Vána

Vala called 'the Ever-young'. Vána is the eternally youthful spirit of the Valar who is happiest when surrounded by flowers, birds and gardens. The sister of Yavanna the Fruitful, and the spouse of Oromë the Huntsman, Vána is the personification of spring. She can be found in her gardens in Valinor which are filled with golden flowers and many-coloured birds.

Vanyar

Of the Three Kindred of Elves who undertook the Great Journey from Middle-earth to the Undying Lands, least is told in the histories that have come to Men of that Kindred which is counted first and whose king, Ingwë, is named High Lord over all the Elven peoples. This race is the Vanyar, who are also known as the Fair Elves. They seem golden, for their hair is blondest of all peoples. They are most in accord with the Valar and are much loved by them; the counsel of the Lord of the Valar, Manwë, and Varda his queen is always theirs.

The Vanyar have had little to do with Men. Only once have they returned to Middle-earth and then it was to fight against Morgoth the Enemy in the War of Wrath, which ended the First Age of the Sun. None of the Vanyar stayed on in Middle-earth; all crossed the sea and returned to the Undying Lands.

What is known of the Vanyar has come to the ears of Men from the exiles – the Noldor who returned to Middle-earth at the time of the Arising of Men. Though they are the least numerous of the Three Kindred, the Vanyar are the most wise and valiant. With the Noldor in their first days in the Undying Lands they built the city of Tirion on the green hill of Túna. This was a great city with white walls and towers, and tallest of the towers of all the Elves was Mindon Eldaliéva, Tower of Ingwë. From it shone a silver lamp over the Shadowy Seas and in the court of the Tower of Ingwë stood a seedling named Galathilion from the tree Telperion, which flourished with the Elven people.

But after a time the Vanyar came to love the Light of the Trees still more, for it inspired them to compose songs and poetry which are their chief loves. So it was that they wished to settle where their full power might be seen. Thus, Ingwë led his people out of Tirion to the foot of Taniquetil, the Mountain of Manwë, the High Lord of the Valar. Here the Vanyar pledged to stay, and there they have remained, though the Trees have faded long ago.

Varda

Vala Queen of the Stars. The greatest and most beautiful queen among the Valar, Varda is the wife of Manwë, the King of Arda. She lives in their palace of Ilmarin on the top of Taniquetil, the tallest mountain on Arda. Varda is often called the 'Queen of the Light' for light is her element. It was she who made and rekindled the stars, lighted the Lamps of the Valar, collected the dew of light from the Trees of the Valar, and placed the Moon and the Sun in the heavens. Varda is the Vala Queen of Heaven, most beloved by Elves, and by them is known by many titles: Tintallë, Elentári, Fanuilos, Snow-white, Gilthoniel, Elbereth and Lady of the Stars.

Vardarianna

The land of Númenor was blessed in its beginning by the gifts of the Valar and the Eldar. Among the gifts of the Elves were the many fragrant evergreen trees that were brought to Númenor by the Teleri Sea Elves from the Lonely Isle of Eressëa and much valued for the heavenly scent of their flower, leaf, bark and wood. Among them was the Vardarianna, which as the name implies was a tree 'beloved of Varda', the Valarian Queen of the Heavens.

Variags

In the land of Khand, south of Mordor, there lived a fierce folk called the Variags during the Third Age of the Sun. They were allied to the evil Easterlings and Haradrim and were servants of the Dark Lord Sauron. The histories of the West tell how twice the Variags came forth at the bidding of Sauron against Gondor. In the year 1944, with the Men of Near Harad, the Variags fought the army of Eärnil of Gondor and were defeated at Poros Crossing. More than a thousand years later the Variags, with the Haradrim and Easterlings, came to the aid of Sauron's armies from Morgul and Mordor in the War of the Ring. But this was the last time they fought Gondor, for an end came to Sauron's power and the Variags made peace with the Dúnedain, and were content with their own land of Khand.

annals of the West and they were not named again in any of the histories of Elves or Men.

Wainriders

Out of the lands of Rhûn in the nineteenth century of the Third Age of the Sun an Easterling people came to make war on the Men of Gondor. They were a numerous well-armed folk with great Horse-drawn wains and war chariots. By the western Men they were named Wainriders and for a hundred years they made war on the Gondor Men. In 1856 the first battle was fought, in which the Wainriders defeated Gondor and her allies, the Northmen. They killed King Narmacil II, took the lands of Rhovanion and enslaved the Northmen who lived there.

The Wainriders ruled Rhovanion until the last year of that century, when the Northmen revolted and Calimehtar, the new king of Gondor, brought his army north. In battle at Dagorlad, the Wainriders were driven east to Rhûn by this new king. But still the Wainriders fomented trouble on the borderlands of Gondor and, with the aid of the Ringwraiths and the Haradrim, in 1944 they made yet another war on Gondor. And so, from both the East and the South, the Men of Gondor were forced to divide their armies. Gondor's King Ondoher went to the East, where his army was broken by the Wainriders and he and his two sons were slain. But the southern army of Gondor defeated the Haradrim army and then marched East. It surprised the victorious Wainriders and annihilated them with an avenging wrath. Their encampment was set alight, and those not slain in the Battle of the Camp were driven into the Dead Marshes where they perished. Thereafter, the name of the Wainriders vanished from the annals of the West and they were not named again in any of the histories of Elves or Men.

Wandlimb

Entwife of Treebeard. Wandlimb the Lightfooted was a female Ent, or 'Entwife', who was beloved of Treebeard of the Fangorn Forest. Wandlimb most resembled a Birch tree, and consequently her Elvish name was Fimbrethil or 'thin birch'. During the Ages of the Sun, the Entwives moved into the open lands and tended fruit trees, shrubs and grasses, while the Ents preferred the deep timbered forests. But late in the Second Age, the gardens of the Entwives were destroyed. Wandlimb and the other Entwives were either slain at this time, or driven far to the East or South of Middle-earth.

Wargs

In the Third Age of the Sun in Rhovanion, there lived an evil breed of Wolves that made an alliance with the mountain Orcs. These Wolves were named Wargs and often when they set off for war they went with the Orcs called Wolf-riders, who mounted the Wargs like Horses. In the battles of the War of the Ring, the Wargs were devastated along with most of the Orc hordes and after that time the surviving histories of Middle-earth speak no more of these wild creatures.

Watchers

In the west hall of Mordor, it is told, there was a narrow passage named Cirith Ungol, where the Great Spider Shelob lived in the Third Age of the Sun. There was also an Orc watch-tower with a great wall that held the road should any bypass Shelob, the fearful guardian.

WAINRIDERS For a hundred years they made war on the Gondor Men.

In the tower's wall were two tall gate-posts that seemed to have no gate. But a gate there was, and though it was invisible it proved very strong. The massive gate-posts were named the Watchers and each was a stone figure seated on a throne. They were triple-faced and triple-bodied, their heads were like vultures' and they had vultures' claws. They were filled with malice and their black eyes glittered with a fearful will, for spirits dwelt within these stone figures. They were aware of enemies visible and invisible, and they barred the gateway with their hatred. For though any army might attempt to force that gate, it could not pass by strength of arms; only by a will greater than the Watchers' malice could a passage be forced. If such a will could be summoned, then the Watchers would raise an alarm from their six vulture heads. They would emit a high shriek and a long cry that brought the Orkish soldiery upon the intruders.

Weather Hills

Within Eriador, just north of the Great East-West Road between Bree and the Trollshaws, are the Weather Hills. This range of hills running northward from its main peak of Weathertop, just above the road, once formed the boundary between Arnor's fiefs of Arthedain and Rhudaur. Although heavily fortified and defended by the Dúnedain during their war with the Witch-king of Angmar, they were overrun by the fifteenth century. By the time of the War of the Ring, the Weather Hills were largely uninhabited.

Werewolves

In the First Age of the Sun there came to Beleriand a race of tortured spirits who were thralls of Melkor. Whether they were Maiar spirits who once served Melkor in Utumno and were shorn by the Valar of their earthly forms, or whether they were evil beings of another kind, is not known. Yet it is certain that these evil spirits entered the forms of Wolves by sorcery. They were a fearsome race and their eyes glowed with dreadful wrath. They spoke and understood both the Black Speech of the Orcs and the fair speech of the Elves.

In the long Wars of Beleriand the greatest number of the Werewolves came, under the banner of Sauron, to the Noldor tower on the River Sirion, and it fell before them. The tower was re-named Tol-in-Gaurhoth, the 'isle of Werewolves', and Sauron ruled there. Beneath Tol-in-Gaurhoth there were deep dungeons, and on the battlements the Werewolves stalked.

In the Quest of the Silmaril, Huan, the Wolfhound of the Valar, came to Tol-in-Gaurhoth and slew many Werewolves. At last one named Draugluin, sire and lord of the Werewolf race, came to fight Huan. There was a great battle, but in the end Draugluin fled to the tower, to the throne of Sauron, his captain. Before Sauron Draugluin spoke the name of Huan, whose coming had been foretold, then he died. Sauron, the shape-shifter, then became a Werewolf himself. In size and strength he was greater than Draugluin, but even so Huan held the bridge and took Sauron by the throat, and by no act of sorcery or strength of limb could Sauron free himself. He therefore surrendered the tower to Beren and Lúthien, whom the Wolfhound served. The evil enchantment fell from Tol-in-Gaurhoth and the Wolf forms of the dread spirits fell from the Werewolves. Sauron fled in the form of a great Vampire Bat and the evil sorcerous power that held the realm of the Werewolves was broken in Beleriand for ever.

WEREWOLVES Drauglin was the Sire of Werewolves whose offspring stalked the battlements of Tol-in-Gauroth, the Isle of Werewolves in the First Age.

Wereworms

In the tales of the Hobbit folk there lived in the Last Desert, in the East of Middle-earth, a race that was named the Wereworms. Though no tale of the Third Age of the Sun tells of these beings, the Wereworms were likened to Dragons and serpents. To Hobbits they were perhaps but memories of those creatures that stalked the Earth during the Wars of Beleriand in the First Age.

West Elves

In the age of the Awakening of the Elves, a great Messenger came out of the West. He was the Vala Oromë, and he beckoned the Elves to a land of Eternal Light. Some chose to make the Journey to the West and were called West Elves or Eldar. Those who chose to remain were named East Elves or Avari, the 'unwilling'. The East Elves dwindled and became lesser spirits, while the West Elves grew mighty and famous in legend and in song.

Westmansweed

In Middle-earth a herb came into use that the Hobbits discovered gave great pleasure if slowly burned and the smoke inhaled. This was the herb nicotiana, which in the Western tongue was called Westmansweed, but most commonly was simply named Pipe-weed. Its use spread from the Shire lands of the Hobbits widely over Middle-earth and was enjoyed, for better or worse, by Men and Dwarves.

White Horn Mountains

The great range of snow-capped mountains that formed the backbone of Gondor was the White Horn Mountains. Sometimes called by their Elvish name Ered Nimrais, or simply the White Mountains, this mountain chain was at least six hundred miles long and ran westward from the Anduin River almost to the sea. The earliest inhabitants of the White Horn Mountains appear to have been the ancestors of the Dunlendings and the Woses, but for most of the Third Age it was primarily inhabited by the Rohirrim and the Men of Gondor. In its northern reaches were found the Rohirrim fortress refuges of Helm's Deep and Dunharrow. On the slopes of the range's easternmost mountain was built Minas Tirith.

White Tower

In the year 1900 of the Third Age, King Calimehtar of Gondor rebuilt the fortress-city of Minas Tirith, and on its citadel, the topmost of its seven defensive ring walls (and each one raised a hundred feet above the other), built a shining White Tower. It was rebuilt and improved in 2698 by the Steward Ecthelion I. The royal court was found here in its great hall and the palantír ('Seeing Stone') was kept in a chamber under the Tower's dome.

Often many of the allies and enemies of Gondor used the term White Tower when they were referring to the whole fortress-city of Minas Tirith and its people.

Wild Men

Long before the coming of the kings of Gondor, a primitive race of woodland hunters dwelt in the Druadan Forest. They were the Woses, whom others called the Wild Men, and they were a tribal people armed with bows and blow-pipes. They were wiser in the ways of the forest than any race of Men in Arda.

Willows

In the Ages of the Lamps when the Great Forests of Arda were made, ancient Willow trees appeared within the forests. The Willow spirits were strong and loved swamp-lands and slow river courses. They lived quietly for a long time and cared neither for the new-come race of Men, nor for the older races of Dwarves and Orcs who hewed and burned wood. Some among the Willows grew sentient and limb-lithe; they were numbered among those named Huorns and their will was bent on destroying all enemies of the forests.

Among Willows, the mightiest recorded in the tales of Middle-earth, is Old Man Willow, who in the Third Age of the Sun lived on the banks of the Withywindle in the Old Forest. He was black-hearted, limb-lithe and filled with a great enchanting power of song. All the land of the Old Forest was held in sway by his will. His great song bent all paths to his feet. Travellers were held in his hypnotic spell; a great song of water and wind on leaves brought them to a deep sleep by his ancient trunk. And with gnarled root or the gaping cavern of his trunk he would capture them, then crush them, or drown them in the river. His power made the Old Forest rightly feared by travellers, and, but for the power of Tom Bombadil, few could have passed safely through his domain.

Wilwarin

During the Spring of Arda, which was in the years of the Lamps, the Valar brought forth forests and many creatures that had no voice, yet were beautiful to behold. Among them was the Wilwarin, which in later times Men called the Butterfly. So content were the Valar with this lovely creature that, when Varda took the silver dew of Telperion to make brilliant the light of the Stars, she also placed the shape of the Wilwarins as a constellation among the wide-wheeling Stars of the heavens.

Window of the Sunset

A cavern refuge of the Rangers of Ithilien which was hidden behind the curtain wall of a spectacular waterfall in north Ithilien. Its waters flowed into the River Anduin near the Field of Cormallen and just south of Cair Andros. Called Henneth Annûn, meaning Window of the Sunset or Window of the West, it was built by Túrin of Gondor in 2901. During the War of the Ring it was often used by Faramir and his Rangers. The Ringbearer, Frodo Baggins, was given shelter here during the Quest of the Ring.

Winged Beasts

In the time of the War of the Ring it is told how those undead spirits called the Nazgûl were carried aloft by Winged Beasts. Swifter than the wind were these creatures that had beak and claw of bird, neck of serpent and wing of Bat. It is said they were fed on Orkish meats and grew beyond the size of any other winged creature of the Third Age. Yet black and evil as the Winged Beasts were, they were not undead beings and wraiths like their masters; rather they were living creatures like Dragons, but more ancient still. They had been bred by Melkor in lurking shadows in the Ages of the Lamps, when Kraken and serpent came from the Pits of Utumno.

Yet, ancient as they were, and though strong and fearsome in their service to Sauron in the War of the Ring, their time on Middle-earth was brought to an end. One Winged Beast was slain by the Elf Legolas, and a second was killed by the sword-maiden Éowyn; those that remained were destroyed in the holocaust that consumed Mordor in the last years of the Third Age.

Witch-king

Nazgûl lord of Ringwraiths. The Witch-king was originally a sorcerer king of the Second Age who was given the first of the Nine Rings by the Lord of the Rings. He became the Lord of the Nazgûl, or Ringwraiths. During the Second Age, he commanded Sauron's forces and fought his battles, but with the downfall of the Ring Lord and the taking of the One Ring, he was swept away into a shadowy limbo. However, since the One Ring was not destroyed, after a thousand years Sauron called him back from the shadows. In 1300 of the Third Age, he rose up in the form of the Witch-king of Angmar. For nearly seven centuries he made constant war on the North-kingdom of Arnor until 1974, when he destroyed its last stronghold in Arthedain. The next year, his own forces were routed and his evil kingdom of Angmar destroyed after the Battle of Fornost. The destruction of the North-kingdom of the Dúnedain having been achieved, in the year 2000 he turned his attentions to the South-kingdom of Gondor. He attacked and took Minas Ithil, and renamed it Minas Morgul. As the Witch-king of Morgul, he fought and harried the realm of Gondor for a thousand years. In 3018, disguised as one of the Black Riders, he led the other Ringwraiths to the Shire in search of the One Ring. At Weathertop, he wounded the Ringbearer, then pursued him as far as the Fords of Rivendell. In 3019, the Witch-king led his vast Morgul army and his Haradrim allies in an attack on the White Tower. In the Battle of Pelennor Fields he slew King Théoden, but – in a strange fulfilment of the prophecy that he could not be slain by the hand of Man – he met his death at the hands of the Rohirrim shield-maiden, Éowyn, and the Hobbit, Meriadoc Brandybuck, armed with a charmed Elven blade.

Witches

In Middle-earth there were beings of many races who wielded sorcerous powers. Among the late-come race of Men, those who gave themselves over to sorcerous power were known as Witches. The most powerful Witches were the Ringwraiths, who were named Nazgûl in Black Speech. For these were the Men who were given Nine Rings of Power by Sauron and who brought so much terror into the World.

Of these nine Witches, one emerged whose power was supreme. In the Third Age of the Sun, he arose in the north of Eriador and made himself an evil realm in Angmar. For many centuries Men spoke fearfully of this Witch-king of Angmar who laid waste the North Kingdom of the Dúnedain. Later, the same Witch-king arose again in the South against the realm of Gondor and took from Gondor a tower that afterwards was named Minas Morgul. There the Witch-king ruled until the days of the War of the Ring, when he was destroyed, and he and the other Witches vanished for ever from the face of Arda.

Withywindle

A small river called the Withywindle flowed through the Old Forest which lay just east of the Shire lands of the Hobbits. Its source was the hills of the Barrowlands and it meandered through the forest until it reached the Brandywine River. Its valley, which was called the Dingle, was filled with willow trees and was the home of that great forest spirit called Old Man Willow. The spirit-being called the River-woman of the Withywindle was the mother of Tom Bombadil's wife, Goldberry the River-daughter.

Wizards

Those whom common Men named Wizards were, as ancient tales reveal, chosen spirits from the Maiar of Valinor. Elves called them the Istari, and under that name the greater part of their deeds in Middle-earth is recorded.

These Wizards came from the West to redress the imbalance that was made by the Dark Lord Sauron in Middle-earth. They came in secret in the form of Men, for it was deemed they could not come forth in the full force of their immortal Maiar spirits but were to be limited to the powers that they might acquire in Mortal Lands. They appeared as old Men dressed in long robes and, filled with the wisdom of the lands, they travelled. They were far-famed as clever conjurors. It is said there were five who in the Third Age of the Sun wandered the lands of Middle-earth, but the histories speak of three only: Saruman the White, Gandalf the Grey and Radagast the Brown.

Wolf-riders

The 'Red Book of Westmarch' records how some among the Orcs of Rhovanion came into the Battle of Five Armies mounted on the backs of the Wolves that were called Wargs. These Orcs were named Wolf-riders by Elves, Dwarves and Men and they formed the cavalry of the Orc legions.

But this alliance of Orc and Wolf was not newly formed in that Age, for both Wolves and Orcs were bred by the evil hand of Melkor the Enemy in the Ages of Stars. Their pact of evil began before the race of Men awoke and the light of the Sun flooded the World. The histories of Beleriand in the last Ages of Stars tell how the Sindarin Elves of Beleriand fought the Wolf-riders many times.

WIZARDS They came in secret in the form of Men, for it was deemed they could not come forth in the full force of their immortal Maiar spirits.

Wolfhounds

From the realms of Melkor the Dark Enemy, in the Ages of Stars, many evil beasts came to torment the people of Middle-earth. Chief among these creatures were the Wolves and Werewolves of Melkor. In defence the Elves of Beleriand bred hunting hounds with which they might destroy these evil beings.

In the histories of Middle-earth, the greatest of these Wolfhounds was one named Huan, who was not born in Mortal Lands. He was bred by Oromë, Huntsman of the Valar, who had given him to the Noldor prince Celegorm in the Undying Lands. The Valarian Wolfhound was an ageless beast that never tired or slept. He was immortal in the manner of Elves and of massive size. By decree of the Valar Huan spoke only three times with words, though he could always understand the speech of Elves and Men. He could not be slain by sorcery nor could spells bewitch him.

Brought to Middle-earth by the exiled Noldor princes, a great doom fell on Huan. In the Quest of the Silmaril he played a large part: for love of Lúthien Tinúviel he went to Sauron's tower on Tol-in-Gaurhoth, the Isle of Werewolves. There he killed many evil beasts on the bridge of the Isle and finally slew Draugluin, lord and sire of Werewolves and chief of Sauron's servants in that realm. Then Sauron himself came forth in Werewolf form and there followed a terrible struggle on the bridge of Tol-in-Gaurhoth between Huan and Sauron. Sauron was a mighty terror in that form, but Huan's power was even greater. He took the greatest of the Maia by the throat and with crushing strength held him, bringing him near to death. And so Sauron gave over the tower to Huan and Lúthien and surrendered the hero Beren who was imprisoned in that place. All the powers of enchantment dropped away from Tol-in-Gaurhoth, the servants of Sauron fled, and Sauron, in the shape of a great Vampire, in fear and wrath flew across the sky.

Yet still another battle lay before Huan, the Wolfhound. This was with the Wolf Carcharoth, the Red Maw, who was the evil guardian of the Gates of Angband. This was the greatest Wolf that ever entered the World and he was raised by Morgoth's hand. By chance the Wolf had swallowed the Silmaril that Beren had taken from Morgoth's crown. The jewel burned within the Wolf and he went mad with the torment. None could stand before Carcharoth's fury, even the warrior Beren fell before his power. And as was foretold Huan came and there was the greatest battle of beast against beast that ever was fought. All the goodness of the Valar was with Huan and all the evil of Morgoth with Carcharoth. The hills sounded with their battle but at last Huan slew Carcharoth, though he himself was mortally hurt by the evil beast, for in the fangs of the Wolf was a dread poison. Knowing death was upon him he came to Beren who was also dying and spoke for the last time with words, saying only 'farewell'.

Wolves

Before the Sun shone, in the Pits of Utumno in Middle-earth many evil beasts were bred that stalked the World with evil Orcs. Chief of the beasts that allied with the Orcs were the Wolves, which first came into the Westlands in the years of Stars. Some of great size served as mounts for Melkor's servants and they were a source of great terror.

In the First Age of the Sun the Werewolf race was bred. The mightiest was Draugluin, their sire and lord. These were not, however, true Wolves but tortured spirits held within the Wolf-form. Their power was great for they were favourites of Sauron the Maia. They came to him in legions and united in the lands of Beleriand. From the Noldor they took the tower of Tol Sirion, which was later named Tol-in-Gaurhoth, the 'isle of Werewolves', and there they made a kingdom of evil.

Though by the Third Age of the Sun Wolves were lesser beings than those of the early Ages, they remained a dreaded race. The 'Chronicle of the Westlands' tells of a race of White Wolves that came out of the Northern Waste during the Fell Winter of 2911 and stained the snows of Eriador with the blood of Men. The 'Red Book of Westmarch' tells much of the Wargs, a breed of Wolf that in Rhovanion made a pact with the Orcs of the Misty Mountains and carried that breed of Orcs, called the Wolf-riders, into battle on their backs. And though indeed the Wargs alone were much feared, this alliance with Orcs was a greater evil yet. Indeed, in the famous Battle of Five Armies, the strongest element of the Orkish forces was its cavalry, mounted on great Wargs.

The greatest Wolf legend is about Carcharoth, the Red Maw, who in the First Age of the Sun was reared by Morgoth on living flesh and filled with great powers. So Carcharoth, who was also named Anfauglir, the 'jaws of thirst', grew to a huge size and his strength seemed without comparison. His eyes were like red coals and his teeth were like the poisoned spears of an Orc legion. Carcharoth was guardian of the Gates of Angband and none could pass him by strength of body alone. The walls of Angband were sheer and dread; chasms of serpents lay on either side of the road and Carcharoth lay unsleeping before the Gate.

In the Quest of the Silmaril, Carcharoth bit off Beren's hand at Angband's Gate and swallowed the Silmaril, which burned him with a fierce fire. In his torment Carcharoth slew Elves and Men as his accursed flesh was consumed by the fire; yet his power became greater still. For Carcharoth's wrath was like the self-destroying unquenchable flame of a shooting Star. But at last he met the one he was long doomed to battle: Huan, the Wolfhound of the Valar. And, though he bit Huan with venomous teeth and thereby ensured that Huan's death would soon follow, Carcharoth was slain by the might of the Valarian Wolfhound near the sweet waters of Esgalduin.

Wood-Elves

In most of the woodlands of Middle-earth, east of the Misty Mountains that had not been wholly consumed by the evils of Morgoth and Sauron, lived the remnant of the Avari, the people who had refused the Great Journey to the West. These people, who were called Wood-elves or more often Silvan Elves, had dwindled with the rising of Morgoth's power in the East. To survive, they became wise in the ways of the sheltering forests and hid themselves from their enemies. They were wise in wood-lore, and their eyes were bright as all Elves' with starlight. They were not a powerful people like their High Eldar kindred, but they were greater than Men or any race that followed them.

Although the histories of Arda tell little of the fate of the Wood-elves and are mostly concerned with the Eldar, many tales are told of two realms of these lesser Elves. In the Second Age of the Sun the Sindar lord Thranduil came out of Lindon and crossed over the Misty Mountains. He discovered many Wood-elves in the forest of Greenwood the Great (which was later named Mirkwood). There Thranduil was made king of the Woodland Realm of these Elves. In a similar way, Galadriel the Noldor noblewoman and Celeborn the Sindar lord came to the Wood-elves of Lothlórien, who made them king and queen of the Golden Wood.

Woodmen

In the Third Age of the Sun there lived in Mirkwood a people who were called the Woodmen of Mirkwood and who were descended from the Northmen. In alliance with the Beornings and the Elves of the Woodland Realm, they fought the evil that had come in that Age to Dol Guldur in the south of Mirkwood. From that place came Orcs, Spiders and Wolves in legion, and the battle to cleanse that great forest was long and dreadful. In the War of the Ring this struggle was named the Battle under the Trees. Through the north ran the Elves, Woodmen and Beornings, destroying the evil minions of Dol Guldur as fire through straw. The Elves of Lothlórien took Dol Guldur, and broke its walls and destroyed its dungeons. So, at the end of the Age, the forest was cleansed and renamed the Wood of Greenleaves, and the lands between the north realm of the Wood-elves and the south woods called East Lórien were given to the Woodmen and the Beornings to keep as their reward and their proper right.

Worms

The most powerful creatures that Morgoth ever bred in Arda were the Great Worms that came out of the Pits of Angband in the First Age of the Sun. Morgoth armed these creatures with scales of iron, mighty teeth and claws, and great powers of flame and sorcery. Men and Elves called these ancient Worms of Morgoth Dragons and they were among the most fearful of beings in all the histories of Middle-earth.

Wormtongue

Northman of Rohan. During the time of the War of the Ring, Gríma Wormtongue was the deformed chief counsellor of King Théoden of Rohan. Secretly, he was a servant and spy of Saruman who steadily undermined the old king and enfeebled him with the Wizard's evil spells. After Gandalf cured Théoden, Wormtongue fled to Isengard, where both he and Saruman were eventually captured and overthrown by the Ents. Afterwards, he travelled with Saruman to the Shire where he turned on his master and killed him. In turn, the pathetic creature was immediately slain by Hobbits.

Woses

In the War of the Ring a strange primitive folk named the Woses came to aid the Rohirrim and Dúnedain in breaking the Siege of Gondor. These wild woodland people lived in the ancient Forest of Druadan, which was in Anórien, below the White Mountains. They knew wood-craft better than any Man, for they had lived as naked animals invisibly among the trees for many Ages and cared not for the company of other peoples. They were weather-worn, short-legged, thick-armed and stumpy-bodied. The Men of Gondor called the Woses the Wildmen of Druadan and believed that they were descended from the even more ancient Púkel-Men. In the First Age of the Sun these were the people who lived in harmony with the Haladin in Beleriand, who called them Drûgs. To the Elves they were known as the Drúedain; to the Orcs they were the Oghor-hai and to the Rohirrim the Rógin.

By the end of the Third Age, Orcs, Wolves and other malevolent creatures often came into Druadan. Though the Woses drove them away, often with poison arrows and darts, the evil beings always returned. So it was that, though the Woses desired no part in the affairs of Men beyond their forest, their chieftain, who was named Ghân-buri-Ghân, offered to help the Rohirrim reach the Battle of Pelennor Fields. For, in a victory for the Rohirrim and the Dúnedain in Gondor, the Woses saw some release from this continual woodland warfare.

When victory did indeed come and the Dark Lord's Orc legions were destroyed, King Elessar of the Reunited Kingdoms of Gondor and Arnor granted that the Druadan Forest would for ever be the inalienable country of the Woses to govern and to rule as they saw fit.

WOSES Wildmen of the Druadan Forest, the Woses were a fair-skinned, pygmy race of hunters. In the War of the Ring they guided the Rohirrim cavalry through their forests to fight in the Battle of Pelennor Fields.

Y·Z

Yavanna

Vala, Queen of the Earth. Yavanna is the spouse of Aulë the Smith, and the elder sister of Vána the Ever-young. Yavanna watches over the growth of all living things. Tall as a cypress tree and always garbed in green she is called Yavanna Kementári, which is 'the fruitful queen of the earth'. She is the mother of the harvest. Yavanna planted the seeds of all plants on Arda, and made the vast forests and pastures of the world. She conceived the protectors of the forests, the 'tree shepherds' called Ents, and made the White Tree of the Eldar in Tirion. Her greatest work, however, was the creation of the incomparable Trees of Light, which for twenty thousand years lit all the lands of Valinor with their brilliance. And it was her powers which brought forth the last flower and fruit of those Trees that became the Moon and the Sun. Yavanna's vast pastures and gardens are to be found in southern Valinor where they border the Woods of Oromë. Her gardens supply the magical flowers from which is made the nectar of the gods, miruvóre.

Yavannamirë

When Númenor was newly made, the Elves of Tol Eressëa came upon their ships bearing gifts. Among the finest of these gifts were many fragrant evergreen trees which gave forth flower and fruit in the Undying Lands. On Númenor there grew up forests of these wonderful, scented trees. Among the finest were the Yavannamirë, named in honour of Yavanna, the Valarian Queen of the Earth. The name means 'Jewel of Yavanna' and besides its fragrant wood, bark and evergreen leaf, the tree produced a luscious, round and scarlet fruit.

Yrch

Near the end of that time known as the Peace of Arda, the Sindarin Elves of King Thingol and Queen Melian found in the East an evil they had not known before. The woodlands and mountains on their borders began to stir with evil beings for which they had no name. These beings were the terrible Goblin people, who were destined always to be the chief servants and harbingers of evil powers. In the Sindarin

YAVANNA Valarian Queen of the Earth. Yavanna was guardian of the harvest, protector of the forest and creator of the Ents. She conceived the incomparable Trees of Light which once lit all the lands of Valinor.

tongue they were named Yrch, in imitation of their own word for themselves: Uruks. In later Ages they became known as Orcs in the common language of Westron.

The Nandor and Laiquendi fled before these dark creatures, who were armed with weapons of steel. But King Thingol, with warriors in bright Dwarf-mail and tall helms, went to war against the Yrch and slaughtered them until the battle grounds were covered with their black blood. The Yrch fled from Beleriand and never crossed the Blue Mountains again until the time of the return of Morgoth the Enemy, their creator and master, from the Undying Lands in the West.

Zirak-zigil

Midway along the Misty Mountain range stands the peak of Zirak-zigil, one of the three great mountains beneath which the Dwarf kingdom of Khazad-dûm was delved. It was also called Silvertine by Men and Celebdil by the Elves. Within the pinnacle of Zirak-zigil – at the top of the Endless Stair – was the chamber called Durin's Tower.

It was here at the end of the Third Age during the Quest of the Ring that the Wizard Gandalf the Grey did battle with the Balrog of Moria. In this Battle of the Peak, the Endless Stair and Durin's Tower were destroyed, but from that great height Gandalf overcame the Balrog and cast him down into the abyss below.

YRCH The Goblin people, or Orcs in the Sindarin tongue, were known as Yrch in the Ages of Starlight in Beleriand. Many were the battles between the Grey Elves and the Yrch legions in those early times.

INDEX OF SOURCES

This index refers the reader from the entries in the Dictionary to Tolkien's original texts.
The following abbreviations have been used:

S – *The Silmarillion*
H – *The Hobbit*
LR – *The Lord of the Rings*
TB – *The Adventures of Tom Bombadil*
UT – Unfinished Tales
BLT (1) – Book of Lost Tales I
BLT (2) – Book of Lost Tales II
LB – Lays of Beleriand
SME – Shaping of Middle-earth
LRD – The Lost Road

Roman numerals indicate parts, and arabic numbers, chapters or sections.

INDEX

E

F

G

H

K

O

P

Q

R

S

T

U

V

W

Y

Z

ACKNOWLEDGEMENTS

Artworks and illustrations have been supplied by the following artists:

VICTOR AMBRUS:	37, 71, 82, 91, 103, 116, 128, 150, 156
SARAH BALL:	222
JAROSLAV BRADAC:	21, 115, 139, 181, 186, 215, 240
ALAN CURLESS:	33,64, 84, 88, 92, 117, 126, 152, 178, 207, 229, 239, 242-243
JON DAVIS:	16, 79, 203, 241
MICHAEL FOREMAN:	43
LINDA GARLAND:	180
DAVID KEARNEY:	131